"Civilizing" Rio

Teresa A. Meade

"Civilizing" Rio

Reform and Resistance in a Brazilian City, 1889–1930

The Pennsylvania State University Press
University Park, Pennsylvania

Library of Congress Cataloging-in-Publication Data

Meade, Teresa A., 1948–
   Civilizing Rio : reform and resistance in a Brazilian city, 1889–1930 / Teresa A.
Meade.

      p.   cm.
   Includes bibliographical references and index.
   ISBN 0-271-01607-8 (cloth : alk. paper)
   ISBN 0-271-01608-6 (paper : alk. paper)
   1. Urban renewal—Brazil—Rio de Janeiro—History. 2. Working class—
Brazil—Rio de Janeiro—Political activity—History. 3. Social conflict—Brazil—
Rio de Janeiro—History. I. Title.
HT178.B72R565 1997
307.76′0981′53—dc20
                                       96-6452
                                        CIP

It is the policy of The Pennsylvania State University Press to use acid-free paper
for the first printing of all clothbound books. Publications on uncoated stock
satisfy the mimimum requirements of American National Standard for Information Sciences—Permanence of Paper for Printed Library Materials, ANSI
Z39.48-1992.

Contents

Illustrations and Tables

Tables

Acknowledgments

The process of writing this book has been long and choppy. Because it is a project that has been put down and picked up many times over, it is with a certain amount of wonder that I find myself even writing these words. Likewise, I realize that this book would not have been completed without the generous assistance and encouragement of many individuals and institutions. It is with pleasure that I can acknowledge them now and offer my thanks.

I first encountered Brazilian history as an undergraduate in Thomas Skidmore's history classes at the University of Wisconsin, stumbling then on this huge and influential part of Latin America that spoke Portuguese and not Spanish. As a graduate student at Rutgers University a few years later, I renewed my interest in Brazil in seminars with Peter Eisenberg. Looking back over the years since graduate school, I realize that many key impressions that I hold about Brazilian history and politics—past and contemporary— were learned in conversations with these men. I am profoundly sorry that Peter died before I could present him with this book. As do many others, I miss Peter's warmth, his wry humor, his incisive comments, his dedication to history, and his love of Brazil. The generosity he and Rosa Eisenberg showed me in Brazil and the encouragement he lent to my work are deeply appreciated. To Tom Skidmore, I want to say thank you for the introduction to Brazil and the continued friendship and collegiality.

The Henry and Grace Doherty Foundation's Fellowship for Advanced Study in Latin America supported the dissertation research that formed the basis for this book. Later funding for research, writing, and travel in the

United States, Brazil, and England came from faculty development grants from Union College (Schenectady) and Towson State University. Further support for travel, conferences, and seminars was provided by the Rockefeller Foundation, the National Endowment for the Humanities, and the U.S. Department of Education.

I appreciate the assistance rendered by the staffs of many archives and libraries, especially the Arquivo Nacional, the Biblioteca Nacional, and the Arquivo da Fundação Getúlio Vargas in Rio de Janeiro; the Arquivo Edgard Leuenroth at UNICAMP in Campinas; the Wellcome Institute for the History of Medicine in London; the U.S. National Archives, the Library of Congress, and the New York Public Library. I have a special debt to the Reference and Interlibrary Loan Divisions of Schaffer Library, Union College, for the many times they promptly and cheerfully helped track down books and sources for this project.

Many friends and colleagues have offered suggestions, advice, and support at various stages of this manuscript, and to all of them I am grateful: Samuel Baily, Bob Baker, Sueann Caulfield, Norma Chinchilla, Catherine Davis, Faye Dudden, Rosa Eisenberg, George Gmelch, Michael Hall, Cindy Himes, Margaret Hunt, Martha Huggins, Adrienne Klein, Robert Levine, Jason Marrero, Carlos Mayo, Nancy Naro, Paulo Sérgio Pinheiro, Gregory Pirio, Alison Raphael, Fernanda Venancio Filho, Paulo Venancio Filho, Mark Walker, Devra Weber, Cliff Welch, and Bob Wells. I am especially indebted to Jeremy Adelman, Timothy Harding, Ira Katznelson, Jeffrey Lesser, and Joel Wolfe, who read the full manuscript or parts of it and offered enormously helpful criticisms and suggestions. Barbara Weinstein, whose own work serves as a model of intellectual clarity, deserves a special thanks for her comments, which were examples of the professional acuity and personal good will for which she is well known.

At Penn State Press, Sanford Thatcher proved to be the fine editor everyone told me he was. Keith Monley was an excellent copy editor. I very much appreciate their help and that of the other staff members, especially Cherene Holland, managing editor, who ushered the book through from manuscript to completed monograph. I also want to thank H. L. Hoffenberg for the photographs and for the opportunity to look through his wonderful collection of Brazilian photos and artifacts in New York.

It is with particular regret that I remember here people who influenced me professionally and personally but have died since I began this project. Warren Dean, Peter Eisenberg, and Warren Susman commented on the dissertation, encouraged me in various stages of research and writing, and most of all taught me that the search for social justice can be an integral part of intellectual inquiry and the scholarly enterprise. They were good friends and I miss them. My sister Rita Meade Dohrmann, who died when I was in graduate school, morally and materially supported my education, my career, and shared my political and social ideals. Her premature death derailed me in ways I have only recently realized.

Finally, Harold Berkowitz, Susan Besse, Sharon Gmelch, Ronald Grele, my mother, Magdalen Meade, and my sisters Mary Mundt and especially Martha Meade served up the necessary prods and praises to keep this and most every other aspect of my life on track. My children, Darren and Claire, have never offered much direct comment on my academic endeavors, but apart from the joy they bring to daily life, their presence is a constant reminder of why we acquire knowledge and seek to pass it on.

My companion, husband, best critic, and best friend, Andor Skotnes, provided so much help in the completion of this manuscript that I scarcely know where to begin. To his formidable theoretical skills, historical insights, good-humored encouragement, computer genius, and loving confidence, I owe too much even to begin to acknowledge. I dedicate this book to him with love and appreciation.

Introduction

In September 1893 "hundreds of agitators" marched down the main streets of Rio de Janeiro, the federal capital of Brazil's nearly four-year-old Republic. Rallying in front of a government building, the crowd attempted to take inside a petition demanding that the officials revoke a recently imposed federal tax on "essential goods." In the eyes of the demonstrators this tax was particularly unjust, not only because it added another burden to already skyrocketing prices on consumer items, but because it was one more cruel reminder of official Rio's disregard for the well-being of the city's residents. Prices were already high, the protesters complained, because speculators preyed on consumers during those times when the government was preoccupied with maintaining order in the distant reaches of the new Republic. In reference to a recent military expedition to the southern state of Rio Grande do Sul, spokespersons for the crowd proclaimed that "when the government's attention is devoted to matters pertaining to the military order, the speculators are most active."[1]

The peaceful march turned ugly when the police prevented the crowd, including even the "respectable citizens" scattered among its ranks, from delivering a set of written complaints to the House of Deputies. What ensued was fairly typical of street demonstrations in those years: the police shoved the crowd; people fought back, hurling rocks at the rows of infantry and cavalry converging on them. In turn the mounted officers charged the gath-

1. *O Paiz*, September 12, 1893, 1, translated by the author, as are all further translations unless otherwise noted.

ering, their clubs swinging and horses' hooves tromping down on protester and bystander alike. Tempers flared, shots rang out, and the peaceful assembly of orderly petitioners turned to melee. Groups from the splintered gathering then rampaged through the downtown streets until nightfall, when exhaustion, hunger, frustration, and relatively indiscriminate incarceration brought an end to the disturbance. What was the outcome? By all accounts, the speculators went back to gouging the urban consumers, pushing food prices ever higher, and the federal tax stayed in place.

Although marches and protests occurred intermittently over the next decade, not until November 1904 did violence again envelop the metropolitan area and touch the lives of many of the city's residents. At that time Rio's residents took to the streets to protest a new law requiring universal vaccination against small pox. Beginning as sporadic rallies on the evening of November 10, the day before the law was to take effect, rioting disrupted the normal operations of the city for the next week, finally ending on November 18. In the course of the week, crowds comprising young and old, men and women, European immigrants and native Afro-Brazilians, hurled rocks from behind barricades and from the tops of buildings. The most militant protesters armed themselves with handguns and other weapons to defend their barricades against the police and army units that were attempting to restore order. Day and night, shouts of "Death to the police!" "Long live the working class!" "Down with forced vaccination!" and "Long live the Republic!" pierced the Rio air.[2]

Similar to the protest of 1893, the demonstration began as a peaceful assembly. On the night of November 10, 1904, as many as five thousand protesters gathered peacefully in the Largo de São Francisco da Paula, a traditional rallying point in downtown Rio de Janeiro. Although the organizers of the November 10 protest (a loose coalition of civilian and military Positivists, socialist trade unionists, and opposition politicians) directed the crowd to disperse and to reassemble in the same location the next day, a few gangs of youths headed out to get a head start on stoning streetlights and overturning public transport vehicles. Most, however, simply paraded about the downtown shouting condemnations of the government and the vaccination law. On the morning of November 11, the first day of the government's mandatory vaccination effort and the day organizers had called for total noncompliance with the new law, protests erupted all over Rio de Janeiro.[3]

2. *Jornal do Brasil*, November 11–12, 14–19, 1904, 1–2.
3. Ibid., November 11–12, 1904, 1–2.

When the riot finally ended more than a week later, the capital lay in shambles. The crowds had overturned and set ablaze streetcars, broken gas and electric streetlights, erected barricades to cut off access to the main arteries in the vital business districts near the docks and trading houses, invaded construction sites to tear apart newly erected walls and floors, and vandalized train stations on lines out to the rapidly expanding *subúrbios* on the outskirts of the downtown. Peculiar targets indeed for a protest against small pox vaccination! Logically, one assumes, in a riot against a health law, the offices of the public health department should have suffered the greatest damage, or the demonstrators should have sought out and tried to punish the doctors and medical personnel responsible for carrying out the vaccination. Instead, the crowds had destroyed the Republican capital's newly constructed downtown offices, government buildings, cultural landmarks, and transit system. Why, one asks, did a people opposed to a public health law set ablaze streetcars and newly renovated buildings? The answer seems to be that the riot had centered on more than vaccination and had unleashed well-grounded fears and hostilities from Rio's poor. Dying daily of malnutrition, dysentery, and tuberculosis, forced by an ambitious urban renewal project from their homes in the center city and out to the disease-infested suburbs, the poor, the working class, and even those struggling into the middle class simply did not believe that the vaccination law would bring them anything but more harm. In effect, the law was part of a general program that was increasingly marginalizing the city's poor geographically, to the distant outskirts of the city, and politically, far from the Republic's priorities.

In the years after the famous riot of 1904, popular protest, sometimes called "collective violence," less often affected the places of commerce and the centers of power in the eventually rebuilt center city of Rio de Janeiro, the heart of the newly proclaimed *cidade maravilhosa* (marvelous city). Nonetheless, protests continued, although in somewhat varied forms and in different places. Not uncommon were minor riots, such as that which erupted on May 4, 1916, on the Estrada de Ferro Central do Brasil (known as the Central), the rail line that in the post–urban renewal years brought workers from their neighborhoods on Rio's outskirts to their workplaces in the center city and South Zone. On the morning of May 4 adults gathered in the stations, ready to push their children past railroad attendants who were to enforce a new policy of charging children who rode during the morning and evening rush hours. Carrying signs demanding that train officials retain the customary free passage for children, adults and youngsters pushed station attendants out of the way and boarded the trains in defiance of the new regulation. Those who attempted to stop the stampede, to collect the fares, or to prevent children from boarding were knocked down and trampled. All along the line, station masters reported to the railroad officers that it was "impossible to enforce the ruling."[4]

These three riots, or incidents of collective violence, that erupted in Rio de Janeiro over a twenty-three-year period appear on the surface as quite distinct historical incidents. They were, moreover, only three cases among many during the First Republic, a period noted for near constant conflict and upheaval. In this book I analyze many of those conflicts and attempt to explain why different social classes, organized in neighborhood groups, labor unions, and affiliated societies, quarreled and fought with the city and federal government from 1890 to 1930. They sparred over the ways public services and housing were allocated, over the continually rising cost of living, over the perpetual lack of decent job opportunities, for a productive and healthy life, and, in some cases, for simple peace and quiet.

On the one hand, this book is a study of the reasons why masses of people sporadically took to the streets in protest. They most heatedly disagreed in the decades at the turn of the century over the massive urban renewal and public health plan that was intended to transform Rio de Janeiro from a disease-infested port city of narrow streets and uninteresting architecture to a thriving metropolis of Parisian-inspired avenues and buildings. When by 1910 the first phase of the urban renewal was largely completed and the poor were removed to working-class suburbs and to the outskirts of the city, the locus of tension shifted to complaints over working conditions and wages, adding to ongoing grievances against high prices, inadequate and unsanitary housing, and the general substandard living conditions that continued to plague the urban poor.

On the other hand, this is a study of the overall outcome of the struggle, not just of what happened after each riot, orderly petition, or militant protest. Since rioting and protest are ubiquitous in history—in both urban and rural areas—what distinguishes the events in Rio from those in other places and times? What do we learn from the Rio case about the form and outcome of collective violence and urban development in general? Did the protesters in 1893, 1904, or 1916 have anything in common? Separated by years, the activities took place in different parts of the city; they were sparked by different events; they often drew together people from separate social classes, of dif-

4. Ibid., May 4, 1916, 1.

ferent ages, genders, and races; and they varied in their purpose (food prices and taxes, health reform and urban renewal, transit fares, living and working conditions). What effect, if any, did these protests have on the way the city developed? In this book I probe those commonalities.

In the first place, the protests took place in Rio de Janeiro, the capital and most important commercial city of Brazil during the Republican government that lasted from 1889 to 1930. To a large extent the social strife in the capital mirrored the broader tensions of Brazilian society. Rio stood at the head of a country in the midst of great social changes and political upheaval: the abolition of slavery in 1888, the massive influx of free immigrant laborers, the final demise of the Empire, and, on November 15, 1889, the declaration of the Republic.[5] But the capital also contained within it the forces that were pulling the country in different directions. It was the city the elite wanted to transform into a showplace of high culture, befitting the capital of an emerging great nation; and at the same time it was the place to which thousands of poor immigrants from Europe and former slaves from the plantations were fleeing in search of a better life. As a result, Rio de Janeiro was, during the First (or Old) Republic, more than a capital and more than an emerging commercial center; it was the site of tension between opposing social classes over the course of Brazil's future. At one pole stood the planter-dominated federal government, including a rapidly expanding government bureaucracy, the increasingly powerful urban manufacturing and commercial elite, and their allies among British financial and merchant groups. At the other pole were the popular classes, including the working class, the marginalized and unemployed urban poor, and a vast array of small shopkeepers, independent drivers, sellers, and street peddlers, a group sometimes called the middle class or, more precisely, the petty bourgeoisie.

Second, the riots and demonstrations in Rio involved more than an internal struggle between opposing social classes. As social conflict, they represented a moment in the collective struggle of a people over who would live in the city, where they would live, and how well they would live. In Rio de Janeiro this fight, over what Manuel Castells calls the "built form of the city" or "allocation of urban space," assumed a configuration that pitted the majority of the laboring poor and the petty bourgeoisie against the smaller

5. Emilia Viotti da Costa, *Da senzala a colonia* (São Paulo: Difusão Européia do Livro, 1966); Robert Conrad, *The Destruction of Brazilian Slavery, 1850–1888* (Berkeley and Los Angeles: University of California Press, 1972); Octavio Ianni, *As metamorfoses do escravo* (São Paulo: Difusão Européia do Livro, 1962); Thomas Holloway, *Immigrants on the Land: Coffee and Society in São Paulo, 1886–1934* (Chapel Hill: University of North Carolina Press, 1980).

group of Brazilian elites and their allies among the foreign merchants, investors, and bankers. The popular classes sought to make their grievances
known in a number of forms: marches, street melees, often riots, and occasionally strikes. Although the poor and working people of Rio de Janeiro
never managed to alter power relations in the city, to change the class structure, or to force a significant reordering in the government's social priorities,
they persisted. In the end, their struggle was an attempt, if a mostly failed
one, to intervene in the spatial molding of their city and to demand a better
share of urban prosperity.

Stated another way, this was a conflict, not unusual in history, in which the
popular classes threw at the ruling class all that they had: themselves.[6] In
fact there were many similarities between the forms that protest assumed in
turn-of-the-century Rio de Janeiro and the much analyzed riots that broke
out in Europe and the United States during the seventeenth, eighteenth, and
nineteenth centuries. Similar to what George Rude documented as the cause
of riots in France, the Brazilian authorities' inattention to demands from the
lower classes caused orderly petitions to escalate into riots and spread from
isolated neighborhoods to districts throughout the city. Usually Rio's demonstrations began as reasonable petitions to municipal and federal authorities for redress of grievances: an end to exorbitantly high food prices or
chronic shortages, a call for street lighting or improved sanitation, and, quite
often, demands for resolutions to the ever-present housing crisis. When rioting did break out, crowds stoned streetlights, burned construction sites,
and even tore up streetcar and railroad tracks, reminiscent of the "machine-
breaking sprees" Charles Tilly described in France.[7]

But different from the crowds of Europe or the United States, Brazilians
who took to the streets to protest unpopular taxes, price hikes, fare increases, economic and political regulations, and destruction of their housing
came up against companies owned by foreign monopolists, taxes imposed to

6. The work here is vast; therefore I refer to only a few of the main sources, including
Edward Thompson, *The Making of the English Working Class* (New York: Random House, 1966);
idem, "The Moral Economy of the English Crowd in the Eighteenth Century," *Past and Present*
50 (February 1971): 76–136; Herbert G. Gutman, *Work, Culture, and Society in Industrializing
America* (New York: Random House, 1977); George Rudé, *The Crowd in History, 1730–1848*
(New York: John Wiley & Sons, 1964), esp. chaps. 14 and 15; Eric Hobsbawm and George
Rudé, *Captain Swing* (New York: W. W. Norton, 1968); Charles Tilly, "The Changing Place of
Collective Violence," in *Workers in the Industrial Revolution,* ed. Peter N. Stearns and Daniel J.
Walkowitz (New Brunswick, N.J.: Transaction Books, 1974), 117–37; idem, *The Contentious
French* (Cambridge, Mass.: Harvard University Press, 1986); Charles Tilly and Louise A. Tilly,
eds., *Class Conflict and Collective Action* (Beverly Hills: Sage Publications, 1981).
7. Tilly, *The Contentious French.*

pay for loans from British banks, and urban renewal projects designed to make Rio look more like London and Paris. Thus, Brazil's dependence on foreign investment and export markets abroad for the vitality of its economy had a profound effect on the particular function of its capital city and on the nature of social protest that erupted in it. During the First Republic coffee planters of the center-south region enjoyed a close alliance with British capitalists, who in turn catered to the needs of the powerful rural oligarchs, miners, and planters, who supplied the coffee, minerals, sugar, hides, beef, rice, and other items for export overseas.[8] Furthermore, throughout the Old Republic, Brazil's urban elite failed to develop as an autonomous power. Urban manufacturers and commercial agents never forged a course at all antagonistic to the rural planters, as did their counterparts in Europe and the United States, nor did they oppose the domination of foreign capital.[9]

Politically, the work of managing the national government was an administrative task reliant on the economic power base among the planters and thus directly subservient to the export-oriented economy. Nine of the ten presidents who served during the Old Republic had direct planter backgrounds or were related by marriage to the oligarchy. Those politicians not related to the planters directly were chosen for political office because of their assurance that they would speak for the well-being of the planters. The result has been that Brazilian industrialization and commercial expansion have emerged alongside massive rural poverty, while agricultural labor relations have remained relatively untouched by the admittedly few democratic reforms affecting urban workers.[10]

This relationship between the city and country, as well as the particular political configuration it engendered, stretches back to the earliest days of Brazil's history as a plantation economy based on a slave labor force im-

8. Edgard Carone, *A República Velha: Evolução política* (São Paulo: DIFEL, 1964), 158–84; Florestan Fernandes, *A revolução burguesa no Brasil: Ensaio de interpretação sociologica* (Rio de Janeiro: Zahar Editores, 1976), chap. 3; Richard Graham, *Britain and the Onset of Modernization in Brazil, 1850–1914* (Cambridge: Cambridge University Press, 1968); Nelson Werneck Sodré, *História da burguesia brasileira* (Rio de Janeiro: Editora Civilização Brasileira, 1976), 210–43.

9. For a fuller discussion of the debates over the transition from feudalism to capitalism in Latin America, see Teresa Meade, "The Transition to Capitalism in Brazil: Notes on a Third Road," *Latin American Perspectives* 5 (Summer 1978): 7–26. The classic debate among Maurice Dobb, Paul Sweezy, and others is in *The Transition from Feudalism to Capitalism*, with an introduction by Rodney Hilton (London: NLB, 1976).

10. Boris Fausto, *Trabalho urbano e conflito social* (São Paulo: DIFEL, 1976), 59–61; Thomas E. Skidmore, "Workers and Soldiers: Urban Labor Movements and Elite Responses in Twentieth-Century Latin America," in *Elites, Masses, and Modernization in Latin America, 1850–1930*, ed. Virginia Bernhard (Austin: University of Texas Press, 1979), 80.

ported from Africa. So long as slavery prevailed (and it did for the first four centuries after European colonization), urban development was stymied, since the availability of the slave, even during the seasonal layoffs from agricultural labor, led the master to use him or her for the production of consumer goods, thereby curbing the demand for urban-produced manufactured goods.[11] In addition, as Mary Karasch shows in her careful analysis of Rio de Janeiro in the early nineteenth century, slaves successfully performed skilled and unskilled tasks and thereby met the limited demand for domestic manufactures in the city itself. The planters were content to import many luxury items from abroad, a practice they maintained after abolition.[12]

The abolition of slavery in 1888 therefore removed an important obstacle to urbanization, and the nation entered a new stage of economic and political relations. Both commercial and artisanal activity increased in the cities as freed agricultural laborers and European immigrants sought work, as well as bought and sold goods there. However, as several studies of urbanization have shown, Brazil's cities grew not so much because of any increase in commerce, manufacturing, and artisanry as because of the sheer number of rural laborers who migrated after abolition. Their livelihood on the countryside no longer ensured, former slaves were forced to migrate to urban areas to find work.[13] The pattern of migration from rural to urban areas in late-nineteenth-century Brazil was not unusual in Latin America during this period, nor has

11. Fernando Henrique Cardoso, "The City and Politics," in *Urbanization in Latin America*, ed. Jorge E. Hardoy (Garden City, N.Y.: Doubleday, 1975), 172–73.

12. Mary C. Karasch, *Slave Life in Rio de Janeiro, 1808–1850* (Princeton: Princeton University Press, 1987).

13. Douglas Butterworth and John K. Chance, *Latin American Urbanization* (New York: Cambridge University Press, 1981), and Martin T. Katzman, *Cities and Frontiers in Brazil: Regional Dimensions of Economic Development* (Cambridge, Mass.: Harvard University Press, 1977), provide good summaries of the urbanization process in Latin America and Brazil and discount the thesis that urbanization in underdeveloped countries is linked exclusively to industrial growth. Several essays in Hardoy's *Urbanization in Latin America* discuss the relation between urbanization and underdevelopment; see Jorge E. Hardoy, "Two Thousand Years of Latin American Urbanization," 3–55; Anibal Quijano, "The Urbanization of Latin American Society," 109–53; Victor L. Urquidi, "The Underdeveloped City," 339–66. For a discussion of city development that accounts for massive poverty among a migratory population, see Susan Eckstein, *The Poverty of Revolution: The State and the Urban Poor in Mexico* (Princeton: Princeton University Press, 1977); Richard M. Morse, "São Paulo: Case Study of a Latin American Metropolis," in *Latin American Urban Research*, vol. 1, ed. Francine F. Rabinowitz and Felicity M. Trueblood (Beverly Hills: Sage Publications, 1971), 151–86; Stanislaw Wellisz, "Economic Development and Urbanization," in *Urbanization and National Development*, vol. 1 (Beverly Hills: Sage Publications, 1971), 39–40. For a review of several studies on Latin American urban history, see John K. Chance, "Recent Trends in Latin American Urban Studies," *Latin American Research Review* 15, no. 1 (1980), 183–88.

it been since: people moved because the land could not feed them, only to end up in cities where prospects were often little better.

While the elite looked abroad for their economic well-being, so too they looked to Europe, mainly France and England, for cultural inspiration in everything from fashion to literature to architecture to the arts. The rest of Brazil's populace—the rural and urban working classes, the tiny petty bourgeoisie and the poor—saw little of the vast wealth from the coffee trade and made a living instead producing, buying, selling, and processing goods for the narrow domestic market. Nor did this majority of Brazilians wait expectantly for the latest fashion from Paris, strain to interpret the opera, or worry about the decidedly non-European facades on Rio's downtown buildings.

Third, these relations between town and country and between Brazil and the world economy affected the types of social conflicts that erupted, and provided a common thread uniting their seemingly disparate causes. For the most part, the urban popular classes—the working class, the poor, and the small middle class—opposed the plans of the domestic and international bourgeoisie, but were never powerful enough to wrest the government away from programs that met mainly the priorities of foreign investors and rural planters. Brazil's precarious economic structure, unstable manufacturing base, and, most of all, want of land reform, which forced thousands of rural laborers to migrate to the city and to compete for the few jobs there, undermined the development of a politically powerful urban labor movement.

In fact, during the Old Republic only a fraction of the working class was even employed on a relatively regular basis. In addition to the small number of reasonably steadily employed workers, Rio's workforce was by and large composed of many casually employed, or "marginalized," workers. This layer of workers, referred to in this study as the "laboring poor" or the "urban poor" for want of a more precise term, made a living in the interstices of the economy (casual workers) and in the informal sector as a part of the "underworld" (gamblers, prostitutes, beggars, and so forth). In other words, the proletariat in Rio shaded into what is sometimes called the *lumpenproletariat*, with no clear line perceptible between these sectors.[14] A worker in a textile mill might be laid off half of the year, during which time he or she

14. Lucio Kowarick, *Capitalismo e marginalidade na America Latina* (Rio de Janeiro: Editora Paz e Terra, 1975), 127–45; idem, "Capitalismo, dependencia e marginalidade urbana na America Latina: Uma contribuição teorica," *Estudos CEBRAP* 8 (April–June 1974), 77–96; Paulo Sérgio Pinheiro, "Classes medias urbanas: Formação, natureza, intervenção na vida política," in *História geral da civilização brasileira*, vol. 9, *O Brasil republicano: Sociedade e instituições, 1889–1930*, ed. Boris Fausto (São Paulo: Difusão Editorial, 1977), 23; Decio Saes, *Classe media e política na Primeira República brasileira, 1889–1930* (Petropolis: Vozes, 1975), 69.

worked as a day laborer, maid, street vendor, numbers runner, or prostitute. Enterprises were so small—in 1889 Rio registered about six hundred factories with only a half dozen employees in each—that layoffs, shutdowns, and slowdowns were more the norm than the exception, forcing large numbers of workers to make their livelihood in creative, new ways.[15] Studies have shown that many of the Carioca [16] lower class fluctuated back and forth across a fine line between legitimate, stable employment and the less respectable world of the street.[17] Just as workers moved from employed to unemployed, from respectable to marginal, the entrepreneurs moved from small owners to street peddlers to the "underworld" figures.

Moreover, a considerable portion of the workforce was casually employed, even in those enterprises located at the hub of the city's economic activity. Virtually all of the labor on the docks was casual, even seasonal, given the importance of coffee exports. This economic instability among all laboring people produced a particular political culture that united small shopkeepers with workers and even the urban poor against the city's elite.

Given the casual and marginal nature of employment in Rio, it is not surprising that it was contention over issues of consumption (fare hikes, food costs, housing problems), rather than point-of-production struggles (wages, working conditions, union recognition), that pushed people into marches and rallies. Manuel Castells's theories on urban development provide an essential framework for understanding this relationship. Just as Diane Davis found in her study of Mexico City, Castells's notion of collective consumption stands as a crucial theoretical concept around which to build a framework for understanding the urban domain in Latin America.[18] Because Rio's development more closely paralleled Mexico City's than that of the cities of Europe or the United States, which have been the object of study for many urban sociologists and historians, Davis's book provides a valuable theoretical and empirical point of comparison for an analysis of Rio de Janeiro. As she remarks, Castells claims that the "provision and administration of collec-

15. Directoria Geral de Estatística, *Recenseamento Geral da República dos Estados Unidos do Brazil en 31 de Dezembro de 1890, Districto Federal* (Rio de Janeiro: Imprensa Nacional, 1895), lxxi.

16. "Carioca," a term of Indian derivation, refers to people and things having to do with Rio de Janeiro.

17. Sandra Lauderdale Graham, *House and Street: The Domestic World of Servants and Masters in Nineteenth-Century Rio de Janeiro* (Cambridge: Cambridge University Press, 1988), chap. 5; June E. Hahner, *Emancipating the Female Sex: The Struggle for Women's Rights in Brazil, 1850–1940* (Durham, N.C.: Duke University Press, 1990), 94–96.

18. Diane E. Davis, *Urban Leviathan: Mexico City in the Twentieth Century* (Philadelphia: Temple University Press, 1994), esp. chap. 1.

tive consumption services, such as transport, housing, and other related infrastructure provided collectively to residents in large agglomerations, are the central axis around which the social and spatial development of cities occurs."[19] Similar to what Davis elucidated in her study of Mexico City, in Rio de Janeiro the size, nature, and boundaries of the city, "the urban domain," have been socially produced. Moreover, that social production has taken place within the struggle over collective consumption—over where and how well people live, eat, move about, and enjoy themselves in a city.

Manuel Castells's argument rests on a number of fundamentals. Primarily, Castells asserts that not only the economic and political characteristics of a city, but also its spatial form, are determined by its function. What cities look like—why their neighborhoods, business districts, slums, and suburbs grew where they did—depends in Castells's terms on whether the city serves primarily as a commercial or an industrial center and on how it functions in the broader world economy. Cities, "like all social reality, are historical products, not only in their physical materiality but in their cultural meaning, in the role they play in the social organization, and in peoples' lives."[20]

Analyzing the "product"—the urban structure and built environment—provides a basic understanding of how some cities develop quite differently from others. Why is it that so many cities in the developing world have evolved as massive metropoles with millions of poor people concentrated on the outskirts, in shantytowns that lack transportation, water, electricity, and health facilities, while the business district and homes of the wealthy cluster in the downtown or in enclaves close to good city services? Castells argues that this "allocation of urban space" has not been accidental. Rather, in most cities of what we call the "developing world," a separation of poverty from wealth and a concurrent isolation of the poor far from city services have been planned. Thus, in Rio, whereas wealth, education, certain cultural refinements, and access to power might have distinguished the rich from the poor, on a more fundamental level it was actually an individual's relationship to the system of imperialism that determined his or her place in the urban matrix. Rio de Janeiro was therefore more than simply a city reliant on foreign investment and markets for its survival or a city with many poor people crowded into substandard houses, forced into jobs that paid less than subsistence wages; rather, it was, and still is, a city in which the occupants have been driven to construct a space and organize a life as though temporary

19. Ibid., 15.
20. Manuel Castells, *The City and the Grassroots: A Cross-Cultural Theory of Urban Social Movements* (Berkeley and Los Angeles: University of California Press, 1983), 302.

builders of their master's estate.[21] In Rio the individual's place on the "estate" depended on his or her class and ability to wield economic and political power.

In addition, this study seeks to shed some light on the conditions under which collective violence erupts. What provokes urban riots? Are they more frequent in some societies than others? Under what conditions and for what reasons do some sectors of the popular classes take to the streets to air their grievances? On the surface, the riots in Brazil resembled in form, in composition of the crowds, and in the targets of the demonstrators the popular rebellions of Europe and the United States usually referred to as "preindustrial," "premodern," or "prepolitical" social movements.[22] Loosely defined, premodern protests are generally local in scope, motivated by a popular resistance to the demands of a central authority, and sometimes backward-looking. Associated with precapitalist stages of production, typical examples of premodern protests are food riots, tax rebellions, and machine-breaking sprees. Modern protest, on the other hand, is "highly organized, more regularly based on associations, more in pursuit or defense of a political program," and correspondent with later stages of capitalist production relations.[23] The most common example is the strike.

Whether these are appropriate terms for the protests in Rio (or even for those in Europe and the United States) is, however, debatable. Outbreaks of violence are so common throughout history, bear similarities over vastly different historical epochs, and even vary widely within the same time period, that attempts strictly to separate premodern bread riots, for example, from modern strikes have raised as many questions as they have resolved. In Rio de Janeiro food riots, tax rebellions, and street melees, commonly considered forms of premodern or preindustrial riot, did not diminish in the face of more orderly and modern strikes as capitalist relations expanded, nor have these forms of collective action receded from the political landscape today.[24] On the contrary, strikes and workplace violence accompanied the continually escalating popular protests against prices, shortages, taxes, and living

21. Ibid., 212.

22. Hobsbawm makes the point that the term "prepolitical" is problematic, as is all of the terminology applied to these social movements, since politics certainly existed before the industrial transformation; however, the "structure, organizations, scope, objectives and perhaps above all the language of politics changed fundamentally during this transformation." Eric Hobsbawm, "Pre-political Movements in Peripheral Areas" (paper presented at the Conferencia sobre História e Ciencias Sociais, Campinas, Brazil, May 26–30, 1975), 2.

23. Tilly, "The Changing Place of Collective Violence," 133.

24. José Alvaro Moisés and Verena Martinez-Alier Stolcke, "Urban Transport and Popular Violence: The Case of Brazil," *Past and Present* 86 (February 1980): 174–92.

conditions, especially in poorer communities during the Old Republic, and, I would argue, they have since become permanent features of popular resistance. If anything, the community-based urban protest movement underpinned and bolstered the fragile trade union movement and replaced it as the preferred form of discourse on more than one occasion.

This distinction, between premodern and modern forms of protest, needs to be abandoned, certainly to understand collective protest in Rio de Janeiro. Furthermore, the existence of distinctly different forms, or types, of protest is dubious in any society. Certainly in the wake of outbreaks of violence in major North and South American cities in the 1960s and more recently in Los Angeles in 1992, one would be hard-pressed to argue that crowds gathering in front of stores and appropriating the goods for themselves are operating in any way fundamentally different from that of bread rioters in eighteenth-century France or protesters in Rio de Janeiro at the turn of the century. Moreover, every form of social protest draws on the experiences, the grievances, the resolutions and failed resolutions of the hundreds of protests that have come before. As Eric Hobsbawm explains, "[S]ignificant 'prepolitical' movements of the present are fusions of the old and new, so are all 'modern' movements, particularly in the peripheral countries."[25] According to Ira Katznelson, urban community protest has been the "major characteristic of political life" in most parts of the West in recent decades. These protests, centered at the place of residence, not at work, have concerned "the delivery of collective services by government and the impact of housing, transport, and social services on the built form of the city and on the quality of life."[26]

If ideologically every form of protest fuses the old and the new, then the single distinction between them rests with the "mechanisms" or the organization of the crowd—the strike and trade union versus the spontaneous street riot. Hobsbawm suggests "it is the discovery that modern organization is better suited to the struggle in a modern society, rather than the discovery of modern ideology," that accounts for the decline of premodern protest in the modern world.[27] Since in even the most advanced capitalist societies there exist pockets where these modern "mechanisms" have never taken root (south-central Los Angeles, for example), classic premodern riots have broken out precisely because there were few other ways of eliciting the response of the political establishment.

25. Hobsbawm, "Pre-political Movements in Peripheral Areas," 8.
26. Ira Katznelson, *City Trenches: Urban Politics and the Patterning of Class in the United States* (Chicago: University of Chicago Press, 1981), 210.
27. Hobsbawm, "Pre-political Movements in Peripheral Areas," 23.

Rio de Janeiro, on the other hand, poses the question of social protest even more acutely. What happens in Rio, or any similar society, where the "mechanisms" of modern resistance (trade unions and electoral politics) remain fragile and undeveloped long after capitalist reorganization of economic relations has triumphed? In Rio during the First Republic and for decades to come, there were few avenues through which the masses could exert political and economic influence. Not only were trade unions loosely organized in the first decades of the century, but the majority of casual workers and urban poor did not hold jobs long enough to consider the option of joining a union even if one existed. Rather than a few enclaves where the conditions of poverty and social alienation predominated, most of Rio de Janeiro was so poor, its growing population so crowded, and the "mechanisms" for redressing grievances so undeveloped that it was in near constant ferment.

In addition, as Michel Foucault has shown in his studies of sickness and health, civilization and madness, sanity and insanity, the realm of social policy has been integrally bound up with multiple institutions in a society.[28] No exception to the rule, the Brazilian Republican elite drew heavily on European notions of civilization, particularly science, to discredit the opposition to their plans for the city's future. Rio's city officials, the engineers and urban planners, never spoke of designing a city to serve exclusively the interests of foreign capitalists, investors, or tourists, nor is it clear that that was their conscious intent. No, in the case of Rio, as with similar projects in other parts of the world in the late nineteenth and early twentieth centuries, the urban renewal and public health plan and the subsequent transportation, communication, and distribution networks that connected the city were justified by a selective use of scientific law as a guide to sanitation and public health. This view of European science was contingent on the lofty assessment of Europe's culture, its society, its cities, the race and culture of its people, all of which the Brazilian elite slavishly emulated. As a result, any opposition to the government's plan to renovate and sanitize Rio de Janeiro in the early years of this century, and complaints against the gross inequalities in living standards and social services that persisted throughout the Old Republic, were dismissed as uncultured, unscientific, superstitious, and, most of all, uncivilized.

From 1890 through the 1920s the thousands of mostly poor occupants were in dispute with the better-off domestic and foreign elite over just how the city should grow, the location of poor and wealthy neighborhoods, and

28. Michel Foucault, *The Birth of the Clinic: An Archeology of Medical Perception*, trans. A. M. Sheridan Smith (New York: Vintage Books, 1975).

the standard of living people could achieve. Visible in Rio's history, therefore, was a connection between the seemingly static notion of allocating space and the dynamic concept of societal conflict, or, said another way, a relationship between the way Rio de Janeiro was transformed and the role (or lack thereof) of the people in producing those structural transformations.[29] Castells's analysis of the relationship between the struggle over collective consumption and the resultant allocation of space serves as the key ingredient for understanding Rio de Janeiro as an urban realm. There was, and is, a tangible, visible outcome to the conflict between classes and groups in a society, as apparent and knowable as the redefined borders and redistributed spoils after a war between nations. The victors in the city struggle "won" access to the essentials of urban life, housing, transport, lighting, water, health, and safety, as well as to such amenities as parks, entertainment, aesthetics, and comfort.

As an analysis of the connection between the place of Rio de Janeiro within the world system and the role of imperialism in shaping the class struggle, a relationship Charles Bergquist calls a "creative fusion" between local history and global structure, this book draws on existing studies of Rio's development. I hope that it complements those works, which have explained the ideologies of the elite, the lives of the urban poor, the tension between the role of domestic servants and the wider city economy, the conflict between whites and people of color, the emergence of Rio's working class and factory system, the transformation of the city during the First Republic, and the importance of science in justifying the social changes of the late nineteenth and early twentieth centuries.[30] While indebted to those works, this book, none-

29. Manuel Castells, *The Urban Question: A Marxist Approach*, trans. Alan Sheridan (Cambridge, Mass.: MIT Press, 1977), 13–23.

30. Charles Bergquist, *Labor in Latin America: Comparative Essays on Chile, Argentina, Venezuela, and Colombia* (Stanford: Stanford University Press, 1986), 384. For Rio in the nineteenth century, see S. L. Graham, *House and Street,* and Thomas Holloway, *Policing Rio de Janeiro: Repression and Resistance in a Nineteenth-Century City* (Stanford: Stanford University Press, 1993); for Rio in the Old Republic, see Jeffrey D. Needell, *A Tropical Belle Epoque: Elite Culture and Society in Turn-of-the-Century Rio de Janeiro* (Cambridge: Cambridge University Press, 1987); June E. Hahner, *Poverty and Politics: The Urban Poor in Brazil, 1870–1920* (Albuquerque: University of New Mexico Press, 1986); Sam Adamo, "The Broken Promise: Race, Health, and Justice in Rio de Janeiro, 1890–1940" (Ph.D. diss., University of New Mexico, 1983); Eileen Keremitsis, "The Early Industrial Worker in Rio de Janeiro, 1870–1930" (Ph.D. diss., Columbia University, 1982); Jaime Larry Benchimol, "Pereira Passos, um Haussmann tropical: As transformações urbanas na cidade do Rio de Janeiro no inicio do seculo XX" (master's thesis, Universidade Federal do Rio de Janeiro, 1982); Nancy Stepan, *Beginnings of Brazilian Science: Oswaldo Cruz, Medical Research and Policy, 1890–1920* (New York: Science History Publications, 1976); Nancy Leys Stepan, *"The Hour of Eugenics": Race, Gender, and Nation in Latin America* (Ithaca: Cornell University Press, 1991).

theless, approaches the history of Rio de Janeiro from a slightly different
angle in hopes of expanding yet further our understanding of both Rio and
of the people who inhabit it. My intent is to sketch the intersection where,
during the First Republic, the demands of the working people of Rio de Janeiro for a decent living and a reasonable share in the city's prosperity col-
lided with the priorities Rio's elite had set for their capital.[31]

31. Labor history has emerged as an increasingly important field of Latin American historiography. For a summary of some of the important contributions to the field, see the excellent
bibliographies edited by John D. French—*Latin American Labor Studies: An Interim Bibliography of Non-English Publications* and *Latin American Labor Studies: A Bibliography of English
Publications Through 1989* (Miami: Center of Labor Research and Studies, Florida International
University, 1989)—as well as the updates French and Guillermo J. Grenier publish in *Latin
American Labor News,* from the Center of Labor Research and Studies.

1

Civilization

To speak of a policed country is the same thing as to speak of
a civilized country.
                    —*O Paiz,* editorial, August 16, 1895

Rio de Janeiro's reputation as one of the world's most stunning cities has
been with it since its founding as a European settlement. Crowded between
the Atlantic Ocean on one side and Guanabara Bay on the other, the city was
at once an ideal port with a well-protected harbor and a tropical paradise of
amazing geographic beauty. Its streets meandered in and out among clusters
of high barren rocks, or *morros*, and at the base of mountains covered with
tropical vegetation. In 1567 the Portuguese entered the bay at its mouth,
between what is today Niterói on the east and Botafogo on the west. Think-
ing they had discovered the mouth to a gigantic river, they named the site
Rio de Janeiro (January River) to mark the month of their conquest. Later
exploration showed that it was not a river at all but a very wide bay, which
subsequently proved to be an ideal harbor. According to some accounts, the
Portuguese Crown reclaimed the site from a band of French Huguenots who
established a trading post there in the early sixteenth century and lived
peaceably with a scattering of Portuguese settlers. Alarmed at the prospect

of French Protestants influencing Portuguese Catholics or, worse, living together cooperatively, as well as impelled to assert Portuguese authority over
potential French claims to the region, the Crown ordered the expulsion of
the Huguenots.[1]

The city grew up along the bay side, and the first narrow streets wound up
from the dock. Along with small shops that sold basic foodstuffs, clothing,
and household wares, commercial establishments lined Rio's crowded arteries. During the eighteenth-century diamond and gold rush and consequent
precious-metal trade, Rio bypassed the northern cities of Recife in Pernambuco and Salvador da Bahia as the most important commercial and financial
center of the country. It was the colonial capital in 1763; in 1808 it became
the site of the Portuguese Court, and in 1822 the capital of the Brazilian Empire. Notably, the momentous events of the late nineteenth century—the
abolition of slavery in 1888, the fall of the Empire, and declaration of the
Republic in 1889—furthered Rio's preeminence as Brazil's most important
city. While the São Paulo coffee planters exerted the major share of the country's economic power, Rio was the main port through which goods entered
and left Brazil in the 1890s, was the setting for some of the earliest industrial
activity, especially in textiles, and was the seat of the government.

Since it was the centerpiece of Brazil's political transformation, the Republic's leaders hoped the city would one day serve as a kind of testimony to the
new nation's transition from a backward monarchy, and an economy based
on slave labor, to a modern, or, as they stated it, "civilized," republic based
on free and, they hoped, immigrant labor. The ruling elite embraced the
notion of "civilization," a term that increasingly punctuated government reports and news articles throughout the nineties and stood as the symbol of
the cultural and economic aspirations for Brazil as a whole. This civilizing
zeal derived as much from a desire on the part of the Republican elite to live
down the stigma of backwardness associated with slavery and the monarchy
as from hopes for building Brazil's commercial and political future.[2]

1. C. J. Dunlop, *Chrônicas, fatos, gente e coisas da nossa história* (Rio de Janeiro: Companhia
Editora Americana, 1972), 39–42; Fernando Nascimento Silva, ed., *Rio de Janeiro em seus quatrocentos anos: Formação e desenvolvimento da cidade* (Rio de Janeiro: Distribuidora Record,
1965).

2. Junta Commercial da Capital Federal, *Relatório apresentado ao Vice-Presidente da República pelo Dr. Fernando Lobo Leite Pereira, Ministro dos Negocios Interiores* (Rio de Janeiro: Imprensa Nacional, 1892), 34–47; Junta Commercial, *Relatório apresentado ao Presidente da República pelo Dr. Antonio Gonçalves Ferreira, Ministro dos Negocios Interiores* (Rio de Janeiro:
Imprensa Nacional, 1895), 68–75; Eulalia Maria Lahmeyer Lobo, *História do Rio de Janeiro: Do
capital commercial ao capital industrial e financeiro* (Rio de Janeiro: Instituto Brasileiro de Mercado de Capitais, 1978), 1:469.

Nevertheless, among the elite there was unanimity neither on the civilizing goal nor on the means to achieve it, just as there was no agreed-upon definition of civilization or view of what it would mean for Brazil. Thus, during the Old Republic, civilization was something of a slogan that never achieved any accepted status or standard among the country's political elite.[3] In addition, the entire issue of civilization in its various contours split rural areas from urban centers. Whereas many rural planters wholeheartedly embraced a modern economic system that granted them healthy profits from their coffee exports, they clung to the traditional cultural values of the slavocracy. After abolition former slaves remained tied to the land, working as debt peons or sharecroppers on the properties of their previous owners. Decades after the May 13, 1888, decree that freed them, many former slaves remained at work on plantations, in debt, unable to leave, and with no possibility of ever owning land or rising above their miserable conditions. The words of an old man on a cacao plantation in Jorge Amado's novel *The Violent Land* capture the predicament of the rural laborer better than most history books: "'I was a lad in the days of slavery,' the old man said as he rose. 'My father was a slave, my mother also. But it wasn't any worse then than it is today. Things don't change; it's all talk.'"[4]

While the power of the *patrão* and all forms of patriarchal authority were felt as strongly in most of Brazil's rural areas as during the era of slavery, the urban bourgeoisie increasingly espoused the cultural standards of the European powers to which all of Brazil was inextricably bound in the import/export trade. But the latter's aspirations for civilization usually stopped short of instituting real material improvements in the lives of the working class and poor. They copied European fashions, adopted the standards of high culture, and focused their attentions on what could be done to make Brazil's cities, especially the capital, look more like the great cities of Europe.

Although there was a deep division between city and country, it was prob-

3. Edgard Carone, *A República Velha: Evolução política* (São Paulo: DIFEL, 1964), 7–132; Fernando Henrique Cardoso, "Dos Governos Militares a Prudente—Campos Sales," in *História geral da civilização brasileira*, vol. 8, *O Brasil republicano: Estrutura de poder e economia*, ed. Boris Fausto (São Paulo: Difusão Editorial, 1975), 15–50. To the Republican liberals "civilization" referred to white European culture as distinguished from the culture that had developed in Brazil, combining African and Brazilian influences. My use of this term does not imply any agreement with its racial implications; I use the terminology of the Brazilian elites to show the extent to which they adopted the views of the European powers. See Nancy Stepan, *Beginnings of Brazilian Science: Oswaldo Cruz, Medical Research and Policy, 1890–1920* (New York: Science History Publications, 1976), 57.

4. Jorge Amado, *The Violent Land*, trans. Samuel Putnam (New York: Alfred A. Knopf, 1945), 85.

ably more cultural than economic or political, at least on the level of the ruling elite. Certainly the latest fashion in ideas and couture took longer to penetrate the countryside than to spread through the parlors and cafés of Rio de Janeiro or São Paulo. On the other hand, the wealthy planters had their connections to life in the city, usually spent much of the year in their urban residences, and were well apprised of the major political and social controversies shaking Europe. At the other end of the class spectrum, although the working poor of Rio may have been marginally more exposed to imports from abroad than their rural counterparts, whose lives were the most isolated of the Republic, rank-and-file urban workers were hardly concerned with the latest fad or developments in Europe. In sum, modernizing and beautifying Rio de Janeiro, a key plank in the Republican civilization agenda, was not part of a national plan to change the prevailing repressive economic and political relationships of either the countryside or the city. Rather, the changes in the port actually consolidated the role of the planters as the suppliers of raw materials, especially coffee, shipped from Brazil. What on the surface may seem ironic was more often the norm: the agricultural countryside, complete with its paternalistic authority over the rural laborers and its power relations little changed from the days of slavery, produced the valuable export commodities that fueled the transformation of the urban centers. Thus, the rise of Rio de Janeiro and São Paulo as cosmopolitan centers was based on the produce of the coffee groves of the surrounding states, just as New York City's growth in the antebellum period, for example, stemmed from the cotton and tobacco production of Alabama and Virginia.

Whereas the culture of the countryside seemed to diverge sharply from that of the city, the economies of the two regions were bound together closely. The glue holding them was their common dependence on the export market and their mutual reliance on the exigencies of their international trading partners. Brazil in the nineteenth century fit into the expanding "single global economy," which, as Eric Hobsbawm explains, was "progressively reaching into the most remote corners of the world" and there creating "an increasingly dense web of economic transactions, communications and movements of goods, money and people linking the developed countries with each other and with the developing world."[5] As the web grew denser, Brazil's dependence on trade and investment, especially with Great Britain, intertwined the class interests of its own ruling circles with those of the English elite. For example, because coffee planters of the center-south region

5. Eric Hobsbawm, *The Age of Empire, 1875–1914* (New York: Pantheon Books, 1987), 62.

based their livelihood on the coffee export market, the planters (and the coffee interests in general) strongly influenced Brazil's domestic urban environment, calling for measures to expand and improve the docks, transportation, and communication lines. Conversely, British capitalists and merchants maintained cordial relations with the planters because the latter furnished the raw materials and agricultural goods that passed through their hands and into Britain's vast imperial network.

Reliance on foreign investors and trading partners had been a common feature of Brazil's development from the earliest years of the colony, and it continued during the nineteenth-century Empire and into the Old Republic. Portuguese colonial merchants from the metropolis, as well as British agents, actively participated in and controlled much of Rio's trade with Europe either through their own import/export houses, the financial network, or direct ownership of the shipping lines. Through the Treaty of Methuen in 1703 Portugal had granted Great Britain a favored position in trade with Portuguese colonies in exchange for Britain's protection of Portugal's shipping lines and the assurance that Britain would buy certain goods from Portuguese colonies. This agreement on the level of empires was then transported to Brazil when Napoléon invaded Portugal and the British fleet in 1808 ushered the Court safely into exile in Brazil.[6] Under the Empire, Portuguese and British merchants obtained a preeminent position in Rio de Janeiro's developing commercial houses. Eugene Ridings notes that Portuguese merchants dominated the trade in sugar, rum, coffee, dress goods, ironware, and wine from 1871 to 1872. After 1831, when Dom Pedro I returned to Portugal, leaving the Empire in the hands of his son, Brazilian nationals achieved some parity in the coffee trade, but the Portuguese still dominated the other fields and continued to control them until the end of the Empire. Whereas the Brazilian nationals hated the Portuguese for their arrogance, they eyed jealously

6. Richard Graham, *Britain and the Onset of Modernization in Brazil, 1850–1914* (Cambridge: Cambridge University Press, 1968), 82. Alan K. Manchester documents the development of the close alliance between Brazil and Great Britain, originating with the seventeenth-century commercial agreements between Great Britain and Portugal, in *British Pre-eminence in Brazil, Its Rise and Decline: A Study in European Expansion* (Chapel Hill: University of North Carolina Press, 1933). See also D.C.M. Platt, *Latin American and British Trade, 1806–1914* (New York: Harper & Row, 1973); Stanley J. Stein and Barbara H. Stein, *The Colonial Heritage of Latin America: Essays on Economic Dependence in Perspective* (New York: Oxford University Press, 1970). For a debate on Britain's role and the role of foreign investment in Latin American development, see D.C.M. Platt, "Dependency in Nineteenth-Century Latin America: A Historian Objects," *Latin American Research Review* 15, no. 1 (1980): 113–30; idem, "The Anatomy of 'Autonomy' (Whatever That May Mean): A Reply," ibid., 147–49; Stanley J. Stein and Barbara H. Stein, "D.C.M. Platt: The Anatomy of 'Autonomy,'" ibid., 131–46.

the advantages the British granted to Portuguese merchants in international and domestic commercial relations.[7]

By the end of the century Great Britain had begun to furnish the largest share of dress goods to the Brazilian market while also assuming a preeminent position in transforming agricultural goods for sale on the international market.[8] Eulalia Maria Lahmeyer Lobo argues that the brief emergence in 1808 of a traditional commercial bourgeoisie, representing Brazil's domestic trading interests, was derailed later in the century during the push to develop transportation and public works that were financed and overseen by the British. Britain's resultant monopoly over key financial and technical aspects of Brazilian growth effectively undermined the latter's autonomous commercial and financial firms. According to Bill Albert, at the turn of the century foreign merchants, mainly British, controlled about 60 percent of the coffee sales abroad. The foreign merchant, operating through a few dozen tightly controlled firms, assumed a powerful position linking the rural planters, who supplied the country's chief exports, with the world of trade abroad. Albert explains that the foreign entrepreneur's "international market contacts, control of credit, and, in the case of coffee, his increasing interest in processing and warehousing" made for an uncontested authority over Brazil's import/export market.[9]

Brazil's economic dependence on both the export market and foreign investors strongly influenced internal class divisions. In the first place, foreign investment allowed for an extremely stable financial return and likewise freed the planters from the risks associated with venture capital investment in the early stages of capitalist growth. In short, Brazilian planters as well as urban entrepreneurs could get very rich very fast by tying themselves firmly to the coattails of powerful British trading houses, investors, and middlemen. Moreover, the national bourgeoisie's struggle during the second half of the nineteenth century to assert its autonomy and stand free from foreign capital later collapsed under the dominance of a new *comprador bourgeoisie*, a class whose emergence was not based on its own capital accumulation but on its function as an intermediary of foreign capital. By the century's end merchant's capital, which is key to accumulation in the early stages of capitalist

7. Eugene W. Ridings, "Business, Nationality, and Dependency in Late-Nineteenth-Century Brazil," *Journal of Latin American Studies* 14, no. 1 (1982): 55–96.

8. Sidney Sérgio F. Solis and Marcus Venício T. Ribeiro, "O Rio onde o sol não brilha: Acumulação e pobreza na transição para o capitalismo," *Revista Rio de Janeiro* 1, no. 1 (1985): 45–59.

9. Lobo, *História do Rio de Janeiro*, 2: 463–510; Bill Albert, *South America and the First World War: The Impact of the War on Brazil, Argentina, Peru, and Chile* (Cambridge: Cambridge University Press, 1988), 21.

market formation, was, in Brazil, functioning as industrial capital. The end result was that Brazil followed a "third road," or variation, on the primitive accumulation process, in which domestic capital accumulated in the coffee trade fused with merchant's capital controlled largely by foreigners.[10]

This heavy reliance on foreign capital for investment did not come without cultural baggage. Albert notes that "the process of external economic subjugation encouraged by the elites was necessarily accompanied and underpinned by the acceptance and promulgation of foreign cultural and intellectual values."[11] However, cultural values did not necessarily follow economic dependence, since it was to France, not to England or Portugal, that the elite looked for inspiration in matters of style and culture. In one of those many ironies in which history abounds, French fashion and culture, despite the Napoleonic invasion of Portugal, continued to enjoy a wide acceptance among the expatriate Portuguese courtiers, a trend that then spilled over to form a major influence on the colonial elite in general. Finding Brazil a physically stunning but nonetheless culturally dreary colonial backwater, Prince Regent João VI set about improving the capital's aesthetic by importing French artists, teachers, artisans, and engineers to build and design botanical gardens, a national library, secondary and professional schools, and to promote the arts, literature, and science according to the French standard. The Crown, and in turn the entire elite class, in the nineteenth century never let their political disagreements with France interfere with their general admiration for nearly every aspect of French high culture.

The Franco-British mania that gripped the elite strata of Brazilian society in the nineteenth century reached its pinnacle during the Old Republic. As Jeffrey Needell's study of belle epoque Rio de Janeiro shows, French culture permeated the schools, theater, and entertainment, the salons, clubs, and cafés of elite society: "For nineteenth-century Brazilians, Civilization was France and England."[12] Wealthy Brazilians copied French culture and fashions and displayed a preference for English business relations. For many, the

10. Albert, *South America and the First World War,* 7–8; Teresa Meade, "The Transition to Capitalism in Brazil: Notes on a Third Road," *Latin American Perspectives* 5 (Summer 1978): 22–24.

11. Albert, *South America and the First World War,* 8.

12. Jeffrey D. Needell, *A Tropical Belle Epoque: Elite Culture and Society in Turn-of-the-Century Rio de Janeiro* (Cambridge: Cambridge University Press, 1987), 28. David Cannadine explains that London's appeal was as a bustling, crowded, commercial city, largely a monument to *private* enterprise, while Paris was a monumental tribute to *state* planning and order. David Cannadine, "The Context, Performance, and Meaning of Ritual: The British Monarchy and the 'Invention of Tradition,' c. 1820–1977," in *The Invention of Tradition,* ed. Eric Hobsbawm and Terence Ranger (Cambridge: Cambridge University Press, 1983), 101–64.

line that separated the civilized from the barbarous was the line that separated the goods and ideas produced in Europe from those indigenous to
Brazil.

But another, far deeper and more profound separation loomed on the Brazilian horizon, bifurcating the nation itself and threatening to derail the civilizing goals the elite crafted in the salons of Rio de Janeiro and other cities.
A vast cultural chasm divided the city from the countryside. The elite constituted a tiny minority of the population, was concentrated in a few cities hud-
dled along the coast, and was hardly significant as the cultural arbiter of life
for the masses of the interior. In addition, several military revolts and widespread social strife in the southern state of Rio Grande do Sul repeatedly
threatened the Republic's ideological hegemony. The price of maintaining
control over distant provinces sorely taxed the new government economically and stretched its military forces, but more important, the uprisings
threatened the legitimacy of the Republic and, in turn, the very concept of
civilization the Republicans were promoting. Nowhere was this more apparent than in the agricultural, poor, and backward Northeast, for it was there
that the major rejection of Republican authority developed. In Ceará, Padre
Cícero Romão Batista, a priest known for his exceptional piety, began a campaign in 1889 to have a local holy woman, Maria de Araujo, declared the
recipient of a miracle because the Eucharist had turned to blood in her
mouth moments after the priest administered her communion. Fueled by
the backlanders' resentment of new taxes, as well as by their suspicion of the
governmental and ecclesiastical central authority, the "miracle" assumed a
political importance in Brazilian life beyond its religious roots. With the politically ambitious and astute Padre Cícero at its helm, the campaign grew
beyond a religious movement to have Maria de Araujo canonized, mushrooming into a full-scale challenge to central authority that haunted the local
and national governments for years to come.[13]

13. Carone, in *Evolução política*, 80–132, describes the political instability of the Old Republic
and the impact of the civil war and strife in the Northeast on undermining the central government. Padre Cícero's campaign is examined by Ralph Della Cava, *Miracle at Joaseiro* (New York:
Columbia University Press, 1970). For a discussion of rural movements during the First Republic, of which Canudos is the most famous, see Duglas Teixeira Monteiro, "Um confronto entre
Juazeiro, Canudos e Contestado," in *História geral da civilização brasileira*, vol. 9, *O Brasil republicano: Sociedade e instituições, 1889–1930,* ed. Boris Fausto (São Paulo: Difusão Editorial,
1977), 39–92. On the background to the Contestado and disturbances in the South at the turn
of the century, see Todd A. Diacon, "Peasants, Prophets, and the Power of a Millenarian Vision
in Twentieth-Century Brazil," *Comparative Studies in Society and History* 32, no. 3 (1990): 488–
514, and idem, *Millenarian Vision, Capitalist Reality: Brazil's Contestado Rebellion, 1912–1916*
(Durham, N.C.: Duke University Press, 1991), chap. 1.

The most significant outbreak of the era, and the most direct assault on the Republic and its civilized image, was the Canudos rebellion in 1897. Antonio Conselheiro (the "counselor"), an intensely religious backlands prophet, and several thousand devoted followers held out in the interior of Bahia against a half dozen regiments of the federal army.[14] Often referred to as one of Latin America's most important millenarian movements, the Canudos uprising was also politically motivated. Conselheiro and his followers angered both local and regional officials for a number of reasons, mostly centering on their refusal to pay new municipal taxes and their rejection of the local landowners' authority. Moreover, the *sertanejos* (backlanders) expressed pro-monarchist sympathies that horrified the Republic's supporters in Recife, Rio de Janeiro, and São Paulo. In a widely publicized incident, Conselheiro, rebuffing an emissary from the Catholic Church sent to convince him to submit to proper political and ecclesiastical powers, explained: "In the days of the monarchy, I let myself be taken, for I recognized the government; but today I will not, because I do not recognize the Republic." Nevertheless, Euclides da Cunha argues that Conselheiro never displayed "the faintest trace of a political intuition; for your *jagunço* is quite as inapt at understanding the republican form of government as he is the constitutional monarchy. Both to him are abstractions, beyond the reach of his intelligence."[15]

To da Cunha, whose brilliant account, *Rebellion in the Backlands,* is still the main primary source on the revolt, Canudos exemplified the contradictory strains within a society torn between its quest for modernity and civilization, on the one hand, and the barbarity that gripped the countryside, on the other. Sent as a journalist from a São Paulo newspaper to cover the army's expeditions against the backlanders, da Cunha for the first time traveled to the interior and there observed a people whose customs, language, and appearance were totally different from those on or near the coast. He likened them to a distant, earlier stage in the evolution of humankind: "What we had to face here was the unlooked-for resurrection, under arms, of an old society, a dead society, galvanized into life by a madman."[16] Although da Cunha claimed that the people of the interior lived in a civilization different from that of the coastal cities, he was not entirely disparaging of their life,

14. Robert M. Levine, *Vale of Tears: Revisiting the Canudos Massacre in Northeastern Brazil, 1893–1897* (Berkeley and Los Angeles: University of California Press, 1992); idem, "'Mud-Hut Jerusalem': Canudos Revisited," *Hispanic American Historical Review* 68, no. 3 (1988): 525–72.

15. Euclides da Cunha, *Rebellion in the Backlands*, trans. Samuel Putnam (Chicago: University of Chicago Press, 1944), 167, 160.

16. Ibid., 161.

observing that the peasants' humility, oneness with nature, and primitive customs represented the "bedrock of our race."[17]

Moreover, da Cunha's adventure in the interior led him to criticize the nation's urban, coastal society he had long taken for granted. Referring to Brazilians' penchant for aping everything European, he surmised that they had all been "deluded by a civilization which came to us second hand," turning the urban elite, himself included, into "blind copyists," adopting a mode of life completely detached from "our rude native sons, who were more alien to us in this land of ours than were the immigrants who came from Europe."[18] Finally, he even cast doubt on the civilization of the conquerors, a people who after brutally defeating the *sertanejos* exhumed the body of Antonio Conselheiro and in a particularly grotesque act of vengeance decapitated the corpse. "That horrible face, sticky with scars and pus, once more appeared before the victors' gaze. After that they took it to the seaboard, where it was greeted by delirious multitudes with carnival joy."[19] Whether this view of the barbarity of the victorious army shook da Cunha's confidence in the accepted premises of civilization is unclear. He did emerge from the experience convinced that coastal Brazil, in its mad dash toward modernity, had left behind in the "centuries-old semidarkness" of the interior "a third of our people."[20]

Euclides da Cunha stands somewhat apart from the other civilization-conscious elite of the era in that he attempted to understand the complexities of Brazil's reality, even if his observations were marred by the "scientific" racism common to his class. Most of the Brazilian elite viewed the inhabitants of the agricultural interior more one-dimensionally: as a barbarous drag on the rest of the country. They pointed to the backlanders' superstition, ignorance, poverty, and absence of cultural and political sophistication as indicative of the problems Brazil had to overcome in order to take its place among the civilized nations of the world. Outraged at the reports of the monarchist sentiments of Conselheiro and his supporters, the Republic's adherents in Rio de Janeiro watched with horror their government's inability to quash the Canudos rebellion, while at the same time they protested the high taxes levied to support the futile expeditions. When news of the failure of the third assault against Canudos reached the capital, "Jacobin" crowds, includ-

---

17. E. Bradford Burns, "Cultures in Conflict: The Implication of Modernization in Nineteenth-Century Latin America," in *Elites, Masses, and Modernization in Latin America, 1850–1930*, ed. Virginia Bernhard (Austin: University of Texas Press, 1979), 11–77.

18. Da Cunha, *Rebellion in the Backlands*, 161.

19. Ibid., 476.

20. Ibid., 161.

ing printers, shopkeepers, and other "persons of property," marched on the seat of government at Catete Palace, attacked monarchist meeting halls enroute, and stoned the offices of pro-monarchist newspapers.[21]

Along with their counterparts in Argentina, Mexico, and other parts of Latin America, Brazil's elite was in the late nineteenth century immersed in a rather brutal self-appraisal and comparison with the civilized European and North American societies.[22] In the mid–nineteenth century the Argentine writer Domingo Faustino Sarmiento, in *Life in the Argentine Republic in the Days of the Tyrants; or, Civilization and Barbarism,* had sought to argue that the prosperous, progressive European civilization thrived in the city, while the backward, primitive agricultural society enveloped the distant provinces. The task of the civilizers was to defeat the values of the reactionary rural society lest they drag down the culture as a whole. Accordingly, he depicted rural society as a place where "dirty ragged children live, with a menagerie of dogs; there, men lie about in utter idleness; neglect and poverty prevail everywhere; a table and some baskets are the only furniture of wretched huts remarkable for their general aspect of barbarism and carelessness." In contrast, "all civilization, whether native, Spanish, or European, centres in the cities, where are to be found the manufactories, the shops, the schools and colleges, and other characteristics of civilized nations."[23]

Ostensibly Sarmiento was writing of the life of Juan Facundo Quiroga, archetypal of the brutal caudillos who ruled the interior of Argentina during the reign of Juan Manual Rosas; but his actual purpose was to contrast the struggle between civilization and barbarism, as the book's subtitle states. Moreover, his judgment was bold and unapologetic, displaying none of da Cunha's ambivalence: city people wear "the European dress, live in a civilized manner, and possess laws, ideas of progress, means of instruction, some municipal organization, regular forms of government, etc."; whereas in the country "people wear a different dress, which I will call *South American*, as

21. *O Paiz*, March 13, 1897. The report in *O Paiz* used the term "Jacobin," without any explanation how this term was interpreted, nor was there any indication that it referred to members of the Jacobin Club of Rio de Janeiro. This club strongly supported Floriano Peixoto's presidency and opposed foreign interests in Brazil, especially the Portuguese business community; see Thomas Skidmore's *Black into White: Race and Nationality in Brazilian Thought* (Durham, N.C.: Duke University Press, 1993), 79–87. Quite possibly, formal "Jacobins" were involved in the demonstration, but most likely those who participated were middle-class, antimonarchist residents.

22. Skidmore, *Black into White*, esp. chaps. 3 and 4, and Burns, "Cultures in Conflict," 11–29.

23. Domingo Faustino Sarmiento, *Life in the Argentine Republic in the Days of the Tyrants; or, Civilization and Barbarism,* trans. from the Spanish (New York: Hafner Publishing Co., 1868), 11, 13.

it is common to all districts; their habits of life are different, their wants peculiar and limited." That Sarmiento is speaking not simply of Argentina but of all of Latin America is likewise apparent in his contrast of political parties in the city and the provinces: "[O]ne of these powers was civilized, constitutional, *European*; the other barbarous, arbitrary, *South American*" (emphasis mine).[24]

In both Brazil and Argentina, the elite drew on the racist theories popular during this period to explain the apparent backwardness of the peasantry. Euclides da Cunha, for example, saw the *sertanejos* as suffering from the effects of the intermingling of Indians, Africans, and Europeans, resulting in a mixed race that supposedly stood at a stage lower than that of whites in the evolutionary hierarchy (a hierarchy that placed white, usually northern Europeans at the top and black Africans at the bottom, with Southern Europeans, Native Americans, and Asians at various stages in between). Whether the backlanders could one day successfully evolve to a stage in keeping with the forward motion of the nation as a whole or would serve as an irremediable drag on the progress of Brazil was yet to be seen. In a sense, da Cunha's equivocalness left open to the elite the hope for some future day of reckoning when Brazil's racial progress marched in step with its national, whiter civilization. This ray of hope in da Cunha's writing may explain why his seemingly pessimistic portrayal of Brazil, with its emphasis on the barbarity of the backlanders and the brutality of the conquering army, achieved such phenomenal popularity among the civilizing elite.[25]

For the cultural and political elite, the writings of Domingo Sarmiento, Euclides da Cunha, and others, such as the Mexican *científicos*, defined the boundaries of late-nineteenth-century Latin American civilization.[26] As E. Bradford Burns observes, Sarmiento, da Cunha, and most of the Latin American intellectuals, as well as almost all the governments in the nineteenth century, aspired after the same goal under a variety of names: "progress, civilization, development, and, retrospectively, modernization." No matter what the name, "the idea was as constant as it was simple: to copy those aspects of Northern European—and, later, United States—culture which most struck the fancy of the elites, thus creating an imperfect and selective process of remolding their nations after foreign models."[27] Significantly, it

24. Ibid., 14, 132.
25. Skidmore, *Black into White*, 109.
26. Alan Knight, "Racism, Revolution, and *Indigenismo*: Mexico, 1910–1940," in *The Idea of Race in Latin America, 1870–1940,* ed. Richard Graham (Austin: University of Texas Press, 1990), 71–113.
27. Burns, "Cultures in Conflict," 28–29.

was on urban life they focused their attention, since, if Latin America was to civilize itself, the most viable site for that improvement was the city, the elite having despaired, at least in the short term, of doing much about the countryside. If the exact process of bringing civilization was unclear, the model was not: they agreed on the superiority of white, European culture, especially as displayed in the great capitals of London and Paris.

It bears remembering that Latin American elites were not alone in their obsession with promoting European civilization or in their preoccupation with issues of race. Nancy Stepan shows that the ideals of racial superiority, encased in theories of biological development, moved from Europe to the rest of the world through the active promotion of eugenics societies.[28] European eugenists divided the world among greater/whiter and lesser/darker races, arguing that the poor, whether people or countries, were poor because they were biologically unfit. This so-called "scientific" racism provided a nice cover for European colonialists and imperialists, especially in Africa and Asia, since it diverted attention from inequities in class society at home and left intact the basic mythology of bourgeois progress attendant on capitalist development. Likewise, in those countries such as Brazil, where the elites were frantically copying European culture, a rationale surfaced that blamed apparent human inequalities on "natural" or "biological" factors rather than on the absence of equal opportunity or social justice. Both the Europeans and their emulators in the developing world thereby shifted the blame for the misery of the poor away from themselves, as well as away from the institutions of class and imperial domination they promoted, and toward biology, about which they could supposedly do nothing.

Biological determinism gave rise to a variety of strategies to promote racial homogeneity. Although Argentina had embarked on a program to eliminate people of African descent from urban areas, and eventually from much of the population, by forcibly relocating blacks from the cities and dispersing them through the countryside or out of the country entirely, a similar strategy was thought to be unworkable in Brazil, given the overwhelming majority of people of African heritage.[29] Some argued that a "whitened" population would emerge after generations of racial mixture between white European immigrants and black, or darker-skinned, Brazilians. One of the best ideological representations of this miscegenationist conception is

28. Nancy Leys Stepan, *"The Hour of Eugenics": Race, Gender, and Nation in Latin America* (Ithaca: Cornell University Press, 1991), esp. chap. 2.
29. Ibid.; George Reid Andrews, *The Afro-Argentines of Buenos Aires, 1800–1900* (Madison: University of Wisconsin Press, 1980), chaps. 5–6; Aline Helg, "Race in Argentina and Cuba, 1880–1930: Theory, Policies, and Popular Reaction," in *The Idea of Race*, ed. Graham, 37–69.

Modesto Broco's late-nineteenth-century painting with the revealing title *The Redemption of Ham*. It approvingly depicts a family that has moved from black to mulatto to white in three generations through the intermarriage between the daughter of a former slave and an Italian immigrant.[30]

In Brazil whitening was an assimilationist strategy intended to forge a dominant ideology to which the subordinate and "other" forces of society had to conform. One of the hallmarks of that conformity was the general acceptance of the superiority of white skin over black, of European over African and Afro-Brazilian values, and the association of whiteness with the elite's definition of civilization. While there have been frequent challenges to the notion of white superiority at various times in Brazilian history, the absence of strong "black power" ideologies and of social movements based on Pan-Africanism are a striking testament to the pervasiveness of the whitening ideal. Thus, whereas whitening has been analyzed, quite correctly, as a racist policy, a counterideology extolling "blackness" has appeared only on the margins of Brazilian society. With the exception of the short history of the Frente Negra Brasileira, which enjoyed some success in São Paulo and Rio during the 1920s and 1930s before it was brutally repressed by Getúlio Vargas, and some efforts recently to build African-Brazilian organizations, there has been little uproar over some fairly blatant racist practices, while derogatory images of blacks go uncontested in movies and in popular culture.[31] Considering that Brazil is a society in which the overwhelming majority of the population can trace its roots to Africa, is a place Luiz Edmundo has spoken of as "more like a corner of Africa than a nation of the New World," the assimilationist ideology has been extremely successful in promoting the white ideal.[32]

30. See the photo in E. Bradford Burns, *A History of Brazil*, 2d ed. (New York: Columbia University Press, 1980); George Reid Andrews, *Blacks and Whites in São Paulo, Brazil, 1888–1988* (Madison: University of Wisconsin Press, 1991), chap. 3. As Hobsbawm concludes, the central role of racism in the intellectual and economic development of the nineteenth century cannot be overemphasized. Therefore, even if whitening, at least to the extent it was promoted, was a uniquely Brazilian phenomenon, similar assimilationist strategies marked other colonialist efforts. For a discussion of whitening, as well as *indigenista* strategies in Mexico and other parts of Latin America, see *The Idea of Race,* ed. Graham, esp. the Alan Knight essay, "Racism, Revolution, and *Indigenismo*: Mexico, 1910–1940," 71–113.
31. The main black nationalist expression in Brazil, centered in the Frente Negra Brasileira, occurred from 1924 to 37. See Florestan Fernandes, *The Negro in Brazilian Society* (New York: Atheneum, 1969), chap. 4; Quintard Taylor, "Frente Negra Brasileira: The Afro-Brazilian Civil Rights Movement, 1924–1937," *Scholarly Journal of Black Studies* 2 (Spring 1978); Teresa Meade and Gregory Alonso Pirio, "In Search of the Afro-American 'Eldorado': Attempts by North American Blacks to Enter Brazil in the 1920s," *Luso-Brazilian Review* 25, no. 1 (1988): 85–110.
32. Quoted in Needell, *Tropical Belle Epoque*, 49.

In late-nineteenth-century Brazil, social Darwinist ideas of the biological superiority of white Europeans combined with the more ameliorated racism of the whitening policy to provide the practical impetus for an ambitious immigration program. Beginning in the 1880s, organizations such as the Sociedade Promotora da Imigracão (Society for the Promotion of Immigration) in São Paulo and the Rio de Janeiro Sociedade Central de Imigracão (Central Immigration Society), in cooperation with the Brazilian government, embarked on an ambitious program to distribute abroad brochures advertising steady work at good wages and even free ship and train passages guaranteed by the Department of Agriculture for anyone willing to immigrate to Brazil's coffee fields. From 1889 to 1934, 4.1 million immigrants entered Brazil; 56 percent of them settled in the coffee fields of São Paulo, 58 percent of whom were directly subsidized by the Brazilian state. The promoters distributed advertisements in European and North American newspapers, and most of the immigrants came from Italy, Spain, Portugal, and Germany, with a lesser number from Syria, Lebanon, and Japan. The overwhelming majority of migrants to Brazil, more than all other nationalities combined, some 690,000 in the 1890s alone, were Italian, though Portuguese immigrants predominated in Rio.[33]

Key to the immigration strategy, and in keeping with the whitening goals of the Republicans, was the admission of white immigrants only. In 1890 the government prohibited Asian and black immigration unless specifically authorized by an act of Congress. On January 6, 1921, the Brazilian Congress passed Article 5 of Federal Decree N. 4247, which specifically prohibited black immigrants from entering Brazil. Notably, the Brazilian government kept its "whites only" policy quiet and was extremely reluctant to admit that it did not accept black immigrants. When blacks sought to enter Brazil, as a number did, they were simply denied visas.[34] One variant on the predominant racism of the immigration strategy was the view that European yeoman farmers would bring the virtues of hard work, thrift, and decency to Brazil

33. Records of the Department of State Relating to the Internal Affairs of Brazil, 1910–29, National Archives, Washington, D.C., Record Group 32, File 832.55/18 (October 9, 1911); File 832.52 27/23 (August 13, 1925). For a discussion of the advertising campaign in the United States, see *Brazilian Business*, the monthly organ of the American Chamber of Commerce for Brazil, 7, no. 6 (1927): 29; Thomas H. Holloway, *Immigrants on the Land: Coffee and Society in Sao Paulo, 1886–1934* (Chapel Hill: University of North Carolina Press, 1980), 36–45; June E. Hahner, *Poverty and Politics: The Urban Poor in Brazil, 1870–1920* (Albuquerque: University of New Mexico Press, 1986), 46.

34. Records of the Department of State Relating to the Internal Affairs of Brazil, Record Group 32, File 832.52/15 (September 4, 1924). See also Meade and Pirio, "In Search of the Afro-American 'Eldorado,'" esp. 104 nn. 9 and 10.

and that these virtues would eventually replace the traditions of the planter aristocracy as the backbone of Brazilian agriculture. Obviously, such an idealistic notion was more popular among urban liberals than rural planters, not to mention that it was unworkable. Most of the immigrants were escaping debt servitude and semifeudal relations of production in Italy and thus hardly arrived imbued with the values of an independent yeomanry.[35] Moreover, the immigration plan was not intended to distribute land to independent farmers, but to supply the coffee plantations with laborers, most of whom worked long hours under brutal conditions for low wages.

Actually, the results of the immigration program provide a revealing picture of the limits of civilization, as far as the Brazilian elite were concerned. In the design of even the most liberal Republicans, civilization, which economically meant capitalism, was never seen as a challenge to the political control of the coffee barons or landowners or as a restructuring of the basic export orientation of the economy. Civilization had nothing to offer the bulk of the population on the plantations and in the desolate backlands, no matter what their color or nationality. Living and working conditions remained deplorable, even little changed from the days of slavery. At the same time, urban liberals were unwilling to replace their own crude paternalism with a stance favoring the political participation of either the rural peasantry or the urban proletariat in the national political process.

On the surface it would seem that the success of the elite's conception of civilization and their attendant civilizing plan depended on the extent to which a sizable portion of the citizenry, of all races, bought into the notion of white, European culture as superior to what existed in Brazil. But the elite constituted a very tiny segment of society, and, as Euclides da Cunha noted, it knew nothing of the culture, the values, or the worldview of the majority of inland people. Nonetheless, the urban elite's influence in shaping the dominant culture was disproportionately large and lasting in relation to its numbers and geographic concentration. As in other areas of the world, in Brazil the cultural legacy of imperialism was, and unfortunately still is, based on the education of a tiny stratum of elites in western European ways, to the extent that they became the literate carriers of the discourse of imperialism, of the clothes, of the customs, of the sense of time and place and decorum. It is in fact this cultural hegemony that explains the peculiar strength of co-

35. Michael Hall, "The Origins of Mass Immigration in Brazil, 1871–1914," (Ph.D. diss., Columbia University, 1969); Maria Tereza Schorer Petrone, "Imigração," in *História geral da civilização brasileira*, vol. 9, *O Brasil republicano: Sociedade e instituições, 1889–1930*, ed. Boris Fausto (São Paulo: Difusão Editorial, 1977), 93–133, esp. 96–97.

lonialism and imperialism, allowing for the grasp of empires to be so vast and so profound, while the exact number of imperialists or colonizers has always been so small.[36]

In the opening decade of the First Republic, the civilizers' attention focused on Brazil's capital, Rio de Janeiro. As a site for this "experiment" in cultural uplift, the capital had great potential. It was geographically well situated to service ships passing from the Brazilian Northeast to Buenos Aires further south; the harbor was wide, deep, and sheltered from the sea on a large bay; and finally, it was breathtakingly beautiful with the blue sea rimming high rocky mountains and lower hills covered with tropical vegetation. Although by the late nineteenth century the state of Rio de Janeiro no longer produced most of the coffee, the majority of the São Paulo crop still passed through Rio's port.

As the capital of the newly formed Republic, Rio de Janeiro hosted foreign dignitaries and travelers from Europe and North America. It was one of the first cities that independent commercial agents and merchants from established European firms encountered in their search for stronger trade relations with Latin America. Brazil, moreover, was trying to communicate to the rest of the world that it was now a country in the midst of change, a "sleeping giant" with enormous economic potential. Much to the glee of the Brazilian elite, a small but nonetheless promising literature extolling their country's virtues, chronicling the beauty of Rio de Janeiro, and discussing Brazil's geography and natural resources was beginning to appear in libraries and bookstores in England, France, and Germany. In order to build on these foundations, and in conjunction with attempts to quell the political crises of the backlands, more and more of the Republic's leaders proposed that the capital city be transformed to bear witness to Brazil's status as an up-and-coming, civilized South American nation.

The transformation would not be easy. Rio had a number of problems that nearly anyone would have acknowledged: it was crowded, unhealthy, unsafe, and lacked basic city services. As the city had grown, as it developed into the

36. Hobsbawm, *The Age of Empire*, 79; Antonio Gramsci, "The Study of Philosophy," in *Selections from the Prison Notebooks*, trans. and ed. Quintin Hoare and Geoffrey Nowell Smith (New York: International Publishers, 1971), 330–33. See also Florencia E. Mallon's provocative comments in *Peasant and Nation: The Making of Postcolonial Mexico and Peru* (Berkeley and Los Angeles: University of California Press, 1995), 1–20. For a discussion of how race interacted with class identity in Brazil, see Marshall C. Eakin, "Race and Identity: Silvio Romero, Science, and Social Thought in Late-Nineteenth-Century Brazil," *Luso-Brazilian Review* 22, no. 2 (1985): 151–74, and Leo Spitzer's study, *Lives In Between: Assimilation and Marginality in Austria, Brazil, West Africa, 1780–1945* (New York: Cambridge University Press, 1989).

center of commerce, manufacture, and government, it had brought with it all
the problems associated with urban growth, including a chronic housing
shortage, inadequate sanitation and public works, and a proliferation of vice.
Because of stepped up in-migration and the influx of European immigrants
in the postabolition period, the population of the Federal District of Rio de
Janeiro had more than doubled in the years from 1872 to 1890 and had increased by 55 percent from 1890 to 1906. Rio proper and the surrounding
migrant settlements numbered 518,290 inhabitants at the start of the Republic and then grew to over one million by 1920.[37]

In some cases, after a few years of grueling work on the coffee plantations,
immigrants escaped to Rio de Janeiro, where they disappeared into the large
communities of recent arrivals who either had settled there legally or had
managed through whatever extralegal means to bypass the plantations entirely. Ironically, the policy the elites had supported to increase the white
(and likewise "whitened" Arab and Asian) population, the policy that formed
the core of their civilizing strategy, brought about changes in the city they
found alarming, and mingled the lines between white and black Rio to the
extent that previous methods of social control proved unworkable. Pedro Antonio de Oliveira Ribeiro, the city's police chief, commented to the minister
of justice in 1891 that "immigration, which we have sought, with its truly notable advantages, has brought us also, in large quantity, the foreigner ruined
by vice, the criminal pursued by authorities in his native country, the adven-
turer capable of all manner of audacity."[38] Blaming the increase in crime on
"insolent vagabonds" and "uncontrollable idle youngsters" who roamed the

37. The census counted the population of the Federal District, which included the Rio de
Janeiro municipality (North, Central and South Zones), the *subúrbios*, and the sparsely populated islands in Guanabara Bay. I have grouped the districts together in the above categories,
corresponding to the North, Central, and South regions but better describing the economic and
social character of the geographic regions. I grouped the islands, Gávea, and Lagôa together
because changes in these areas are not covered in this study. Though Gávea and Lagôa at this
time had several furniture and textile factories, as well as working-class housing, the major
growth of these districts mostly occurred after 1930. Directoria Geral de Estatística, *Recenseamento da População do Imperio do Brazil a que se Procedeu no Dia 1 de Agosto de 1872* (Rio de
Janeiro: Imprensa Nacional, 1873–76), 58; idem, *Recenseamento Geral da República dos Estados
Unidos do Brazil em 31 de Dezembro de 1890, Districto Federal* (Rio de Janeiro: Imprensa Nacional, 1895), lxxiii; idem, *Recenseamento do Rio de Janeiro Realisado em 20 de Setembro de 1906*
(Rio de Janeiro: Imprensa Nacional, 1907), 180–261; idem, *Recenseamento do Brazil Realisado
em 1 de Setembro de 1920, População do Rio de Janeiro (Districto Federal)* (Rio de Janeiro: Imprensa Nacional, 1923), vol. 2, pt. 1, xxvi.
38. Ministerio da Justiça e Negocios Interiores, *Relatório apresentado ao Ministro da Justiça
e Negocios Interiores, Barão de Lucena, pelo Secretária da Policia da Capital Federal, Pedro Antonio de Oliveira Ribeiro* (Rio de Janeiro: Imprensa Nacional, 1891), 3.

MAPA DAS PARÓQUIAS

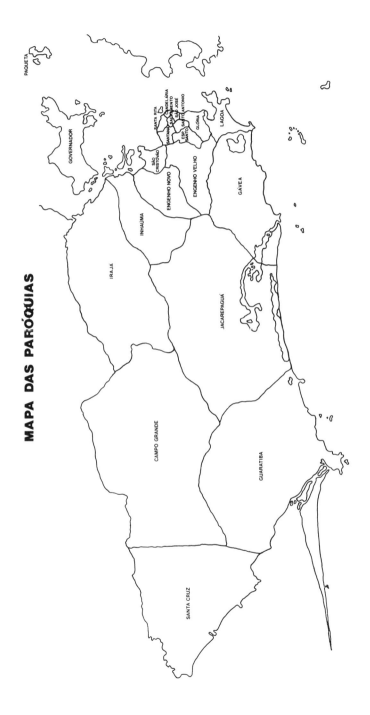

The districts of Rio de Janeiro. From Eulalia Maria Lahmeyer Lobo, *História do Rio de Janeiro: Do Capital Comercial ao Capital Industrial e Financeiro*, vol. 1 (Rio de Janeiro: IBMEC, 1978).

downtown commercial district, the chief called on the government to grant the security forces broader powers so as to "ensure respect for the principle of authority." Oliveira echoed the period's most familiar theme as he explained that this respect for authority was the "means through which this great center of people and riches can assure the progress and civilization of the cultured (people)," though forced to live with a "deprived and unstable population all about us."[39]

The city's business and political leaders were appalled at the proliferation of vice, including petty crime, prostitution, vagrancy, gambling, and begging. And without a doubt, the city's topography, wedged between jutting *morros*, the ocean, and the bay, made it difficult to police. But there are indications that the city's elite then, as now, was less concerned with an increase in vice so long as it remained contained to the poorer neighborhoods. The real problem in Rio was that the city had grown so rapidly and haphazardly that congested areas brought the diverse social classes and races into close proximity. A press report in 1895 proclaimed that "reporters for this newspaper have related police statistics showing the extraordinary and frightening development of robberies, assaults, and other transgressions against private property. . . . these ostentatious assaults occur in plain day in the busiest and most public places of the city." Moreover, the editor warned of the "very pernicious effects these crimes can cause us, the future embarrassment that they can create for us." Ending with a call for greater vigilance by the municipal authorities, he evoked the issue of crime and its control in the terms most common to the era: "It is already well known that to speak of a *policed* country is synonymous, is the same thing, as to speak of a *civilized* country."[40]

During the opening years of the Republic more and more of the city's respectable citizenry expressed their fears of an increase of unruly and undesirable elements throughout the city and especially in the downtown. Crime came to be seen not as an act of violence or a threat to property but as a disturbance of the public order and thus as a social threat instead of a personal one.[41] Several of Rio's daily newspapers carried regular features deploring the increased number of beggars "dragging themselves through the streets in the nauseating rags of their miserable state."[42] Distressed by this sight, newspapers representing the opinions of wealthy residents proposed

39. Ibid., 4.
40. *O Paiz*, August 16, 1895, 1.
41. Sandra Lauderdale Graham, *House and Street: The Domestic World of Servants and Masters in Nineteenth-Century Rio de Janeiro* (Cambridge: Cambridge University Press, 1988), 132.
42. *O Paiz*, October 15, 1900, 1.

that the police be more adamant in removing beggars from the well-traveled streets, where they could easily be seen by visiting dignitaries, businessmen, and travelers. Mendicancy and vagabondage (which term, applied to women, meant prostitution) deeply disturbed the city's elite. The growth of these practices struck at the very heart of the contradiction between civilization and barbarism as pertaining to Rio's development, and it called into question the direction in which the city was proceeding. If the end of slavery had meant the end to the personal accountability of the master over the slave, or the *patrão* over the worker, who then was responsible for the disposition of this "troubling class of people who had no legitimate social place" or at least not one apparent within the confines of the existent order? [43] One frank observer, comparing the city's pretensions with reality, called Rio a "supercivilized capital, metropolis of garbage and of wealth, of sumptuous palaces in Botafogo and Laranjeiras . . . alongside the permanent display of cancers and putrid open sores on beggars." Noting the combination "of innumerable charitable institutions and of thousands of vagabond children," the observer concluded that Rio displayed the characteristics of "barbarity with the varnish of wealth." [44]

A good number of "sumptuous houses" in Catete and Lapa housed prostitutes who serviced the respectable gentlemen of the city, while ladies who charged less and catered to laborers and sailors worked the side streets near low-cost housing units. In Vivaldo Coaracy's *Memórias da Cidade do Rio de Janeiro,* a colorful account of the downtown urban life before the renovations, the author describes both the physical details and the social hierarchy of the prostitute market in the old Largo do Rossio between Riachuelo and Espírito Santo Streets, not far from Flamengo Beach. From behind the venetian blinds, almost always closed on order from the police, one could make out the silhouettes of women whispering their lascivious invitations to the men passing on the sidewalk. At night, Coaracy continued, the traffic in this district was intense. The prostitutes, whose French names suggest their elite clientele, enjoyed a minor celebrity status in the bars of the Largo do Rossio. A few of the best-known ladies, and the establishments for which they worked, were Margarida Gauthier of the Dumas bar, Fille Elisa of the Goncourts, Boule de Suif, and Nana (the last three names were actually "vocational" monikers). As Coaracy put it, in "the Rio de Janeiro of that time, the hierarchy of meretriciousness started with the *cachaça* (a popular cheap rum) in the São Jorge Street and ended up with the obligatory champagne

43. S. L. Graham, *House and Street,* 132.
44. *O Paiz,* September 12, 1901, 2.

of the *pensões chiques* in Catete" and the surrounding areas.[45] Interestingly, the hierarchy in prostitution, like everything else, moved from Brazilian women and rum up to French women and champagne.

Since prostitution was an accepted male indulgence, it was not unusual to find it practiced in the most respectable locales of the city.[46] Reportedly, even members of the national legislature and important foreign merchants were propositioned on their way to work.[47] Nonetheless, as Sueann Caulfield notes, "respectability" and "respectable society" were gendered categories, since the social space available to men was far ampler than that accorded to "respectable" women.[48] Coaracy describes the curious turnover in the clientele of the Confeitaria Colombo during a typical weekday. From midday until 4:30 the elite women of the city stopped at this elegant café for tea and ice cream or a small lunch. At 4:30 the café emptied completely, except for a smattering of men from the literary set who sat sipping sherry. Then at five o'clock sharp the café began again to fill up with men from the most respectable class, but this time they were joined by some of the city's most famous madams and prostitutes. Coaracy notes that, "generally, the first to arrive was the 'battalion' of Suzana, a while later that of Vallerie, and then the others."[49]

The elite show at the Confeitaria Colombo had its counterpart in the bars and walkways of the Largo do Rossio near the São Pedro Theater. There a veritable "market of women" flourished nightly; there the toughs of the city, sailors, and poorer men "bought and sold, traded or rented" women, negotiating between the pimps and the clientele the importing of "merchandise" from one plaza of the city to another. According to Coaracy, an active "white slave trade" prospered in the hands of mainly European "merchants" who peddled Brazilian, Polish, German, and Russian women in the city's main thoroughfares.[50] It is, however, difficult to know whether Coaracy had verifiable evidence for the nationalities of the women or was, following the tra-

45. Vivaldo Coaracy, *Memorias da cidade do Rio de Janeiro*, vol. 88 of *Coleção documentos brasileiros* (Rio de Janeiro: Libraria José Olympio Editora, 1955), 136–37.

46. June E. Hahner, *Emancipating the Female Sex: The Struggle for Women's Rights in Brazil, 1850–1940* (Durham, N.C.: Duke University Press, 1990), 95.

47. Gastão Cruls, *Aparencia do Rio de Janeiro: Noticia histórica e descritiva da cidade* (Rio de Janeiro: Livraria José Olympio Editora, 1965), 2:551.

48. Sueann Caulfield, "In Defense of Honor: The Contested Meaning of Sexual Morality in Law and Courtship, Rio de Janeiro, 1920–1940" (Ph.D. diss., New York University, 1994), 86.

49. Coaracy, *Memórias da cidade*, 138.

50. Ibid., 139. See also Donna J. Guy, "Medical Imperialism Gone Awry: The Campaign Against Legalized Prostitution in Latin America," in *Science, Medicine, and Cultural Imperialism*, ed. Teresa Meade and Mark Walker (New York: St. Martin's Press, 1991), 75–94.

ditional stereotype, labeling prostitutes who were not Brazilians Jews, the code words for which were "Poles" and "Russians." Jeffrey Lesser's study of Jewish immigrant communities in Brazil notes that turn-of-the-century anti-Semitic spokespersons sought to limit Jewish immigration by linking it with an influx of prostitution but that there were in fact Jewish prostitutes and pimps in Brazilian cities. Indeed, Lesser details some fascinating cases of Jewish organizations in Rio and São Paulo formed by prostitutes and of a synagogue in Rio whose president was one of the city's most well-known pimps.[51]

Coaracy for his part accepted prostitution as "a universal fact," if indeed a "social eyesore," dwelling little on its destructive treatment of young women except to call attention to the "shame" of the Largo do Rossio.[52] Caulfield notes that the Republican Penal Code never criminalized prostitution but that persons "encouraging" or "profiting" from prostitution could be subject to one to two years in prison. The extent to which this part of the code was ever enforced is not known.[53] Obviously there was a link between the ideological view that prostitution was a "shame," if a "necessary" one, and the reluctance to prosecute offenders, since, as Caulfield notes, "cultural norms" that justified prostitution for men (in a city where men slightly outnumbered women) mandated the practice and even contributed to its increase. All that could be hoped for, then, was to contain the physical boundaries of the prostitutes' field of operation.[54]

Indeed, some of the moralizers and civilizers of the day descried just this intermingling of legitimate and illegitimate entertainment. One member of Rio's elite proclaimed that "an immoral and offensive public decorum exists because these women sit meretriciously in the windows and doors of houses in which they reside in the main streets of the city." As a consequence, he continued, the "honest population" is forced "to tolerate this unpleasant spectacle, particularly apparent because they [prostitutes] occupy ground-level houses, conspicuous in their licentious and completely immoral interior designs." He went on "to urge the council to adopt measures that prohibit

51. Jeffrey Lesser, *Welcoming the Undesirables: Brazil and the Jewish Question* (Berkeley and Los Angeles: University of California Press, 1995), 34–37.

52. Coaracy, *Memórias da cidade*, 139. Caulfield provides evidence that physicians and other male professionals argued that prostitution was a "necessary evil" that protected the virtue of women, since men had more developed sexual instincts and needed prostitutes with whom they could vent their excessive sexual energy; "In Defense of Honor," 90

53. The law became stricter after Brazil agreed to the 1904 International Accord for the Repression of the Trade in Women and Children, which went into effect in Brazil as a part of Lei no. 2992, September 25, 1915; Caulfield, "In Defense of Honor," 92.

54. Ibid. 97.

the practice of prostitution in pavement-level houses situated in the central streets of the city transversed by street cars." Drawing on a familiar rationale, the writer begged "the illustrious council" to take under consideration his suggestion, which he saw as a "measure that would benefit the public of this civilized capital."[55] At issue here, of course, was who constituted the "honest" population of the "civilized capital": the respectable gentlemen in the Confeitaria Colombo, the crude white slavers and their customers in the streets behind the Largo do Rossio, or even the women themselves?

If barbarity was afoot, then there was nothing more barbarous than the way the poor, the immigrants, and the migrants from the countryside, black and white, entertained themselves. The late nineteenth century was a time when rollicking café concerts, nightclubs, and cabarets proliferated especially in Catete, Lapa, and the areas of Flamengo bordering on the center city. The most famous clubs were the Moulin Rouge, the High Life, the Guarda-Velha, the Eldorado, the Maison Moderne, and the Cassino. The Moulin Rouge, on the corner of Espírito Santo Street in the Largo de Rossio, the area noted for prostitution, was actually an amusement park with a shooting gallery, Ferris wheel, roulette tables, a carousel, and other entertainments. Customers moved from the covered café at the entrance to the open-air amusement park in the rear and back again, lubricating their luck at the gambling table or rides on the Ferris wheel with the cheap beer served at picnic tables. The Moulin Rouge and other cabarets in the center city were places where nightly many people gathered in loud and raucous entertainment, places where the drinking went on until dawn and not infrequently fights broke out.[56]

One of the most notable features of the Lapa district, however, was that it concentrated a broad swath of the city's social classes. Coaracy makes particular mention of the Café Suíço and the Stadt Munchen, near the Praça Tiradentes in Lapa and a few blocks from the Largo do Rossio, as only two of the most notable cafés and restaurants that filled the area. The Stadt Munchen was the favored watering hole for the bohemian crowd that crammed the café after the last show at one of the many theaters in the district. On any night after the performance and on into the early morning hours "it was difficult to find an empty table in either the beer hall in front or the restaurant in the rear."[57]

55. Ao Secretária de Policia da Corte de Manoel Jose Espinola, Chefe de Policia, November 13, 1888, Arquivo de Patrimonio Histórico e Artístico do Estado do Rio de Janeiro (hereafter APHA-RJ), 1.

56. Coaracy, *Memórias da cidade*, 128–29.

57. Ibid., 134. See also Needell, *Tropical Belle Epoque*, 34–35.

Rio, however, was not only a place of cross-class socializing but a racially heterogeneous city as well. In the Old City whites and blacks, immigrants, longtime *libertos* (persons of color who had been free before 1888), and recent migrants from the plantations intermingled. As Sidney Chalhoub has noted, the new Republican elite viewed with apprehension the demographic, economic, and cultural predominance of what they saw as "the black city."[58] Following on the heels of the abolition of slavery in 1888, "Black Rio" represented an odd threat to the Republican government. First, although the demise of slavery and the Empire came at nearly the same historical moment, pro-monarchist forces won the allegiance of many blacks by successfully exploiting the fact that it was under the reign of Pedro II, Brazil's last emperor, that slavery was abolished. Signs of that loyalty appeared in the monarchist symbols of the carnival parade, in a display of respect for both African kings and Brazilian emperors in black religious and ceremonial icons, and even in a scattering of anti-Republican demonstrations.

Second, the legacy of slavery in Rio had left a world in which blacks, both former slaves and *libertos*, moved freely about the center city and, in the paranoid eyes of the white elite, dominated the streets. Police records from the 1880s and 1890s reveal numerous cases of Afro-Brazilians apprehended in downtown Rio for drinking on the street, congregating in front of kiosks and bars to socialize, or simply walking around at night. Men were interrogated for meeting, escorting, or picking up women, indicative of the extent to which both black men and black women intermingled in the downtown street life.[59]

In a curious way one of the remarkable features of old Rio de Janeiro was the relative democracy of its popular culture, in spite of the extreme inequalities that divided social groups and classes. Although members of different classes and races lived separately and worked or took their leisure in slightly varied locales, and in some cases at distinct times, the physical overlap of these vastly unequal social strata was striking. A government official, a merchant, a teacher, a coffee planter, or even a visiting dignitary stopped off at a bar or restaurant a block or two from the Moulin Rouge, where a carpenter, a street peddler, a quarry worker, or a local ruffian caroused. Moreover, it was not unheard of for everyone and anyone to stop by the Moulin Rouge and similar nightspots. In Coaracy's description, the places of entertainment, including even the Confeitaria Colombo, hosted the elegant ladies of the city

58. Sidney Chalhoub, "Medo branco de almas negras: Escravos, libertos e republicanos na cidade do Rio," *Revista Brasileira de Historia* 8, no. 16 (1988), 83–105.
59. Ibid., 93–95.

Fig. 1.   Rua do Ouvidor in the Old City, c. 1885. Photograph by Marc Ferrez, Jennings Hoffenberg Collection.

elite as well as prostitutes, though at very separate hours. With the exception of the women of the elite class, whom social convention required assiduously to guard their respectability and stay clear of late night entertainments, the city was nearly wide open. By century's end, as Chalhoub makes clear, the racial issue, or what he calls "white fear," began to wind its way into the cultural awareness of the Republican elite. In the time of slavery the government had from time to time taken steps to fix the lines between slaves and free persons in sometimes futile attempts to reinforce social control, but now, under the postabolition Republic, the old rules and the old boundaries no longer applied.[60]

It was this overlap—this relative democracy of shared raucous entertainment, all-night cabarets, and, during carnival, the wild pranks, or *entrudos,* and street dances—that the renovations would destroy. By the end of the first decade of the twentieth century, almost all of the cabarets and bars where the popular classes occasionally rubbed shoulders with the elite in Lapa and Catete fell under the ax of Mayor Pereira Passos's renovations. Thus the campaign against decadence and vice, which particularly targeted the amusements of the urban poor, had as a by-product the regulation and transformation of the cultural values of the middle and upper classes as well, particularly the men.[61] Vivaldo Coaracy's accounts of life in old Rio de Janeiro hint at the ambivalence of the civilizers themselves. He writes with no slight tinge of nostalgia for the agitated nightlife of Lapa and the other areas of the Old City in the days before the renovations, and then, as though checking himself, he casts aside his own lament by proclaiming that the renovation was necessary in the name of "civilization and progress."[62]

Here lay the crux of the issue. The concern with civilizing Rio had to do with more than the fear that a few bawdy nightspots or beggars and prostitutes in the main streets of the city discouraged foreign investors and harmed Brazil's prospects as a developing world power. Whatever obstacles these social conditions presented, they paled in comparison with the overriding issue of social control. Entertainment, vice, and social strife overlapped in Rio's downtown, while the potential arose for violent conflict in new and frightening forms.

60. Ibid., passim.

61. This was certainly not unique to Rio de Janeiro. Gareth Stedman Jones describes the attempts to close London's music halls as a part of the moralizing impulses of the late nineteenth century, attempts that had an outcome similar to that in Rio; "Working-Class Culture and Working-Class Politics in London, 1870–1900: Notes on the Remaking of a Working Class," *Journal of Social History* 7, no. 4 (1974): 460–508.

62. Coaracy, *Memórias da cidade,* 283.

As the century drew to a close, riots, demonstrations, and strikes involving migrants from the countryside, immigrant workers, and the laboring poor signaled the emergence of groups that were contesting the elite's economic, political, and cultural priorities. Violence and social conflict were no longer isolated in the distant interior. Although the coastal elite had read with alarm Euclides da Cunha's account of the *sertanejos* and of social and cultural life in the backlands, they had taken comfort in the notion that social strife and, in their view, barbarism at its rawest were characteristics of the countryside. By the end of the nineties it seemed that urban chaos and disorder also promised to increase and intensify along with the industry, commerce, and population of the capital city. As Charles Tilly observes, violent outbreaks of class conflict and collective protests typically occur in societies undergoing a disruption in previous methods of producing and exchanging goods, alterations in social class relationships, and the transfer of political power.[63] Rio de Janeiro was no exception.

63. Charles Tilly, "The Changing Place of Collective Violence," in *Workers in the Industrial Revolution,* ed. Peter N. Stearns and Daniel J. Walkowitz (New Brunswick, N.J.: Transaction Books, 1974), 122.

2

The Features
of Urban Life

Today the people eat worse and it costs more.
        —*O Paiz*, February 18, 1890

Crime, vagabondage, prostitution, mendicancy, and poverty, or what one historian has called the "corrupting features of urban life," [1] distressed the city's elite not only because these visible signs of vice and decay were so apparent on a day-to-day basis throughout Rio de Janeiro, but also because they threatened the inevitable march of progress the modernizing forces were expecting. By the late nineteenth century, calls for social control, containment, and even repression of the ever-growing mass of poor people drowned out the entreaties of those reformers who had argued for improving the lot of the urban poor. Social control was seen as synonymous with civilization and as a program for improving the city's deteriorating image. Moreover, and much to the alarm of the new Republican leaders, violence was not confined to the

1. Gareth Stedman Jones, *Outcast London: A Study in the Relationship Between Classes in Victorian Society* (New York: Oxford University Press, 1971), 16.

countryside (if it ever had been), but was more the resort of a broad cross section of working people, many of whom lived not far from Brazil's government offices. Whereas street demonstrations and various peaceful and not so peaceful *reclamações* had been constant features of Brazil's urban and rural landscape throughout its history, during the early years of the century the number of capital residents speaking out against their deplorable living and working conditions reached new heights.

That the Carioca citizenry took to the streets to express their grievances against an escalating cost of living, substandard and inadequate housing, and abysmal working conditions was certainly nothing unique in urban political culture. There is no doubt that resistance is as old as authority itself, that people have always joined together in spontaneous, as well as organized, demonstrations against unfair policies, or those deemed unfair, in opposition to laws and regulations, changes in market conditions, and inadequate living and working conditions. James Scott has noted the existence of pervasive resistance to authority in many societies, which, as a "hidden transcript," has not always been acknowledged by those wielding the power. If historians look below the surface to find the constant and often hidden resistance, that new record dramatically alters the "official transcript." Moreover, as Susan Eckstein comments in the introduction to a collection on recent popular protest movements in Latin America, theories that draw on an analysis of grievances, organizations, and leadership have proven inadequate to explain the range of ways common folk have devised to defy the social order and to demonstrate dissatisfaction with their lot. The shortcomings of existent theories aside, Eckstein admits that riots, strikes, social movements, and all forms of protest tell us as much about the priorities and the workings of a society as they tell us about the actions and the protesters themselves. Most important, social upheaval did not erupt without good cause.[2]

By the turn of the century Rio de Janeiro had become an arena for a new and heightened stage in a struggle that challenged the old order's class relationships. Abolition had transformed the previous methods of social control, while the impetus to grow, to build an industrial base, to market goods around the world, and to Europeanize the culture meant that Brazil's capital was more than a city with neighborhoods, commerce, workers, and owners. It was a city in tremendous flux. Rio's absolute demographic growth, alter-

2. James C. Scott, *Domination and the Arts of Resistance: Hidden Transcripts* (New Haven: Yale University Press, 1990); Susan Eckstein, ed., *Power and Popular Protest: Latin American Social Movements* (Berkeley and Los Angeles: University of California Press, 1989), 1.

ations in customary methods of social control in the latter half of the nineteenth century, and, closely related to these two, increase in poverty because of the unstable economic situation and periodic depressions arose as the key factors that determined its character during this crucial era of transformation.[3] The following pages describe the bearing of each of these factors on the capital's development.

After 1888 the city grew by an average rate of 2.9 percent yearly as migrants from the countryside fled the drudgery of the plantations in hopes of better prospects in the city, where they joined thousands of immigrants arriving from Europe. Rio went from a modest 266,831 inhabitants in 1872, the year of the last census under the Empire, to 518,290 in 1890 and reached 1,124,572 by 1920. In the period of the Old Republic alone, the capital's population increased approximately 117 percent. By 1890 recent arrivals from Europe and from the agricultural interiors of the south-central states of Rio de Janeiro and São Paulo, combined with a smattering from the rest of Brazil, accounted for 55 percent of Rio's population.

Although Brazil as a whole experienced a large increase in immigrant population, the influx of Europeans during the Old Republic was not unusual for Rio. As the seat of the Portuguese court in 1808 and the center of international trade throughout the nineteenth century, Rio had always had a high percentage of foreigners. Immigrants, 70 percent of whom were from Portugal, accounted for approximately 27 percent of the city's population in 1872 and increased to 29 percent in 1890, the year of the highest immigrant influx. The remaining 26 percent of the recent arrivals were migrants from the countryside who, along with the majority of the city's population, were native-born Brazilians. If slightly more than a quarter of Rio's population comprised native-born recent migrants to the city and another 29 percent were immigrants, the demographic transformation underway was profound. As the century drew to a close, a majority of the capital's residents hailed from Brazil's remote agricultural regions or distant nations.[4]

Also, the growth in the absolute size of the city, combined with the extreme dislocations brought on by the abolition of slavery in 1888, threw into

3. For a discussion of the breakdown in methods of social control by the 1870s and the fluctuations in the slave system after the Law of Free Birth in 1871, when slaves were able to purchase their freedom in considerable numbers, see Sidney Chalhoub, "Slaves, Freedmen, and the Politics of Freedom in Brazil: The Experience of Blacks in the City of Rio," *Slavery and Abolition* 10, no. 3 (1989): 64–84.

4. Sam Adamo, "The Broken Promise: Race, Health, and Justice in Rio de Janeiro, 1890–1940" (Ph.D. diss., University of New Mexico, 1983), 15–17.

Table 1   Population of Rio de Janeiro (Federal District), 1872–1920

Area	1872	1890	1906	1920
Center city [Renewal area]				
Sacramento	26,909	30,663	24,612	27,370
Candelária	9,818	9,701	4,454	3,962
São Jose	20,010	40,014	44,878	29,697
Santa Rita	30,865	43,803	45,929	38,164
Sant'Anna	38,446	67,533	79,315	91,333
Glória	22,135	44,105	59,102	70,027
Santo Antonio	20,629	37,660	42,009	52,472
Total	168,812	273,479	300,299	313,025
North Zone [Poor/working-class area]				
Espírito Santo	13,793	31,389	59,117	79,297
Engenho Velho	15,428	36,988	91,494	140,930
São Cristóvão	10,833	22,202	45,098	59,979
Engenho Novo	—	27,873	62,898	98,979
Total	40,054	118,452	258,607	378,538
Subúrbios [Outskirts of city]				
Irajá	5,782	13,130	27,410	99,591
Jacarepaguá	7,993	16,070	17,265	23,156
Inhaúma	7,220	17,448	68,557	133,213
Guaratiba	7,091	12,654	17,928	23,609
Campo Grande	9,686	15,950	31,248	52,405
Santa Cruz	2,631	10,954	15,380	16,506
Total	40,403	86,206	177,788	348,480
Other areas				
Lagôa	13,447	28,741	47,992	57,558
Gávea	—	4,712	12,750	15,270
Islands	4,115	6,700	7,899	11,701
Total	17,562	40,153	68,641	84,529
Total population	266,831	518,290	805,335	1,124,572

SOURCES: Directoria Geral de Estatística, *Recenseamento Geral de República dos Estados Unidos do Brazil em 31 de Dezembro de 1890, Districto Federal* (Rio de Janeiro: Imprensa Nacional, 1895), lxxiii; idem, *Recenseamento do Rio de Janeiro Realisado em 20 de Setembro de 1906* (Rio de Janeiro: Imprensa Nacional, 1907), 180–261; idem, *Recenseamento do Brazil Realisado em 1 de Setembro de 1920, População do Rio de Janeiro (Districto Federal)* (Rio de Janeiro: Imprensa Nacional, 1923), 2:xxvi.

chaos the previous methods of ensuring public order. Despite their roots in Portugal or the Brazilian countryside, many people in the city, and most of the poor, were culturally estranged from one another, unfamiliar with their environs, and passed long hours crowded into the least hospitable living and working conditions the city offered. At the same time, the unstable economic and political climate of the early Republic enhanced the possibilities for outbreaks of rioting and social tension. Moreover, the government did little to meet the challenges the demographic explosion produced. On the contrary, in a city whose resources were already inadequate, scapegoating the newly arrived migrants began to pass as official policy. In 1899 Epitacio Pessoa, repeating the sentiments of the minister of justice a few years earlier, argued that "those from the states of the union and from foreign countries" have been the cause for the increase in crime, vagrancy, and idleness, necessitating the "special attention of the public powers." The population boom was causing the city's borders to be extended outward, and clusters of houses were springing up overnight in the mountain valleys and beginning to climb the ridges of the city's Zona Norte (North Zone). Accordingly, the "extensive area and the accident of topography" made it difficult for the police "to guarantee the security of individuals and to safeguard the property of the citizenry."[5]

But more than the "accident of topography" or population increase was at issue. The end of slavery had definitively altered class relationships, not only freeing thousands of people to sell their labor on the market but likewise transferring from the *patrão* to civil society responsibility for social services and, in the capitalist order, social control. Sandra Lauderdale Graham argues that the state in the years immediately following abolition attempted but failed either to elaborate a new set of laws to govern servants who had previously lived and worked under the close eye of their owners or to fix new rules of authority for society in general. Officialdom continued on a pragmatic course; and given the strength of customary rules that infused the master-servant relationship in particular, and given the dearth of options open to former slaves, the previous pattern of informal contracts and casual arrangements prevailed.[6] Nonetheless, the "tolerable sense of order" that predominated in the transitional period declined precipitously as free labor outnumbered slave. To meet the challenge, by the 1870s a professional police

5. Ministerio da Justiça e Negocios Interiores, *Relatório apresentado ao Ministro da Justiça e Negocios Interiores pelo Dr. Epitacio Pessôa* (Rio de Janeiro: Imprensa Nacional, 1899), 74.

6. Sandra Lauderdale Graham, *House and Street: The Domestic World of Servants and Masters in Nineteenth-Century Rio de Janeiro* (Cambridge: Cambridge University Press, 1988), 130.

force emerged that extended the system of "state-sponsored" control previously exercised over people as property to the entire mass of urban poor. As
Thomas Holloway demonstrates, the veneer over patron-client relationships,
which the police had polished before abolition, disappeared in the years after
it, leaving only the police, along with the military, as the real enforcers of a
new bourgeois order designed to control and subdue the urban masses.[7]

The immense changes in the city, brought on by the new waves of internal
and international migrants and by the expanding job opportunities in manufacturing and services, meant that the Rio of 1900 or 1905 operated under
social norms dramatically different from those prevalent in the wake of abolition. In population alone, Rio de Janeiro was by 1900 or 1906 no longer the
medium-sized metropolis it had been in 1888. There were more people, and
more of them were poor. Immigrants arrived with very few resources,
crowded into the tenements near the docks, and sought work as laundresses, construction workers, day laborers, or factory workers. Brazilian
census data actually show that the proportion of the economically active
population dropped from 66 percent in 1870 to 41 percent in 1920. Despite
an expansion in manufacturing, the industrial sector moved only from 29 percent of the population in 1870 to 33 percent in 1920, while the commercial
sector grew from 16 percent to 19 percent.[8] The only sectors that increased
appreciably were "liberal professions" and public-sector employment, which
might be an indication of the instability of the workforce more than an exact
measure of the number of people employed. For example, the census noted
a drop in the number of domestic servants over this time period, but that
seems illogical given the absolute increase in the population and the absence
of data showing that Brazilians stopped relying on maids. Therefore, these
figures indicate high levels of casual employment, labor mobility, and instability. Frequent swings in the economy, periods of recession followed by
higher productivity, meant that a worker might be a servant sometimes, a
textile worker at other times, idle or "self-employed" the rest of the time.
Census data reflected this transience, but for the Carioca laborers the reality
behind the numbers was a cruel poverty.[9]

For former slaves who migrated from the countryside or those with longtime residency in Rio, life was often worse. Statistical comparisons of hous-

7. Thomas H. Holloway, *Policing Rio de Janeiro: Repression and Resistance in a Nineteenth-Century City* (Stanford: Stanford University Press, 1993), 231.

8. Eileen Keremitsis, "The Early Industrial Worker in Rio de Janeiro, 1870–1930" (Ph.D. diss., Columbia University, 1982),16.

9. See the sources cited under Table 1. Keremitsis offers these statistics, but does not draw the same conclusions; "Early Industrial Worker," 16.

ing, nutrition, health, and incomes for whites and for people of color in Rio from 1890 to 1940 indicate that the white immigrant population fared better in every category than did mulattos and blacks. Even those black workers who had longer-term residency in Rio lost positions to immigrants, and those who arrived from the countryside with few marketable skills assumed the worst jobs at the lowest pay.[10] Even excepting the particular racial oppression that affected the recently freed slaves and people of color in Rio, the working class in general was poorly remunerated, lived in dilapidated and unsanitary housing, fell ill and died in great numbers during the frequent epidemics that swept the city.

Throughout the First Republic, periodic spurts of economic growth, which brought on brief spates of prosperity, alternated with years of stagnation and accompanying declines in wages. For all consumers and laborers in Rio, however, periods of prosperity usually meant higher prices, not wage increases, whereas, when exports fell off and prices declined, wages were cut and workers laid off. The Republican government, mired in perpetual crises and a series of ineffectual financial policies, did little to check skyrocketing prices on essential consumer goods. In particular, the relative prosperity of the late Empire, which high coffee prices had sustained, collapsed in the first years of the Republic when the world price and demand for coffee began to fall off and then dropped sharply during the worldwide depression toward the end of the decade. Since coffee prices suffered extreme fluctuations, Brazil's long-standing practice of relying on export earnings for most of its revenue continuously placed the economy in financial straits. Coinciding with the fall in coffee prices, the Republican government's attempt to consolidate the vast reaches of the territory wreaked havoc on the national treasury. In particular, the civil war in the South and the expeditions against Canudos depleted the Republic's already meager resources.[11]

From 1889 through 1894 the government embarked on a futile effort to

10. Adamo, "The Broken Promise," 40–42, 73–76, 110, 122–28, 143–47, 158, 168. George Reid Andrews, in his work on São Paulo, offers the fullest account of this discriminatory hiring practice, and added to Adamo's evidence, that work supports the presumption that a similar pattern operated in Rio; *Blacks and Whites in São Paulo, Brazil, 1888–1988* (Madison: University of Wisconsin Press, 1991), chap. 3.

11. Government summaries of the disturbances throughout Brazil, urban and rural, and their interconnection are reported in Ministerio da Justiça e Negocios Interiores, *Relatório apresentado ao Presidente da República de Antonio Luiz Affonso de Carvalho, Chefe da Policia da Capital Federal, Dezembro, 1890* (Rio de Janeiro: Imprensa Nacional, 1891), 6; idem, *Relatório apresentado ao Presidente da República pelo Dr. Antonio Gonçalves Ferreira, Ministro da Justiça e Negocios Interiores* (Rio de Janeiro: Imprensa Nacional, 1895), 13; idem, *Relatório apresentado ao Presidente da República pelo Dr. J. J. Seabra, Ministro da Justiça e Negocios Interiores* (Rio de Janeiro: Imprensa Nacional, 1905), vol. 1, app. G, 3.

raise funds by printing money, which in turn set off an inflationary spiral and wild speculation in bogus business ventures, further undermining existing problems in the production and distribution of essential goods. Even the modest increase in industrial output during the first half of the 1890s was insufficient to sustain a positive growth rate.[12] Salaries increased slightly from 1889 to 1894, but so too did rents, food prices, and the cost of essential items. The government embarked on a plan to replenish the treasury mostly through a regressive sales tax on basic consumer items. However, raising taxes was probably the worst tactic the government could propose, especially given its lack of credibility in controlling speculation on essential items and rents, as well as its failure to arrest chronic inflation. A tax hike in this context only served to anger just about everyone and laid the foundations for a series of demonstrations against the Republic's policies that drew together the working class, the petty bourgeoisie, and the marginally employed urban poor.

But with its economic priorities firmly wedded to protecting the export market, the government refused to elaborate domestic measures that benefited anyone but the most privileged ranks of the domestic urban bourgeoisie and foreign merchants.[13] It as much as proclaimed that the capital of the new Republic was a city that served the interests of the financiers, foreign investors, and the planters whose goods the urban merchants marketed, rather than a place for ordinary Brazilian people to earn a decent living, eat, sleep, relax, and move about in some modicum of comfort. On the other hand, the immediacy with which ordinary people responded to price or tax increases, cuts in wages, and layoffs indicates that they had not surrendered completely to the whims of the planter government, nor did they intend to concede without a fight.

The capital's consumers throughout the 1890s took to the streets to vent their frustrations with a government that was devoting huge resources to quelling disturbances in the countryside while at the same time ignoring mounting problems in the capital. Price increases on food and transportation, as well as shortages and monopoly price-gouging, gave rise to some of

12. The period of wild speculation and inflation was named the Encilhamento ("saddling-up"), and it stretched from 1888 to 1894. Luiz Antonio Tannuri, *O Encilhamento* (São Paulo: Editora Hucitec, 1981), 39–68; Mauricio A. Font, *Coffee, Contention, and Change in the Making of Modern Brazil* (Cambridge, Mass.: Basil Blackwell, 1990), pt. 1; Caio Prado Jr., *História econômica do Brasil* (São Paulo: Editora Brasiliense, 1945), 219–24.

13. Eulalia Maria Lahmeyer Lobo, *História do Rio de Janeiro: Do capital commercial ao capital industrial e financeiro* (Rio de Janeiro: Instituto Brasileiro de Mercado de Capitais, 1978), 2:501–7.

Fig. 2. Praça da São Francisco, c. 1890s. A favorite location for rallies and demonstrations during the First Republic. Photograph by Marc Ferrez, Jennings Hoffenberg Collection.

the city's more violent protests. On February 17, 1890, "hundreds of workers" claiming to represent "thousands" of others marched on the Ministry of Commerce, calling on the government to prevent speculators from artificially causing shortages and inflating prices. Some from the city's elite and conservative business community noted apprehensively that the crowds included not only the usual "troublemakers" from the downtown tenements but also residents from the newly emerging working-class neighborhoods cropping up on the outskirts of the Old City.[14] Shaken by this outpouring of anger and appalled at the specter of mobs of workers from the outlying areas descending on the downtown, *O Paiz*, the newspaper that spoke for the business community, warned the Republic's officials to find solutions to the crisis of inflation and shortages while it was yet possible to handle the discontented masses peacefully. "Whatever the cause, today the people eat worse, and it

14. *O Paiz*, February 17, 1890, 1.

costs more," the editor proclaimed. Worse yet, the paper predicted, these "problems" (high prices on scarce goods) will be opposed "with the greatest violence."[15]

It was not just the violence of the crowds that *O Paiz* viewed as threatening. Rather, the conservative daily feared that official intractability on social policy was actually encouraging the working poor to oppose the government in violent confrontations that drew participants from all of the city's neighborhoods and sometimes ended in rampages through the downtown. Their worst nightmare came true in the September 1893 march described briefly in the opening pages of this study. The agitation began as a rather modest demonstration of "hundreds" of Rio's residents in protest over taxes, especially on consumer items. But the implications were more far-reaching, since the crux of the agitators' grievance rested on two factors. One, there were reportedly "respectable citizens" in the ranks of the marchers, and, two, the protesters complained that the government was refusing to pay attention to the problems of the city and was instead preoccupied with distant civil disorders. For a march to turn to melee was not unusual in Rio during this period or at any time, but to lose the support for the Republic from the "respectable" citizenry did not bode well for the new government.[16]

The warning from *O Paiz* three years before had apparently gone unheeded, at least by the police department. The government, for its part, had then pleaded lamely for the business community and especially the working poor to have patience. The shortages, it explained, were a temporary matter caused by "the drought that whipped through the most productive regions of the country last year, deficiencies in the Rio de la Plata harvest, the enormous buying and shipping of cereals and other goods to the drought-stricken northern provinces."[17] Even without the hindsight of history, these explanations rang hollow. Continued shortages and price increases, along with repeated demonstrations throughout the 1890s proved beyond all doubt that the high prices confronting Rio consumers had not resulted from a single drought or the temporary breakdown of the distribution network; rather, these were problems endemic to the structure of capitalism as it was developing in Brazil.

An end to the military campaigns in the South in 1896 and against Canudos in 1897, along with some stimulation of local rice and basic foodstuff produc-

15. Ibid., February 18, 1890, 1, and March 21, 1890, 1.

16. Ibid., September 12, 1893, 1.

17. Ibid., March 21, 1890, 1. A similar explanation had appeared in the same newspaper earlier in the year; see ibid., January 29, 1890, 1.

tion in the state of Rio de Janeiro, brought consumer prices down and temporarily curbed speculation. President Manuel Ferraz de Campos Sales (1898–1902), the second civilian president after Prudente José de Morais Barros and the second export-oriented Paulista, showed little interest in addressing domestic problems.[18] As a result, prices did not fall adequately to make up for an offsetting deflationary trend in wages, giving little relief to those workers who were already at the bottom of the wage scale. Even this slight decline was short-lived, since consumer prices followed the rollercoaster ride set by the world market price for coffee. When coffee sales plummeted, as they did in 1905–6, 1912–13, and in 1916–17, for example, domestic prices rose.

On the other hand, reliance on the export economy alone should not have caused such massive inequality in the system. Countries have certainly prospered on the basis of agricultural exports: Australia and, in the late nineteenth century, Argentina, for example. In Brazil, however, corruption and favoritism permeated the economic and political system, effectively preventing the population as a whole from sharing somewhat evenly in the good times and from suffering disproportionately in the lean years. Faced with a decline in world coffee prices and a shortage of capital, planters, cattlemen, and other members of the powerful agricultural sector prevailed on the federal government to subsidize domestic produce, essentially stabilizing and even increasing the prices of basic foodstuffs and necessities for urban consumers.[19] Brazilian capitalists, no different from their counterparts anywhere else except in extremity, exalted the benefits of the "free market" until, of course, the market turned against them, and then they rushed to the government for their subsidies. Such policies, and the choke hold the planters held on the government, minimized incentives to look for alternatives to exports as a way of accumulating capital.

For example in order to assure high profits for wholesalers supplying the Rio market, the government sanctioned a monopoly that sold meat through designated stores.[20] The monopolies on fresh meat particularly angered Rio's

18. June E. Hahner, *Poverty and Politics: The Urban Poor in Brazil, 1870–1920* (Albuquerque: University of New Mexico Press, 1986), 161.

19. Eulalia Maria Lahmeyer Lobo, Octavio Canavarros, Zakia Feres, Sonia Gonçalves, and Lucena Barbosa Madureira, "Evolução dos preços e do padrão de vida no Rio de Janeiro, 1820–1930: Resultados preliminares," *Revista Brasileira de Economia* 26 (October–December 1971): 256; Lobo, *História do Rio de Janeiro,* 2:504.

20. Paulo Sérgio Pinheiro, "Classes medias urbanas: Formação, natureza, intervenção na vida política," in *História geral da civilização brasileira*, vol. 9, *O Brasil republicano: Sociedade e instituições, 1889–1930*, ed. Boris Fausto (São Paulo: Difusão Editorial, 1977), 2:27–28.

consumers, since they undermined competitive pressures that otherwise might have brought down retail prices on meat and other foodstuffs. Consequently, over the years a semilegal black market developed whereby slaughterers from Niterói and Cachoeira sold meat to butcher shops outside the official monopoly at a 20 percent discount. The discount meat markets were widely accepted, and until 1902 butchers and retailers operated with few restrictions despite government regulations. Pressed to uphold profits to monopoly producers during a particularly lean period in May 1902, municipal authorities moved to close down the extralegal network and confiscate the nonmonopoly meat.

When news of the government's action spread through working-class neighborhoods in early May, angry consumers gathered in front of Rio's butcher shops. Crowds erected barricades to prevent monopoly wholesalers from distributing their meat to the butchers, and a few bold folks broke into the monopoly shops in hopes, no doubt, of "confiscating" or just taking the meat.[21] Fighting erupted when police attempted to disperse the crowd and confiscate and burn the illegally supplied goods. Skirmishes with the police, fighting in front of butcher shops, and even gun battles stretched from May 29 through June 2. The calm that returned in early June meant at least a partial victory for the demonstrators. First, there seemed to be no arrests despite the fact that newspaper accounts had placed the number of demonstrators in the hundreds. In addition, authorities reported that they would temporarily relax their enforcement of the ban on the sale of nonmonopoly meat.[22]

Labor's actions against government policies, or strikes, walkouts, and slowdowns against employers, moved more slowly and occurred more sporadically in these years than did consumer-based protests. The textile industry was growing, but the mills were concentrated in the suburban areas rimming the Old City, and workers were housed nearby, thus keeping whatever worker discontent that erupted in the factories from spilling over into the downtown. Initially the mill owners simply allowed workers to pitch their shacks on company land; later they constructed housing that they rented to families, several of whom lived packed into a single unit. Forced to accept whatever wage the owner paid, and to pay rent at whatever rate the mill owner charged, entire families of immigrant workers lived isolated in the *vilas operarias* (more aptly named *vilas misérias*) and passed long days in the mills. Despite miserable conditions, organization among the workers

21. *Correio da Manhã*, May 29, 1902, 1; *Gazeta de Notícias*, June 1–2, 1902, 1.
22. *Gazeta de Notícias*, June 2, 1902, 1.

was difficult, and labor agitation, when it did occur, generally affected only those workers at a single factory or workplace. Of the strikes between 1890 and 1910 that Eulalia Maria Lahmeyer Lobo and Eduardo Navarro Stotz calculated in their statistical studies of economic cycles and the labor movement, few were in basic manufacturing. Most involved dockworkers and workers in transportation, municipal service, and skilled trades. Out of twelve of the most important strikes between 1899 and 1905, four involved streetcar drivers or conductors on either private or municipal services.[23]

Why these particular sectors as opposed to mill workers or others in the small manufacturing sector? First, service-sector, transportation, and utility workers were acutely affected by the overall economic instability of the period, since their wages were drawn from either the municipal coffers or from firms whose assets were largely based on foreign loans.[24] The continual financial crises of the early years of the Republic subjected this sector to cuts and delays in their wages, forced layoffs and cutbacks in the workforce, and resulted in a generalized disillusionment with the new government. To illustrate, municipal trolley drivers struck to increase their wages and shorten their working hours in mid-January 1900. Meeting intransigence from the Republican administrators, a group of three hundred strikers marched on the president's residence at the Catete Palace, shouting "vivas" for the monarchy and "Death to the Republic!"[25] Seven different infantry battalions, three cavalry regiments, and one artillery unit cut off the marchers short of the official residence. Ultimately, the government relied on the military to disperse demonstrations around the city and crush the strike.[26]

Despite this clear indication of the government's lack of receptivity to labor's demands, transportation and public-sector workers continued to agitate over the next decade. In 1901 municipal garbage collectors struck after going three months without being paid. Pronouncing the strikers' demand "respectable and just," the usually antilabor *O Paiz* called on the municipal coun-

23. Eulalia Maria Lahmeyer Lobo and Eduardo Navarro Stotz, "Flutuações cíclicas da economia, condições de vida e movimento operario—1880 a 1930," *Revista Rio de Janeiro* 1 (December 1985): 67.

24. Keremitsis notes that trolley drivers had unique bargaining strength among the Rio workers because they were an essential service and drove every day, as opposed to factory laborers, who were frequently faced with layoffs and shutdowns; "Early Industrial Worker," 186. Hahner argues that authorities responded more quickly and harshly to strikes by transport workers or stevedores than to walkouts at small textile plants and other factories. The former jeopardized the important export trade, whereas strikes in domestic factories posed less of a threat to the overall economy. Hahner, *Poverty and Politics*, 264.

25. *O Paiz*, January 16, 1900, 2.

26. Ibid., 1.

cil to pay the back wages. The workers, the paper contended, were owed a "genuine guarantee of their rights, liberty, and dignity of work."[27] The strike ended when municipal authorities promised to restore back pay. But soon after the workers had returned to their jobs, they found that management was demanding that the garbage men put in longer days at the same pay and, worse, that the most militant rank and filers had been dismissed. The garbage collectors walked out again, but this time the city officials called in police and cavalry units to break up picket lines and prevent any demonstrations in support of the strike. When the strike became violent, as a result of attacks by the police, *O Paiz* quickly changed its sympathies, reneged on its previous support for the drivers' cause, and labeled the entire episode an "anarchist provocation."[28]

A second feature of this period was that government policies could as easily be opposed by organized worker resistance, usually in the form of strikes and demonstrations, as by occasional outbreaks of popular protest against taxes or the continually rising cost of living. The convergence of worker demands with those of consumers came about because both sectors were given little share in the profits during periods of prosperity and likewise suffered more during the cyclical depressions. Their shared oppression brought about the use of shared "mechanisms" of resistance. The solidarity was most apparent when riders and employees faced off against the powerful transportation companies.

Profiteering by streetcar companies and hostile responses from both workers and passengers were long-standing. In the 1880 Vintem Riot over five thousand people gathered on the Campo de São Cristóvão near the imperial palace in protest over the imposition of a tram tax. Lasting four days, the 1880 riot set the stage for the many subsequent protests that spanned the years from 1890 through 1904.[29] These worker/consumer actions, which involved streetcar drivers and wagoners but drew support from riders as well, illustrate the way consumers, some of them from the middle class, joined with workers to protest the policies of the arrogant transportation companies. When in June 1901 the Companhia São Cristóvão raised the fare on its trolley lines in an effort to collect more revenue to finance expanded service in Rio's central business district, it was met with a riot. Angry passengers, "ostensibly of all classes," including students, workers, and "respect-

27. Ibid., January 14, 1901, 1.
28. Ibid., January 15, 1901, 1.
29. Sandra Lauderdale Graham, "The Vintem Riot and Political Culture: Rio de Janeiro, 1880," *Hispanic American Historical Review* 60, no. 3 (1980): 431–49.

able passengers," responded to the fare hike by stoning, overturning, and setting ablaze several cars.[30] Announcing that it was impossible to continue the service, because of the continual attacks on the lines, streetcar drivers walked off the job.

Following the usual procedure for crushing a strike, mounted police stormed the crowds of demonstrators, who had already succeeded in destroying two streetcars. The angry crowd retreated but showered the cavalry with rocks and, according to the police, even a few gunshots. Sporadic rioting continued on the second day and spilled over to a third. The vehemence of the protest, the widespread involvement of both passengers and drivers, and the fact that rioters were attacking cars on nearly every stretch of the line forced the São Cristóvão management to restore fares to their preriot level. At the end of June victory marches filled the streets of Rio de Janeiro and São Paulo, where students had supported the Rio protesters. Crowds yelled "triumphant acclamations" in support of the working class, against the streetcar companies, and against the government.[31]

The cross-class alliance that marked the Rio protests was one of their most notable features. In Rio, as in any other large urban area, workers' strikes against streetcar companies inconvenienced passengers and always risked drawing the hostility of the most affluent passengers toward the workers and away from the companies. On the other hand, strikers could tap the passengers' ready reserve of hostility toward the companies, as happened in two important Rio protests.

Taxi drivers and streetcar operators who owned or leased their own vehicles struck in January 1902 and again in January 1904 over a new municipal tax added to the cost of an operator's license. Originally passed on December 19, 1901, the tax was assessed on each mule or traction animal the driver operated. In the face of vehement protests from the drivers, the tax was not immediately enforced.[32] However, in January 1904 the city government resolved to renew efforts to tax new and even existing licenses in hopes of shoring up an expanding revenue shortage in the city treasury brought on by the extensive renovation works. In spite of the drivers' threatened strike, the city needed to collect more money from the capital's residents to meet the mounting costs of the renovation, which was not only depleting city funds but also federal reserves. In response, drivers for the Companhia São Cristóvão, Companhia Vila Isabel, Empresa de Transportes e Carruagens,

30. *Jornal do Brasil*, June 21, 1901, 1.
31. Ibid.
32. Ibid., January 14–15, 1901.

and Companhia da Gaz walked off the job. Immediately the minister of justice dispersed 169 infantry and 108 cavalry among the police stations, offices
of the transport companies, and health department offices to stave off violent
demonstrations.[33]

For nearly a week strikers battled scabs and the police throughout the city,
successfully paralyzing traffic. They barricaded the tram lines, set small fires
on or near the tracks, and pulled strikebreakers from the cars in attempts to
ensure that the lines came to a complete halt. In one case, striking drivers
ambushed a scab-operated funeral wagon during the procession to the cemetery. They chased off the driver, overturned the wagon, and, to the dismay
of the onlooking mourners, left the casket, wagon, and presumably the
corpse in the street. In another incident, strikers apprehended a wagon full
of stray dogs belonging to the city dog catcher. The assailants sent the driver
running, freed the dogs, and dumped the wagon in the Mangue Canal.[34]

Several daily newspapers carried a statement in which the drivers justified
their struggle, complaining that they were already overburdened with taxes
on barn rent, sanitation taxes, and cuts in their wages to pay assistants. They
called on the mayor to lift the new head tax on traction animals, stating that
they had no choice but to pass the increase onto the passengers and other
consumers in the form of a higher car fare, a move the strikers considered
unjust but necessary. Arguing that they were not opposed to paying municipal taxes, they nonetheless objected to paying at the exorbitantly high rate
the government was demanding. Finally, the strikers complained that users
and workers on the city's transport services were being forced to pay for the
city's current financial crisis and for the renovation works that were depleting the city's coffers. Instead, they stated, the tax burden should be shifted
to the owners of the large transportation lines.[35]

The drivers' message quickly garnered the support of streetcar passengers, especially the demand to lower fares. Disgruntled with the service and
with repeated attempts by the companies to raise the fares, passengers
joined strikers in a march through the streets near Praia Formosa and in
Engenho Velho near Nova do Livramento and Gamboas. Bands of strikers
and passengers threw rocks at streetlamps and engaged in skirmishes with
police. Over three hundred strikers and protesters were arrested or detained
briefly before the job action ended in defeat on January 12, 1904, four days
after it had begun.[36]

33. Ibid., January 10, 1904, 1–2.
34. Ibid.; *Correio da Manhã*, January 10, 1904, 1, and January 12, 1904, 2.
35. See note 34 above.
36. See note 34 above.

Although the strike and accompanying demonstrations fit into a general pattern of hostility and violence against transportation companies in Rio de Janeiro, the breadth of support for the strikers was significant. The poorest rung of urban society could occasionally afford to ride public transports, but not regularly. Most of the passengers were from the ranks of the white- and blue-collar working class as well as shopkeepers, government functionaries, students, and other entrepreneurs. Therefore, it can be assumed that a large number of the protesters who supported the drivers, themselves a part of the more stable workforce of the city, were workers and middle-class. Likewise it can be assumed that the riders' support derived as much from their discontent with the companies as from solidarity with the workers. That is, the cross-class alliance that characterized this and other demonstrations, culminating in the antivaccination riot at the end of 1904 and in subsequent strikes in later years, resulted from a widespread and, to the horror of many officials, growing dissatisfaction with the condition of city services, as well as with the methods and priorities set for improving them.

In the long term, resolutions to these wider problems, and thus to the social conflict ripping the capital, eluded the Republic's leaders. Reliant on the export trade, and refusing to curb the political control of the coffee barons, leaders refused to end monopoly price-gouging, to recognize the just demands of the city's poor and working majority, or even to address the mounting complaints from middle-class consumers. While debt, inflation, high prices, and low wages remained endemic to Brazil's economy throughout the First Republic, officials continued to greet protests with repression.

It bears mentioning that the violence, the strikes, and the protests were not unique to Rio de Janeiro in the early years of the Republic. Roderick Barman's analysis of the Quebra-Quilo riot that rocked the Northeast in late 1874 and 1875 and Lauderdale Graham's examination of the Vintem Riot in Rio in 1880 both show that ongoing tensions could explode when sparked by the enactment of seemingly minor laws or the imposition of unjust and unexplained taxes. Both the famous Canudos rebellion in Bahia at the end of the century and the lesser-known Contestado rebellion that swept through Santa Catarina and Parana from 1912 to 1916 brought together devout followers of mystical prophets with protesters against taxes and, in the latter case, opponents of a proposed route for a new railroad line. Riots and rebellions, in the most urban area of Brazil or in the remote backcountry of Pernambuco and Santa Catarina, were a consequence of national political events and the country's continual financial problems, which remained unresolved throughout the Old Republic. Whether in the country or in the heart of the developing

cities, protests, strikes, and popular rebellion disrupted the Republicans'
plan to showcase Brazil as the emerging center of South American order,
progress, and civilization.[37]

In addition, the upheaval in turn-of-the-century Brazil very much resembled the actions of crowds in France and England during similar periods
of economic and political transition. In the late seventeenth and eighteenth
centuries in Europe, an emergent market economy and reliance on wage
labor replaced the authoritarian, if more paternal, feudal order, forcing thousands of rural poor into urban centers. No doubt the crisis of vagabondage,
the instability of the market economy, and the chaos of the cities were even
more extreme under the conditions of disintegrating feudal relations in Europe than after abolition in Brazil. After all, Henry VIII of England had 72,000
vagabonds hanged by way of forcing the idle poor to expend their lives in
the textile sweatshops.[38] Two centuries later in Rio de Janeiro the elite were
maybe more adept at convincing the poor to work and to mind the laws of
capitalist society; but again their goal did not come easily, or without resistance. In Rio, as in France, England, and later in the United States, crowds
gathered in front of stores to protest marketing regulations, high prices, the
tyranny of the speculators, and the general inattention of the authorities to
the needs of the poor. For example, in 1902 in New York City, the same year
as the Rio riot, crowds congregated in front of stores to denounce the monopolies that controlled the sale and distribution of meat. Women, according
to Herbert Gutman, "battered butcher shops, carrying out slabs of meat
'aloft on pointed sticks . . . like flags.'"[39] There is a kind of tragedy in the
realization that strikes and protests over the same issues erupted continents
apart, at the same time or separated by centuries, but the participants knew
nothing of each other during the events or of what they shared as like-
minded comrades in similar historical moments.

37. Roderick J. Barman, "The Brazilian Peasantry Re-examined: The Implications of the
Quebra-Quilo Revolt, 1874–1875," *Hispanic American Historical Review* 57, no. 3 (1977): 401–
24; S. L. Graham, "The Vintem Riot and Political Culture"; Robert M. Levine, *Vale of Tears:
Revisiting the Canudos Massacre in Northeastern Brazil, 1893–1897* (Berkeley and Los Angeles:
University of California Press, 1992); Todd A. Diacon, *Millenarian Vision, Capitalist Reality:
Brazil's Contestado Rebellion, 1912–1916* (Durham, N.C.: Duke University Press, 1991). In his
work on the development of the Brazilian civil service, Lawrence S. Graham states that the case
of Canudos more than any other demonstrates the "ineffectiveness and inability of the central
government in Rio to enforce policy during the Old Republic"; *Civil Service Reform in Brazil:
Principles Versus Practice* (Austin: University of Texas Press, 1968), 21.

38. Karl Marx and Friedrick Engels, *The German Ideology*, ed. R. Pascal (New York: International Publishers, 1947), 51–52.

39. Herbert G. Gutman, *Work, Culture and Society in Industrializing America* (New York: Random House, 1977), 62.

By the turn of the century, the Republic's newly articulated strategy for implanting civilization and progress in Rio de Janeiro began to center on the debate over public health, an issue that likewise was closely tied to the question of social control. Since the city was notoriously unhealthy, a place where epidemics were frequent and sanitary conditions abysmal, some worried that discontent over sanitation would escalate into rioting to match that now troubling the capital over prices, shortages, monopolies, wages, and other issues.

Rio was especially unhealthy not just because it was in the tropics but because it rested on a few strips of land wedged between sharply rising hills, the ocean, and the bay. The land flooded during the rainy season, when water from the bay rose above the retaining walls and poured into the streets, but it remained marshy even after the water receded, because the drainage system was so inadequate. Worse, this battle between land and sea meant that for much of the year pools of stagnant water stood in the downtown areas, providing an ideal breeding ground for mosquitoes carrying yellow fever and malaria.[40] A British traveler described Rio in the late nineteenth century as a "labyrinth of narrow streets, some not more than seven yards wide. West and north of the busy and squalid port area the city is built around marsh and swamps. Here where the poorer inhabitants congregate, is a happy hunting-ground for the yellow fever scourge."[41]

Yellow fever, smallpox, and other epidemics periodically ravaged the city, particularly the poor districts. In 1850 a massive epidemic of yellow fever left 90,000 ill and 4,160 dead. Between 1850 and 1908 the disease returned to claim another 60,000 victims, 15,179 of them in major epidemics between 1890 and 1898. In 1891, a year of major immigrant influx, four terrible epidemics struck—yellow fever, malaria, smallpox, and influenza—leaving 4,454 dead from yellow fever alone. In addition, typhoid, malaria, dysentery, and tuberculosis continued to devastate the populace in the years when the most destructive epidemics stayed away.[42]

---

40. For the best descriptions of Rio's physical and social characteristics during this period, see Vivaldo Coaracy, *Memorias da cidade do Rio de Janeiro,* vol. 88 of *Coleção documentos brasileiros,* (Rio de Janeiro: Libraria José Olympio Editora, 1955); Luiz Edmundo, *O Rio de Janeiro do meu tempo* (Rio de Janeiro: Imprensa Nacional, 1938), 207; Brasil Gersón, *História das ruas do Rio de Janeiro* (Rio de Janeiro: Editora Souza, 1954); Fernando Nascimento Silva, ed., *Rio de Janeiro em seus quatrocentos anos: Formação e desenvolvimento da cidade* (Rio de Janeiro: Distribuidora Record, 1965), esp. the history section written by Claudio Bardy; Francisco Ferreira da Rosa, *Rio de Janeiro* (Rio de Janeiro: Edição Official da Prefeitura, 1905), 16–17.

41. Alured Gray Bell lived in Brazil at the end of the nineteenth century and into the first decade of the twentieth; *The Beautiful Rio de Janeiro* (London: William Heinemann, 1914), 20.

42. The figures cited are most likely lower than the actual count. Even after the sanitary code was passed in 1903, mandating notification of all diseases to the Department of Public Health, many cases continued to go unreported. Lobo, *História do Rio de Janeiro,* 2:470; Directoria

Although wealthy residents were able to escape the city during epidemics, they became increasingly distressed by the severity of yellow fever and the damage that the presence of all disease was doing to Rio's reputation among foreign business circles. The elite's civilization plans hinged on Rio's ascendance as a leading commercial and trading center, closely tied to Brazil's general economic growth. Because future prosperity was reliant in large part on the export of raw materials and the importation of capital goods, the health and efficiency of the capital and major port assumed heightened importance. The nation's trade, and thus this delicate balance between imports and exports, was threatened because shipping companies, aware of the prevalence of yellow fever and smallpox, refused to dock their vessels at the port. Since ships usually stopped in Rio and Santos, the port for São Paulo, before traveling on to Montevideo and Buenos Aires, captains risked carrying disease to other ports and infecting personnel over a wide stretch of the continent. During the epidemic seasons officials at the ports of neighboring countries refused entry to any ship whose last stop was Rio, which was enough to keep most shipping companies from docking in the city during the hot summer months, from December through March. Rumors circulated among government and business leaders in 1894 that because of the danger of disease a number of important British commercial houses were reluctant to open offices in Rio.[43]

More than just threaten commerce and foreign trade, the decrepit state of

---

Sanitária da Capital Federal, *Relatório do Instituto Sanitário Federal ao Presidente da República* (Rio de Janeiro: Imprensa Nacional, 1895), 214–16; idem, *Relatório ao Presidente da República pelo Dr. Antonio Gonçalves Ferreira, Ministro dos Negocios Interiores* (Rio de Janeiro: Imprensa Nacional, 1896), 243, 314–15; idem, *Relatório ao Presidente da República pelo Dr. Amaro Cavalcanti, Ministro dos Negocios Interiores* (Rio de Janeiro: Imprensa Nacional, 1897), 248–49. For a summary of the effects of the epidemics, see Directoria Geral de Saúde Pública, *Relatório apresentado ao J. J. Seabra, Ministro da Justiça pelo Director Geral de Saúde Pública, Annexos ao Relatório do Director Geral de Saúde Pública* (Rio de Janeiro: Imprensa Nacional, 1904), app. N1, 80–83. On cholera and other epidemics of the nineteenth century, see Donald B. Cooper, "The New 'Black Death': Cholera in Brazil, 1855–1856," *Social Science History* 10, no. 4 (1986): 467–88.

43. Ferreira da Rosa, *Rio de Janeiro*, 15. Major yellow fever epidemics struck the Rio de la Plata region in 1857 and 1871. At its height, in April 1871, the death rate reached 563 persons a day in Buenos Aires, alarming political leaders and spreading panic throughout the city. With the onset of cooler weather in May and the start of the Argentine winter, yellow fever subsided, leaving behind a record of 14,000 dead. James R. Scobie, *Buenos Aires: Plaza to Suburb, 1870–1910* (New York: Oxford University Press, 1974), 122–24. For a detailed description of the yellow fever epidemic, its social and medical effects, see Miguel Angel Scenna, *Cuando murió Buenos Aires, 1871* (Buenos Aires: Ediciones La Bastilla, 1974). For a discussion of the 1871 epidemic's effect on the black population in Buenos Aires, see George Reid Andrews, *The Afro-Argentines of Buenos Aires, 1800–1900* (Madison: University of Wisconsin Press, 1980), 91–92.

sanitation seemed to epitomize the ineptness of the Republic and to call into question what, if anything, had been gained under the new government. Possibly inspired by pro-monarchist sentiments, one irate Carioca commented: "From a practical and utilitarian point of view, the population of the city of Rio de Janeiro has not gained any advantage from the Republic; on the contrary, life here has become much more difficult." Pointing to a series of failures, he noted that "there has not been a single material improvement amidst the many improvements begun years ago by the Department of Hygiene and by various engineers. Nor have some of the projects initiated by the monarchist government moved ahead." No doubt echoing the sentiments of many residents of the city, his list combined complaints over poor sanitation with those over rising crime: "There has been no improvement in the water-supply service, no efficient provisions for cleaning out the sewers; insubordination continues to flourish among the ranks of the armed forces, both those on land and at sea. Pocket picking is increasing day by day; public security is on the same level as it was during the worst days of the monarchy." However universal the problems of petty crime and sanitation were, the writer summarized the views of his class toward the new government: "There aren't any houses, and the prices of the few there are have been raised; the cost of imported goods and of those goods produced within the country has gone up by almost 50 percent; there aren't any servants, and those there are are impossible; there is no municipal administration, or a decent police force, or a regular health system."[44]

The government was therefore feeling the squeeze from two sides—fears of spreading violence from the poor and growing discontent from the literate, propertied citizenry. The latter was filling the pages of the daily papers with letters, petitions, and notices of their meetings denouncing the failures of the municipal and Republican governments. Most of their complaints centered on poor sanitation and lack of water. In June 1892 the residents of Andrades Street, between Senhor dos Passos and Hospício, sent a letter to the Department of Public Works stating that their neighborhood had been without water for over three days. "It seems incredible that there is a shortage of this precious liquid, considering how much it has rained," the complainants declared.[45] A decade later occupants of Bento Lisbôa Street, almost in the shadow of the Palace of Catete, complained that they were frequently without water, that sewage piled up along the streets, that garbage collection was irregular, and that they were "unsure from one day to the next if water would

44. *Jornal do Brasil*, April 15, 1891, 2.
45. Ibid., June 20, 1892, 1.

be available for washing and drinking."[46] And when the "distinguished residents" of Meier congregated at the house of Captain Antonio Ferreira de Barros in February 1903, they resolved to form a "commission" so that they could formally communicate to the Department of Public Works the fact that they were more than six days without water. Despite their personal reply from the inspector general for Public Works assuring them that their problems would be corrected promptly, very little was accomplished on a citywide basis.[47]

One of the main reasons for the government's paralysis was that overpopulation was pushing an inadequate system of public works and limited housing to the breaking point. From 1869 to 1888 the number of collective housing structures, including pensions, one-night boarding houses, and tenements, as well as hotels, grew enormously in the center city. In the postabolition period the long-standing problem of overcrowding worsened and eventually reached crisis proportions as migrants and immigrants poured into the capital. The center city became a magnet from 1888 to 1890, drawing to it former slaves from the countryside and from the desperately poor towns of the interior. No matter how crowded the conditions in downtown Rio, there were job opportunities, or rumors of opportunities, that simply did not exist in the countryside.[48]

In the early 1890s most of the working class and urban poor who resided in the city of Rio de Janeiro lived in the downtown tenements, disparagingly called *cortiços*, meaning "beehives." The *cortiços* earned their name from their ramshackle construction, each dwelling rather precariously attached to and piled on top of the other, resembling a beehive. These dwellings dotted the zones of the central district near the docks and downtown commercial houses in Sant'Anna, Sacramento, São José, Santa Rita, and the *morro* of Santo Antonio. In 1888 the *cortiços* accounted for 3.96 percent of the city's buildings and housed 11.72 percent of the population, or about 31,272 people out of a total population of 266,831. In 1890 it was estimated that the *cortiços*, along with other rooms and collective houses, contained more than 100,000 people. And although the number of dwellings, most of them additions tacked onto existing buildings, tripled, the expansion did not keep pace with the growing numbers of occupants. The density rate in 1888 was already at 2.6 per room, well above the 1.5 that was considered acceptable. In 1890 the

46. *O Paiz*, February 14, 1902, 1.
47. Ibid., February 16, 1902, 2.
48. Jaime Larry Benchimol, "Pereira Passos, um Haussmann tropical: As transformações urbanas na cidade do Rio de Janeiro no inicio do seculo XX" (master's thesis, Universidade Federal do Rio de Janeiro, 1982), 352–62.

housing inspector noted that the parishes of Sacramento, São José, Santa Rita, São Cristóvão, Glória, Lagôa, and Engenho Velho all grew at rates in excess of available housing, and in the cases of Sacramento, Santa Rita, and São José at rates of three or four times those of capacity. On average, therefore, two or three families often lived piled into very small rooms, and in the most densely populated parishes this number could have been higher.[49] The apartments were notorious for their lack of light and ventilation, and considering that they were illuminated with kerosene lamps, the absence of windows presented a particular danger of asphyxiation from the fumes, not to mention the danger of fire. Sewage systems were inefficient or sometimes lacking; bathrooms were shared by one to two hundred persons; water was frequently in short supply and often cut off entirely. Health officials recorded disease and mortality rates higher than those in other parts of the city. In 1895 a report from the public health inspector related that death from yellow fever, tuberculosis, and all other diseases was consistently higher in those districts with the poorest population crowded into collective housing units.[50]

Residents of the *cortiços* included quarry workers, day laborers on the docks, construction and municipal workers, peddlers, domestic servants, and anyone who was making a living servicing the downtown commercial establishments. Most were casual laborers—people who contracted for jobs by the day or week, many of whom were seasonally employed or had jobs only when ships docked. In addition, most of the city's washerwomen lived in these tenements, since they were constructed with the living quarters surrounding courtyards where laundry tubs were provided to tenants for a fee. Finally, the *cortiços'* proximity to the hub of the city meant they were popular dwellings for the prostitutes, beggars, and pickpockets who practiced their trades in the business and tourist community in the city center.[51]

49. Directoria Geral de Estatística, "Estatística Predial," in *Apuração das Cadernetas Empregadas no Recenseamento Geral da República dos Estados Unidos do Brazil en 31 de Dezembro de 1890, Districto Federal* (Rio de Janeiro: Imprensa Nacional, 1895), 424–25; Sidney Sérgio F. Solis and Marcus Venício T. Ribeiro, "O Rio onde o sol não brilha: Acumulação e pobreza na transição para o capitalismo," *Revista Rio de Janeiro* 1, no. 1 (1985): 52; Benchimol, "Pereira Passos," 360.

50. Antonio Martins de Azevedo Pimentel, *Quaes os melhoramentos hygienicos que devem ser introduzidos no Rio de Janeiro para tornar esta cidade mais saudavel* (Rio de Janeiro: Imprensa Nacional, 1895), 188. Pimentel completed an extensive study for the public health division, detailing many of the living conditions in the city and the measures that needed to be taken to resolve the health and housing crisis, and criticizing many measures already in effect.

51. Directoria Geral de Estatística, "População Classificada Segundo as Profissões," *Recenseamento Geral da República dos Estados Unidos do Brazil em 31 de Dezembro de 1890, Districto Federal, 1890* (Rio de Janeiro: Imprensa Nacional, 1895), 408–21; idem, "Profissões," *Recenseamento do Rio de Janeiro Realizado em 20 de Setembro de 1906* (Rio de Janeiro: Imprensa Nacional, 1907), 180–389.

Aluizio Azevedo's novel *O Cortiço* (in English translation, *A Brazilian Tenement*) provides insight into the living conditions and social interaction of the crowded urban world in which women, men, and children of different classes, races, and nationalities, speaking Portuguese or Italian and working at a variety of conventional and unconventional jobs, lived literally on top of each other. Indeed the cooperation and conflict that such intimacy necessarily entailed form the central tension of the novel. In it the tenement's proprietor, João Romão, a hardworking Portuguese, lives with Bertoleza, a former slave whose freedom Romão supposedly purchased from her blind owner with the slave's own money. With earnings from Bertoleza's lucrative *quitanda*, from which most of the neighborhood bought manioc porridge, fried fish, and liver, added to "every copper brought in by his bar," the wily Portuguese built the *cortiço*. As a "master hand at scant measure and short weight, buying for a song what unfaithful slaves stole from their masters, cutting closer and closer his own expenditures, piling privation on privation, working himself and the negress like a yoke of oxen," João Romão managed to buy a major part of the quarry that adjoined the back of his shack.[52] The quarry workers and their companions/wives, who work as laundresses, live in the cramped "hives" the tight-fisted Portuguese has built out of lumber and materials stolen at night from construction sights around the city.

In addition to the intrigues among the tenement dwellers, the plot of Azevedo's novel involves a rivalry between João Romão and the wealthy Miranda, "a Portuguese merchant with a wholesale dry-goods business downtown on Rua Hospicio."[53] Because the bar/quarry proprietor and tenement landlord refuses to sell a strip of property that would have allowed Miranda's mansion a respectable distance from the bar, the washtubs, and makeshift shacks, the vast social chasm between the residents of the *cortiço* and the adjacent big house does not exist at all geographically. The mansion towers over the courtyard, forcing the bourgeois Miranda and his family to partake of the noises, smells, and social life of the *cortiço*. Thus, in addition to the portrait Azevedo draws of the humanity that survived among the poor despite the ravages of vice, crime, and poverty, he shows the hypocrisy of the elite, who in late-nineteenth-century Rio found themselves forced to share the ills of urban life and, most disturbing, to stand vulnerable to its effects.

If art mirrored reality, Rio's elite had no intention of keeping it that way.

52. Aluizio Azevedo, *A Brazilian Tenement*, trans. Harry W. Brown (New York: Robert M. McBride, 1928), 9.
53. Ibid., 10.

As more and more migrants poured into the city, and as the demand for housing was met in the haphazard, individual way depicted in Azevedo's fiction and reproduced in real life for the majority of the city's residents, the municipal government saw itself in danger of losing all regulatory control over habitation in the center city. Beyond the issues of misery and crowding in the *cortiços*, city officials also feared that crime was increasing along with the population, while morality was declining proportionately. Dr. Agostinho José de Souza Lima, inspector of public health, reported in 1891 that the *cortiços* promoted a "complete absence of moral virtue" among their inhabitants. "Crowded together in sordid promiscuity," the inspector noted, tenement occupants were living a life where "horrendous nudity" and "licentious behavior" were commonplace.[54] The *cortiços* earned a reputation as schools of crime and immorality and were considered directly responsible for the proliferation of vice in the downtown district. Added to this, the fact that laundresses were washing and drying clothes in the *cortiço* courtyards meant that diseases that might have remained contained to the city's poor were being spread to the wealthy as well. If in 1884 the Brazilian Academy of Medicine denounced the *cortiços* as "'nests' of yellow fever, of all infectious diseases, of vice and crime," certainly by 1890, considering how much they had grown over that six-year period, the medical community considered the dwellings worse.[55]

Finally, the *cortiços* themselves, as physical structures, were dilapidated and unsightly. Their very presence was an eyesore in the downtown and particularly worrisome to the city's elite, who were attempting to promote a gentrified image. The *Revista da Semana*, a weekly glossy magazine read by the cultured elite, decried the proliferation of these "parasitic neighborhoods" as a stain on the otherwise glorious aspects of this "great metropolis." The magazine, and others like it, argued that the *cortiços* should be eliminated for the harm they did to the city's aesthetics and thus the danger their presence posed in the elites' quest to attract foreign visitors and investors.[56]

Despite their miserable condition, the *cortiços* still had advantages over other housing available to a low-income Carioca family. The tenements were close to the downtown and accessible to jobs and to the few existent city services, including water, lighting, some paved streets, sidewalks, and public

54. Directoria Sanitária da Capital Federal, *Relatório apresentado ao Ministro dos Negocios Interiores de Agostinho José de Souza Lima, Inspector Geral de Hygiene* (Rio de Janeiro: Imprensa Nacional, 1891), 53.

55. S. L. Graham, *House and Street*, 127.

56. Adamo, "The Broken Promise," 35.

transportation, regardless of the sorry state of these services. The *cortiço* in Azevedo's novel is "the most convenient point in Botafogo for working people."[57] While the downtown district was hardly modern, it did have rudimentary services that were completely lacking in the industrial zones to the north and west of the downtown and in the *subúrbios* that were mushrooming on the outskirts of Rio de Janeiro. Migrants to Rio who arrived after 1890 for the most part settled in the Zona Norte, especially Engenho Velho, São Cristóvão, and Engenho Novo, and in the *subúrbios,* which stretched from Irajá and Inhaúma on the border of the city out to Santa Cruz.[58]

The *subúrbios* included the vast shanty districts near expanding industries; these districts were populated by families who worked from dawn to far past dusk mainly in textile mills. Moreover, textile workers had little choice in where they lived. Mill owners constructed barracks near the mills, which they rented to their employees for 15, 20, or 30 milreis per month, usually simply deducting the amount from the workers' pay.[59] In February 1902 workers at the Tijuca textile mill went out on strike, demanding that the company terminate a policy that required workers to live in company-built housing and to buy their food and other essentials at the company store. The company, *O Paiz* reported, collected 50 milreis a month on a house for a married couple or family and 25 milreis on rooms for singles and required a worker to pay half the rent on a single dwelling even if he or she did not live in it. Payment for housing was mandatory, whether a worker used it or not. In addition, the strikers complained that prices for goods from the company store and for company-built housing were much higher than those for nearby rental units and shop goods. Despite their proclamation that they would not return until "the factory directors allowed their employees the freedom to live and to make their purchases wherever they desired," the strike proved inconclusive, and the workers settled for less.[60]

57. Azevedo, *A Brazilian Tenement*, 21.

58. Because of the rapid expansion of Rio de Janeiro, both the districts of the North Zone and the towns outside Rio commonly were called *subúrbios*. I use the term *subúrbios* in the Portuguese to distinguish it from its English translation "suburb." *Subúrbios* are poor, working-class districts on the outskirts of Rio de Janeiro, whereas suburbs are middle- and upper-class residential districts in the United States, also on the outskirts of cities. Janice E. Perlman, *The Myth of Marginality: Urban Poverty and Politics in Rio de Janeiro* (Berkeley and Los Angeles: University of California Press, 1976), 19. In the epidemics before 1893, mortality was highest in São José and Sant'Anna, districts in the center city, where many *cortiços* were located, and in the northern industrial zone of São Cristóvão. Directoria Sanitária da Capital Federal, *Relatório do Encarregado do Serviço de Estatística Demografo-Sanitário* (Rio de Janeiro: Imprensa Nacional, February, 1893), 24.

59. Solis and Ribeiro, "O Rio onde o sol não brilha," 46.

60. *O Paiz*, February 13, 1902, 2.

Since the *subúrbios* grew up as extensions of these company towns under the control of the factory owners, conditions there matched the unhealthy state of the mills. Bereft of city services, the *subúrbios* had mud streets, were sometimes cut off from the rest of the city because of the absence of transportation lines, and had only a few stores that sold dried meat, vegetables, rice, and beans. Public health, administrative, and government officials hardly ventured into the *subúrbios* to provide any kind of service. During the epidemics wagons parked on some of the main streets and collected the sick who were willing to go to isolation centers, but attempts to provide any kind of medical service were rare. These vast makeshift settlements stood pretty much apart from the authority of official Rio de Janeiro, similar to *favelas* today.[61] And, like *favelas* today, they were the fastest growing sections of the capital district. From 1890 to 1920 the *subúrbios*, most of which barely existed before 1890, grew by over 100 percent. The housing options available to a recent immigrant or migrant to Rio de Janeiro at the turn of the century were all equally abysmal; nonetheless, some were probably better than others.

As the nineteenth century drew to a close, government officials, along with members of the business and cultural elite, began in earnest to search for a solution to the many problems facing the city. Although calls, and some projects, to promote public works and to rid the city of disease dated back to the early days of the Empire, the combination of changes in Brazilian society at the end of the century helped to consolidate the disparate and incomplete efforts of the past into a single plan that included controlling disease, renovating the center city, removing the "residuum" from the watchful eye of foreign visitors and native elites alike, and alleviating the conditions that gave rise to urban rioting. Thus, urban renewal and changes in the current housing situation began to assume an importance equal to that of public health proposals. Attention focused on the *cortiços*.

The *cortiços* and their occupants conflicted with the civilizers' plans for

61. *Favelas* are defined by the Instituto Brasileiro de Geografia e Estatística as clusters of fifty or more huts that are not served by the city public works departments and are not included in the network of street, numbering, and feeing system divisions. The first *favela* appeared on the hill behind the War Ministry building in the early 1900s. Seeking compensation and pension payments that the government owed them, army veterans of the Canudos campaign took up a vigil on the hill and petitioned army officials. They named the slope on which they camped after Favela Hill in Bahia, from which the final assault against Canudos was launched. Subsequently the name came to be applied to the shanty towns that sprang up on the mountain slopes throughout the city, which became major centers of population after 1920. Andre Pearse, "Some Characteristics of Urbanization in the City of Rio de Janeiro," in *Urbanization in Latin America* (proceedings of a seminar of the United Nations Bureau of Social Affairs, ECLA, and UNESCO, Santiago, Chile, July 6–18, 1959), ed. Philip M. Hauser (New York: International Documents Service, 1961), 191–92.

Table 2. Population Changes in Rio de Janeiro, 1872–1920

Area	1872–90		1890–1906		1906–1920		1890–1920	
	Pop. Chg.	% Chg.	Pop. Chg.	% Chg.	Pop. Chg.	% Chg.	Pop. Chg.	% Chg.
Center city [Renewal area]								
Sacramento	3,754	13	−6,051	−19	2,758	11	−3,293	−10
Candelária	−117	−1	−5,247	−54	−492	−11	−5,739	−59
São Jose	20,004	99	4,864	12	−15,181	−33	−10,317	−25
Santa Rita	12,938	41	2,126	−1	−7,765	−16	−5,639	−12
Sant'Anna	29,087	75	11,782	17	12,018	15	23,800	35
Glória	21,970	99	14,997	34	10,925	18	25,922	58
Santo Antonio	17,031	82	4,349	11	10,463	24	14,812	39
Total	104,667	62	26,820	12	12,726	4	39,546	17
North Zone [Poor/working-class area]								
Espírito Santo	17,596	127	27,728	88	20,180	34	47,908	152
Engenho Velho	21,560	139	54,506	147	49,436	54	103,942	281
São Cristóvão	11,369	104	22,896	103	14,234	31	37,130	167
Engenho Novo	—	—	35,025	125	36,081	57	71,106	255
Total	50,525	195	140,155	118	119,931	46	260,086	219

Subúrbios
[Outskirts of city]

Irajá	7,348	127	14,230	108	72,181	263	86,461	658
Jacarepaguá	8,077	101	1,135	7	5,891	34	7,086	44
Inhaúma	10,228	141	51,139	292	64,656	94	115,765	663
Guaratiba	5,563	78	5,274	41	5,681	31	10,955	86
Campo Grande	6,264	64	15,298	95	21,157	67	36,455	228
Santa Cruz	8,323	316	4,426	40	1,126	7	5,552	50
Total	45,803	113	91,532	106	170,692	96	262,274	304
Other areas								
Lagôa	15,294	113	19,251	66	9,566	19	28,817	100
Gávea	—	—	7,858	166	2,700	21	10,558	224
Islands	2,585	62	1,199	17	3,802	48	5,001	74
Total	17,879	128	28,308	70	16,068	23	44,376	110
Total population	218,874	71	287,045	55	319,237	39	606,282	117

SOURCE: Directoria Geral de Estatística, *Recenseamento do Brazil reclisado em 1 de setembro de 1920, População do Rio de Janeiro (Districto Federal)* (Rio de Janeiro: Imprensa Nacional, 1923), 2:xxvi. *Note:* For consistency with the 1872 and 1890 census , I rely on the 1920 recalculation of the districts, which counted Gambôa, Andarahy, Tijuca, and Meier as a part of Engenho Velho and Engenho Novo.

Rio's urban development and disrupted the carefully demarcated system of class privilege through which the Republican government maintained order. The fact that members of all classes lived in close proximity, crowded in a few blocks near the downtown docks, meant that grievances overlapped, especially those pertaining to housing and sanitation. Health Inspector Souza Lima captured the prevailing sentiments of the elite when in 1891 he called for the destruction of the *cortiços* "in the interest of freeing the central city from vice and *visible* poverty" (emphasis mine).[62] Although he likewise justified tearing down the *cortiços* "in the interest of preventing the spread of disease," was it an accident that he placed this "interest" second? The inspector called for the construction of sanitary workers' housing in the *subúrbios* to replace the downtown tenements, thus explicitly detailing what was to happen to the center-city residents.

The inspector's remarks were a preview, conscious or not, of the plan that was eventually adopted for resolving Rio's housing and health crisis, with the notable exception of the construction of worker housing, which was never built in significant numbers to replace buildings demolished in the renewal. Beginning in 1902 Rio embarked on an urban renewal and public health plan that resulted in the relocation of the poor from the downtown to the suburban outskirts. In addition to making the capital a healthy and beautiful place, the renovation plan fit nicely with the civilization goals of the elite: it enhanced Rio's reputation abroad as a major Latin American port city; it resolved the question of social control; and it forced on the working poor the inconvenience and, notably, the expense of cleaning up the city.

62. Directoria Sanitária da Capital Federal, *Relatório apresentado ao Ministro dos Negocios Interiores de Agostinho José de Souza Lima*, 53.

3

Sanitation and Renovation

When dawn broke there were no stones left standing.
—Vivaldo Coaracy, *Memórias da Cidade
do Rio de Janeiro*

The many improvements that were introduced as a part of the public health and urban renewal campaign in the first decade of the twentieth century were often revisions of projects that had been initiated decades earlier. Lacking in adequate venture capital to finance expensive public works, Rio's administrators had turned to British and North American firms during much of the nineteenth century for funds and expertise. Several foreign-owned or -financed companies played key roles in the three main aspects of the Rio de Janeiro renovations: sanitation, housing, and transportation.

Since sanitation was the longest-standing problem, it attracted the most attention. As early as April 26, 1857, the Visconde do Bom-Retiro, minister of the Empire, signed a decree charging John F. Russell with the task of constructing a sewage disposal system. Operating through the English bank of Glenn and Mills and Co., in 1862 Russell contracted an English company incorporated as the Rio de Janeiro City Improvements Company, Limited, to plan and build the system. The company, which everyone called simply the City, installed a system of sewers in the central business district and moved quickly to hook up all the downtown buildings to its lines. The 1872 census reported that thirty thousand of the downtown residences were connected to the City's system, or about 42 percent of the buildings in Rio. By 1890 the figure had grown to almost 60 percent of the dwellings in the downtown and in a number of neighboring suburbs.[1]

The City Improvements Company came under fire from the very beginning both for the shoddiness and expense of its work and for the way it used its connections with the local government to extend its reach into all aspects of the urban renovations. First, the sewage and drainage system was insufficient for Rio's growing needs and was poorly adapted to its climatic conditions. During the torrential rains, the canals designed to carry water runoff overflowed, and filthy water, human and animal excrement, garbage, and even animal carcasses gushed down city streets. Moreover, since the receptacles for collecting and distributing fresh water were too small or insufficient in number, drastic water shortages occurred during periods of light precipitation, which prevented the operation of the hydraulic pumps that were designed to drive the water-powered system. Consequently, once the rains stopped, sewer water stood in stagnant pools about town. Defenders of the English system pointed to its effectiveness in Europe; however, it apparently did not suit a wet tropical climate and mountainous terrain.[2]

In 1877 Candido Barata Ribeiro, on the faculty of the College of Medicine of Rio de Janeiro, pointed to the inadequate sewage disposal system as a principal cause of the frequent outbreaks of disease, especially yellow fever.[3] Another critic noted that the City was at fault, "not because it has badly carried out its duties, rather more simply because a project of this type cannot be definitively completed in a short period, and the scarcity of water has impeded the satisfactory operation of the plan."[4] Health officials reported

---

1. Antonio Martins de Azevedo Pimentel, *Quaes os melhoramentos hygienicos que devem ser introduzidos no Rio de Janeiro para tornar esta cidade mais saudavel* (Rio de Janeiro: Imprensa Nacional, 1895), 118–20; Sidney Sérgio F. Solis and Marcus Venício T. Ribeiro, "O Rio onde o sol não brilha: Acumulação e pobreza na transição para o capitalismo," *Revista Rio de Janeiro* 1, no. 1 (1985): 48.

2. Pimentel, *Quaes os melhoramentos hygienicos*, 118–20.

3. Candido Barata Ribeiro, *Quaes as medidas sanitárias que devem ser aconselhadas para impedir o desenvolvimento e propagação da febre amarela na cidade do Rio de Janeiro* (Rio de Janeiro: Imprensa Nacional, 1877), 69–74.

4. Pimentel, *Quaes os melhoramentos hygienicos*, 189.

that during the summer months the air above the sewer along Rivoli Street was as contaminated as the air in the sewer itself. Since the sewers contained in undiluted and unprocessed form "human excrement, food wastes and cleaning water, bathing water from hospitals and water used to launder hospital patients' clothing, contents from the intestines of cadavers from the morgues, and water used to groom both sick and healthy animals," the danger to those in the street was reportedly high.[5]

Rio actually had a very long list of engineers, companies, proposals, and counterproposals respectively commissioned, contracted, tried, and rejected for dealing with the problem of collecting and distributing water. Indeed, the remedies were as old as the problems, and the international coterie of experts who had lent their services was equally impressive. In 1876 the government contracted an Italian engineer, Antonio Gabrielli, who designed a system based on reservoirs to be built on various high plateaus to collect rain water, which would then be flushed through pipes down the hillsides when the rains subsided. Gabrielli's plan, although identical to one he had installed in Vienna, was actually an extension of the work a Spanish engineer had begun in Rio a few years before. However, after Gabrielli's plan proved ineffective, a Brazilian engineer stepped in to propose that the original plan (the Spaniard's) should be preserved, leaving the water piped from the reservoirs but adding a system of fountains at various points in the city as the final distribution mechanism. Despite the internationalism of the expertise, almost none of these projects was completed, although a few of the fountains were. The reason nothing was finished was probably that either the funding or the will to see the project through was insufficient, especially in the waning days of the Empire.[6]

Thomas Holloway's study of the changing patterns of policing in Rio during the nineteenth century illustrates the transitional nature of civil administration as political power shifted to the republicans. Gangs of street thugs expert at the deadly marshal art of *capoeira*, which had been imported from Africa and perfected by runaway slaves as needed protection, challenged the authority of the military and civilian police. In the transitional period demarcated by the abolition of slavery in May 1888 and the declaration of the Republic in November 1989, *capoeira* gangs broke up pro-Republican rallies

5. Directoria Geral de Saúde Pública, *Relatório apresentado ao Dr. Cruz pelo Delegado Alvaro Graça*, 9 Districto Sanitário, vol. 5, app. 11 (Rio de Janeiro: Imprensa Nacional, 1907), 7–8.
6. Vivaldo Coaracy, *Memorias da Cidade do Rio de Janeiro*, vol. 88 of *Coleção Documentos Brasileiros* (Rio de Janeiro: Libraria José Olympio Editora, 1955), 250–51.

Fig. 3. Aqueduct bringing water to the city from Corcovado Mountain in the last decade of the nineteenth century. Photograph by Marc Ferrez, Jennings Hoffenberg Collection.

and sought to intimidate oppositional forces, no doubt at the behest of powerful monarchical interests.[7] Although a criminal code had been in place since 1830, not until the establishment of a new penal code under the Republic in October 1890 did the police have the authority to repress systematically the *capoeiragem*. Despite the many differences between the way the state used police power to control public order and the way it implemented sanitation codes to control disease, it was apparent that as the government moved from one center of political power to another, the pendulum swung back and forth between laws and their enforcement. What Holloway shows existed in the case of the police can be extended to sanitation and other aspects of public administration. The national government might have been charged with overseeing policies throughout the country, but its impetus was to create the apparatuses to transform Rio "because of the city's position as the national capital, major port, and obligatory point of entry for foreign businessmen, diplomats, and tourists."[8]

Given the dire state of sanitation in most Brazilian cities, one of the first actions of the newly formed Republican government was passage of a comprehensive public health and sanitation bill on December 18, 1889. Although the 1889 law was only partially implemented, it marked a change in the previously chaotic methods of combating disease in Brazil. It centralized plans to change sanitation codes, prophylactic and medical care, and it took the first steps in implementing the controversial beautification and renovation campaign in the capital. The measure authorized the City Improvements Company to begin widening and paving streets, to excavate a dump, and to develop a system for the collection and incineration of garbage. Finally, the most significant aspect of the 1889 legislation was that it promoted the work of a number of private companies, in addition to the City, under government auspices, thereby allowing the powerful foreign-capitalized transportation firms a direct say in the way Rio de Janeiro was to allocate its space.[9]

The four main transit companies—Companhias Jardim Botânico, São Cristóvão, Vila Isabel, and Carris Urbanos—oversaw the extension of electric trolley lines (called *bondes* after the English word ["bonds"] for that

---

7. Thomas H. Holloway, *Policing Rio de Janeiro: Repression and Resistance in a Nineteenth-Century City* (Stanford: Stanford University Press, 1993), 269.

8. Ibid., 274.

9. Pimentel, *Quaes os melhoramentos hygienicos*, 188; Directoria Geral de Saúde Pública, Placido Barbosa e Cassio Barbosa de Rezende, *Os serviços de saúde pública no Brazil especialmente na cidade do Rio de Janeiro de 1808 a 1907* (Rio de Janeiro: Imprensa Nacional, 1909), 1:56.

which financed their construction) from the center city to the suburbs. The North American based Companhia São Cristóvão, successor to the Rio de Janeiro Street Railway Company, extended its mule-pulled *bonde* lines from downtown out to Tijuca, São Cristóvão, Saco do Alferes, Catumbí, Cajú, and other points in the northern industrial zones. By 1900 the Companhia Jardim Botânico, which began as the Botanical Garden Rail Road in 1868, had constructed lines linking the center city with the wealthy, beachfront zones in Jardim Botânico, Ipanema, and eventually Copacabana.[10]

Differences in the development of the wealthy Zona Sul (South Zone) and the working-class Zona Norte demonstrate the collusion of the various transportation companies with the City. The first and most obvious example involved the work of the Companhia Jardim Botânico. In 1901 it built a trolley line from the center city out to the Vila de Ipanema, a vacant property owned by the Baron of Ipanema, one of Brazil's wealthiest and most prominent citizens. Within the next five years, the City Improvements Company completed a sewage system, electrical power lines, and a network of streets in Ipanema, which, added to the efficient trolley connections with the center city, greatly enhanced the lovely beachfront area's value—all this, despite the fact that Ipanema's population was not significant enough to be listed in the federal census until 1920 and the municipal records show that it had only ninety-six buildings. Similarly, Copacabana was added to the Companhia Jardim Botânico route when the tunnels connecting the south beach area with Botafogo were opened in 1892 and 1906. And as with Ipanema, the trolley lines and accompanying lighting, sewage, and public services were added before the people. Copacabana registered no population on the censuses of 1872, 1890, and 1906 and then grew to 22,761 by 1920.[11]

In contrast, by 1906 the City had made no improvements in the northern districts of Inhaúma, which had 67,478 people, or more than 3.5 percent of the population of the entire city; in Campo Grande, which had 31,248, more

10. Sylvia F. Padilha, "Da 'Cidade Velha' a periferia," *Revista Rio de Janeiro* 1, no. 1 (1985): 17–19; Solis and Ribeiro, "O Rio onde o sol não brilha," 49–50.

11. Directoria Geral de Estatística, *Recenseamento do População do Imperio do Brazil a que se Procedeu no Dia 1 de Agosto de 1872* (Rio de Janeiro: Imprensa Nacional, 1873–76), 58; idem, *Recenseamento Geral da República dos Estados Unidos do Brazil en 31 de Dezembro de 1890, Districto Federal* (Rio de Janeiro: Imprensa Nacional, 1895), lxxiii; idem, *Recenseamento do Rio de Janeiro Realisado em 20 de Setembro de 1906* (Rio de Janeiro: Imprensa Nacional, 1907), 180; idem, *Recenseamento do Brazil Realisado em 1 de Setembro de 1920, População do Rio de Janeiro (Districto Federal)* (Rio de Janeiro: Imprensa Nacional, 1923), 2:xxvi; Solis and Ribeiro, "O Rio onde o sol não brilha," 49.

than 3 percent; or in Santa Cruz, which had 15,380, about 2.5 percent of the city's population. The thousands of isolated residents of these areas had no sewage system, no lighting, no streets, and no transportation lines to connect them with the rest of Rio. By 1920 Inhaúma had a stop on the Central rail line but still no lighting and inadequate sanitation, but its population had reached 131,886; Copacabana, with less than one-sixth the population, had a full range of lighting, sewage, and transportation services. It is worth noting that during the opening decades of the century Ipanema and Copacabana were exclusive locales to which the wealthy retreated in their *bondes* or own private coaches. Therefore, the trolley lines to the South Zone were built primarily to bring in servants and guests, whereas the poor of the North Zone, with no means of transportation, were forced to walk long distances to await the train.[12]

Another example of the favoritism accorded the wealthier neighborhoods was the form of transportation the companies built. While *bonde* lines criss-crossed the downtown and stretched south, it was the railroad that extended to the distant northern *subúrbios*. Since the trains were already in existence to transport coffee from other parts of Brazil to the docks, in 1897 the Leo-poldina Railway Company and in 1903 the Estrada de Ferro Central do Brasil (the Central, or EFCB) both added passenger trains to meet the growing commuter needs. Rather than build comfortable passenger commuter trains or trolley lines to service riders from the Zona Norte, as they had for those from the South, the transit companies simply added seating cars to the coal-dust-laden freight trains on the existing lines, all of which were notoriously dirty, noisy, and slow.

Finally, the rail lines connected certain northern zones but bypassed oth-ers, regardless of the number of residents in need of the service. For ex-ample, the rail lines extended to Inhaúma, Irajá, Vicente de Carvalho, Coelho Neto, and Pavuna, all areas with nuclei of small producers and shopkeepers who either provided foodstuffs for the city's markets or produced shoes and textiles they sold in other parts of the city. On the other hand, districts that produced nothing but were rapidly growing, such as Jacaré, Faria, Timbo, and Manguinhos, districts with thousands of shanty dwellers, received no transportation lines at all. Moreover, since the railroads had a long-standing relationship with the coffee planters, and indeed existed to transport cof-fee from the interior to the coast, the use of the train lines to transport

12. See note 11 above.

people and some domestic goods served to subsume all of Rio's production, and even the mobility of its working population, to the coffee production system.[13]

In sum, the urban renewal plan affirmed the hegemony of both foreign investors and coffee exporters by inserting their control into the internal workings of Rio's settlement, as well as locked the fragile domestic economy into a position of subservience. No individual smallholder in Inhaúma, for example, could transport his goods to market without paying freight rates to the powerful Central railroad. Moreover, if the domestic producers objected to the rates, as they did, there was nothing to prevent the transit companies from shutting down the stop entirely or threatening to do so. As Sidney Solis and Marcus Ribeiro report in their discussion of capital investment and the role of the Rio de Janeiro City Improvements Company, "The City demonstrated that the 'exploitation of the city' could be an excellent source of wealth for other business transactions."[14]

The availability of affordable housing closely paralleled the status of the city's transit. On the one hand, the transportation companies had an interest in the urban renewal plan beyond just the establishment of new rail and *bonde* lines. Ultimately their profits depended on the daily movement of large numbers of people and goods from the outlying regions to the center city and back again, an enterprise that was only possible if the downtown no longer housed the working poor. Conveniently, on the other hand, the City Improvements Company, along with the Companhia Evoneas Fluminense and the public health department, under the auspices of the municipal council, were able to order the destruction of unsafe or unsanitary structures. Not surprisingly, the downtown *cortiços,* which housed the bulk of the city's poor, were first on the list.

Certainly the City, as well as any private or public agency, could make a strong case for condemning structures universally considered "dirty, ugly, and miserable."[15] However, the controversy centered on where the occupants would live once their houses were torn down. Indeed, the history of plans to replace the *cortiços* with better housing dated back to Law 719,

13. Solis and Ribeiro, "O Rio onde o sol não brilha," 49–50. For an explanation of the power coffee producers exerted in Brazil's economic life, see Thomas H. Holloway, *The Brazilian Coffee Valorization of 1906: Regional Politics and Economic Dependence* (Madison, Wis.: State Historical Society, 1975), 5–26.

14. Solis and Ribeiro, "O Rio onde o sol não brilha," 49.

15. Luiz Edmundo, *O Rio de Janeiro do meu tempo* (Rio de Janeiro: Imprensa Nacional, 1938), 370.

passed in 1853, in which the imperial government had called for the construction of "hygienic housing" for the "poor classes." But nothing much was ever done. Some critics of the government's lethargy on this issue argued that contractors were actually more interested in building additional tenements than in replacing or upgrading existing ones, because the buildings were cheap to put up, hardly maintained at all, and extremely profitable. Although the government amended Law 719 in 1845 to penalize owners of unsanitary housing, there are no indications that tenement owners were ever fined or that the fine was of any consequence.[16]

Appended to the laws mandating new sanitary and affordable housing were the numerous concessions to companies authorized to build them, including one to Arthur Sauer in February 1888, another to the Companhia de Saneamento do Rio de Janeiro a few months before the end of the Empire, granted on June 4, 1889, and one to the Companhia Fluminense in 1890. Altogether the imperial government granted at least twelve concessions to various companies to build housing, but no more than a few dwellings in São Cristóvão were ever completed.[17]

In the first decade of the Republic, housing plans, along with all aspects of the renovations, had fared little better than they had under the Empire. Graft and incompetence among the licensed companies combined with dissension in political circles to hold back progress. Above all, the task of maintaining order in distant areas of the country and chronic financial crises during the 1890s diverted political energies and revenues away from the urban renewal project. In particular, the massive cost of the project appeared prohibitive. The picture changed in the early years of the twentieth century as greater interest, along with financial resources, focused on urban development.

After the election of Francisco de Paula Rodrigues Alves as president of the Republic in 1902, the renovation of the Brazilian capital became a top priority. During his tenure as the governor of the state of São Paulo,

16. Robert Moses Pechman and Luís César Queiroz Ribeiro, "A Companhia de Saneamento do Rio de Janeiro," *Revista Rio de Janeiro* 1, no. 1 (1985), 107.

17. *Estatutes da Companhia de Saneamento do Rio de Janeiro*, June 4, 1889, APHA-RJ, chaps. 1–2, 7. For documentation on various plans to build workers' housing, see Requerimiento do coronel de engenheiros Paulo José Pereira a Presidente e Ministros da Camara Municipal, October 23, 1881, APHA-RJ; Decreto Legislativo, N. 9511, October 17, 1885, APHA-RJ (concedindo to Luiz Raphael Vieira Souto, a civil engineer, the right to draw up plans for workers' housing), Códice 46-4-56, 29; Decreto Legislativo, N. 8789, 1884–1892, APHA-RJ; Luiz Raphael Vieira Souto to Prefeitura of the Federal District, 1885, 1889, and 1892, APHA-RJ, 2–6; Luiz Barbosa Madureira Freire and Antonio Augusto Fuya to Prefeitura of the Federal District, January 21, 1891, APHA-RJ, 2–3.

Rodrigues Alves had directed the successful renovation of the state capital, including a lighting system and network of electric streetcars installed by the São Paulo Tramway, Light, and Power Company and a widespread sanitation and public health program under the auspices of the municipal government.[18] As a native of the main coffee-producing area of the country, Rodrigues Alves understood the pivotal role of Rio de Janeiro in promoting the import/export market and establishing Brazil's reputation abroad as an attractive center of commerce and capital expansion. Well situated as a conservative politician under both the Empire and the Republic, as well as a member of a prominent planter family in São Paulo, the president was likewise personally motivated for pushing the reforms. He had lost a child in one of Rio's yellow fever epidemics. Rodrigues Alves was, in sum, "representative of the old and new forces at play and self-consciously their instrument."[19]

The year after his inauguration the president authorized the beginning of the massive public works project, paid for by loans from English firms, the house of Rothschild, new taxes, and bonds. Most important, he drew together a team that regularized the existent but chaotic urban renovations, put forward a plan based on the famous urban renewals of Buenos Aires, Paris, and London, and joined into a single project the dual notions of sanitation and civilization. The team is by now well known, their accomplishments amply documented. Headed by the aged prefect Francisco Pereira Passos, Rodrigues Alves's personal appointee to oversee the renovation and beautification of Rio's central business district, joined by the engineer Lauro Müller, minister of transport and public works, Paulo de Frontin, and Francisco de Bicalho, the works proceeded at an astonishing pace.[20]

In a little over a year, from 1903 until 1905, 590 buildings in the center of Rio de Janeiro were demolished, including many of the *cortiços*. The Avenida Central (later renamed Avenida Rio Branco) became the centerpiece of the renovations, lined with institutions of cultural refinement sporting the best of Parisian beaux arts architecture: the Municipal Theater, the Monroe Palace, the National Library, the Academy of Fine Arts, the Grunle Hotel, the

---

18. Gerald Michael Greenfield, "Lighting the City: A Case Study of Public Service Problems in São Paulo, 1885–1913," in *Essays Concerning the Socioeconomic History of Brazil and Portuguese India*, ed. Dauril Alden and Warren Dean (Gainesville: University Presses of Florida, 1977), 118–49; Joseph L. Love, *São Paulo in the Brazilian Federation, 1889–1937* (Stanford: Stanford University Press, 1980).

19. Jeffrey D. Needell, *A Tropical Belle Epoque: Elite Culture and Society in Turn-of-the-Century Rio de Janeiro* (Cambridge: Cambridge University Press, 1987), 33.

20. June E. Hahner, *Poverty and Politics: The Urban Poor in Brazil, 1870–1920* (Albuquerque: University of New Mexico Press, 1986), 162.

Fig. 4.   The district of Glória as seen from the seawall promenade in Flamengo;
mule-drawn trolley at right, c. 1890. Photograph by Marc Ferrez, Jennings
Hoffenberg Collection.

military and naval clubs, and the new offices of the city's main daily newspapers, the *Jornal do Commercio, Jornal do Brasil,* and *O Paiz.*[21] The personal
triumph of Paulo de Frontin, the new avenue was modeled on the main
streets of Paris and displayed the Brazilian variant of French civilization
down to the choice of institutions it showcased (fine arts, academia, journalism, the state, commerce, and tourism) and the precision of the facades.
Copying Georges Eugene Haussmann, the famed baron of the Parisian
Great Works, Frontin worked from a central plan, sought to achieve a unified
style, submitted each architect's design to a jury selection process, and restricted each building to a stipulated height and width.[22]

The results were lauded as nothing short of astounding. European observ-
ers in particular extolled the downtown as "a comprehensive project boldly

21. Francisco Ferreira da Rosa, *Rio de Janeiro* (Rio de Janeiro: Edição Official da Prefeitura,
1905), 16–20, 248–59.
22. Needell, *Tropical Belle Epoque,* 40.

Fig. 5.   Ceremony opening the demolition of São Bento Hill for the construction of
Avenida Central (now Rio Branco), 1904. Photograph by Marc Ferrez, Jennings
Hoffenberg Collection.

conceived and brilliantly executed." British traveler Alured Grey Bell ex-
claimed that "ugly specimens of architecture without art and habitations
without hygiene" were torn down and replaced with "many elegant shops,
several 'Picture palaces,' and scores of business buildings, banks, shipping
offices, import houses and others." [23] At the opening ceremonies for the Avenida Central, the Carioca elite boasted that their accomplishments even surpassed the recent reforms in Buenos Aires, that paragon of European civilization in Latin America. The precise model for the Rio works may be the
subject of some dispute, simply because there were so many urban renewal
projects in the late nineteenth century from which to draw; nonetheless,

23. Alured Grey Bell, *The Beautiful Rio de Janeiro* (London: William Heinemann, 1914), 21–23.

whether Buenos Aires, Paris, or London, Rio's engineers, government, and urban elite had firmly agreed on a European cultural and architectural foundation for their newly civilized downtown.[24]

Over the course of the more or less six-year span of the Rio renovation project, marshland was filled, water channeled, a boulevard and seaside promenade built, streets widened and opened to the sea breeze, and, possibly most important of all, the port facilities were modernized and connected by rail with the countryside. One of the most ambitious of the renovations was the construction of a higher retaining wall against the sea, topped by a promenade that started at the south end of the Avenida Rio Branco, just behind the Monroe Palace, and stretched to Praia Vermelha (Red Beach) at the northern edge of Copacabana. According to Bell, though the majority of the city's population made little use of the several-mile-long promenade, it was quite popular with British visitors and businessmen as a place to stroll, be seen, and greet friends. Probably steadfast in his belief that Brazilians would one day pattern their lives completely after the British, Bell explained that the Beira Mar promenade was not built for the Rio of the present anyway, but for "the Rio of the future."[25] Curiously, it was a future in which the poor were quite literally held in the dark. By 1905 the new promenades and avenues of the center city were electrically lighted, while most of the poor northern areas had yet to be connected even to the existing system of gas illumination.

Work on the construction of new docks began in late 1903 and was finally completed in 1911. The improvements included new warehouses, wider and deeper berths for ships, British-style cranes for unloading, new piers and landfills. The importance of the harbor and dock renovations should not be underestimated. Though surpassed by Santos in later years as the leading port for the export of coffee, 41 percent of Brazil's imports still entered the country through Rio as late as 1906. Finally, it was in Rio that foreign visitors and businessmen disembarked and formed their impressions of Brazil's investment potential. The modern port, it was felt, only enhanced the already breathtaking entrance to the city through the mouth of Guanabara Bay.[26]

The second aspect of the renovation/sanitation plan was the offensive against disease and the epidemics that periodically ravaged the city. Despite

24. June Hahner states that the renovators were most conscious of competing with Buenos Aires in designing the city, whereas Jeffrey Needell sees their inspiration as coming directly from the Parisian model. Hahner, *Poverty and Politics*, 161; Needell, *Tropical Belle Epoque*, chap. 1.

25. Bell, *The Beautiful Rio de Janeiro*, 23.

26. Ferreira da Rosa, *Rio de Janeiro*, 259.

Fig. 6. Avenida Central, the main street of the renovated downtown, c. 1908. Photograph by Augusto Malta, Jennings Hoffenberg Collection.

the passage of health laws, opinion was divided over what caused the epidemics and, as a result, how to stop them. Insufficient prophylactic measures resulted from insufficient scientific knowledge and the concomitant haphazard approaches to disease control that continued during the late nineteenth century. Some medical authorities, such as Luis Pereira Barreto, a leading São Paulo physician and public health advocate, held that yellow fever was transmitted by germs in water. Others argued that it spread through bad air, "humors," or smells.[27] In a step toward systematizing the existing public health program and ending the controversies over what caused Rio's epidemics, Rodrigues Alves on July 12, 1902, annulled a September 1892 law that

27. Nancy Stepan, *Beginnings of Brazilian Science: Oswaldo Cruz, Medical Research and Policy, 1890–1920* (New York: Science History Publications, 1976), 56.

had placed responsibility for public health in the hands of the municipal administration. Instead, he consolidated all matters pertaining to the capital's public health in the hands of the federal government. In March of the following year he appointed Oswaldo Gonçalves Cruz director general of public health.[28]

Oswaldo Cruz was well qualified to head the public health program and to implement the most effective method to combat disease. Born in a small town in the state of São Paulo, Cruz received his medical degree from the Faculty of Medicine in Rio de Janeiro in 1892 at the remarkably young age of twenty. He studied microbiology and experimental pathology for two and a half years at the Pasteur Institute in Paris, the foremost center of microbiological research in the world. In addition to receiving specialized training in microbiology, however, Cruz's stay in Paris exposed him to the broader intersection between issues of disease control, sanitation, and urban planning, whose interconnection nineteenth-century modernizers were then hotly debating. On the one hand, working with scientists studying conditions in French colonies in Africa and Southeast Asia, Oswaldo Cruz was exposed to the most advanced theories on methods to control tropical diseases, and he became convinced that certain diseases were transmitted through parasites. On the other hand, while studying in Paris, Cruz observed the results of Haussmann's Great Works and witnessed firsthand the philosophical underpinnings for this nineteenth-century model of planning and architecture, for the allocation of urban space.

After his return to Brazil in 1899, Cruz headed a campaign to stop the spread of bubonic plague in the port city of Santos. The success of his efforts in Santos, his reputation as a modern, progressive scientist and advocate of public health, and his vocal concern that disease was harming Rio's reputation abroad brought Cruz's name to the attention of Rodrigues Alves's closest advisors. Impressed with the young doctor's expertise, the president gave to Cruz full authority to carry out the sanitation of the capital.[29]

Along with the sanitation of Havana, New Orleans, and other tropical and semitropical cities, the full-scale assault on yellow fever in Rio de Janeiro stands as a landmark in the record book of disease prevention and control. Basing his plan on the findings of Carlos Finlay and the successful program

28. *O Paiz*, July 13, 1902, 1; Stepan, *Beginnings of Brazilian Science*, 88.
29. Donald B. Cooper, "Oswaldo Cruz and the Impact of Yellow Fever on Brazilian History," *Bulletin of Tulane University Medical Faculty* 26 (February 1967): 49–52; Stepan, *Beginnings of Brazilian Science*, 87–88.

undertaken by Walter Reed's commission in Havana, Cruz outlined a proposal to eliminate yellow fever, smallpox, and plague from the city. The campaign against yellow fever involved destroying the breeding grounds for the
Aedes aegypti mosquito and its larvae and ordering the drainage of pools of
stagnant water. Plague was to be eliminated by killing rats and using vac-
cines and serums against the disease in victims. His public health crews, who
earned the name "mosquito inspectors," moved throughout the city, spraying, killing rats, ordering the demolition of all unsanitary housing, and systematically implementing the various aspects of the code, including, for a
while, the registration and isolation of fever victims. The final component of
Cruz's plan was mandatory vaccination of all residents against smallpox. Although by this time rather common in other parts of the world, compulsory
vaccination was considered so controversial in Brazil that the measure was
not included with the original bill in 1903. Nonetheless, Cruz lobbied for it
over the next year and, with Rodrigues Alves's backing, won the addition of
an obligatory vaccination provision to the public health code in October
1904.[30]

The city exploded in riot on November 11, 1904, the day the vaccinations
were to begin. While the vaccination was feared in and of itself, the intensity
of the riot cannot be explained as opposition to vaccination alone; rather, it
must be viewed within the broader context of the entire renovation plan.
After all, vaccination was merely the most tangible aspect of a sanitation
drive many different social groups had opposed for years, implemented
through a health department that meted out different treatment for rich and
poor; and finally, the compulsory law had come from a government many in
Rio sorely distrusted.

Who then opposed the public health plan, and why did that opposition
ultimately center on the vaccination law? Some residents of the Zona Norte
and *subúrbios* were early opponents of the plan because, as they had argued
for years, few of the highly publicized services that were improving life for
residents of the Zona Sul and the center city were reaching the populous
industrial districts. Why should they believe that vaccination, a painful, in-
convenient, and frightening measure, was necessary for public health, when
the health authorities seemed little interested in the general sanitation of the
city's most populous and poorest neighborhoods? During the heavy rains of

---

30. Tratamento de variolosos, Decreto do Instituto Vaccinogenico, 1888–1906, APHA-RJ, Art.
1–14, 17; Directoria Geral de Saúde Pública, "Reorganização dos serviços de hygiene adminis-
trativa da União," Decreto N. 1, *Os serviços de saúde pública no Brasil,* (Rio de Janeiro: Imprensa
Nacional, 1904), 2:895–97.

the summer months, children, animals, and even adults were drowned or swept away in the rushing water of the rivers that formed along the dirt roads that connected these makeshift villages with the rest of the city.[31] While supposedly spraying mosquitoes and larvae was a key component of Cruz's plan, a physician pointed out in an article in the widely read *Jornal do Brasil* newspaper that the mosquito inspectors never ventured into Cascadura, Madureira, Rio das Pedras, and Jacarepaguá. "Is it possible," he asked, "that the pernicious mosquitoes that transmit disease are only those of the city and that those of the *subúrbios* are inoffensive!"[32]

Likewise the poor in the center city, far from the dangerous *subúrbios*, feared vaccination just as they had opposed many aspects of the health code to date. After all, it was their houses that were miserably unsanitary; it was their water that was the most contaminated; it was their streets that were the darkest, most dangerous, and most polluted. When the epidemics struck, it was mostly the poor who contracted the diseases and, as a consequence, were ordered to the isolation centers, where a most certain death awaited, while their tenement houses fell to the ax of the sanitation engineers. In short, the public health measures did not seem to improve the health of the poor; rather, they appeared to make matters worse. Long before the passage of the 1903 law, Rio's health department already had a history of disregarding the feelings, if not the lives and property, of the *cortiço* residents and of incurring their wrath. In July 1901 health officials had forcibly entered an apartment and ordered sent to an isolation center a child suspected of having smallpox. When the inspection teams failed to heed the protests of the child's parents, the entire tenement met and resolved never again to allow the health officials access to their homes.[33] Notably, even the fear of smallpox in the tenement did not justify, in the eyes of the family and their neighbors, the callous disregard of the health officials.

The practice of isolating fever and smallpox victims, which Cruz considered essential, was in fact one of the most disputed aspects of the 1903 Sanitary Code. Since the isolation facilities were notoriously unsanitary and primitive and since isolation often meant death except for the unusually lucky victim, most people preferred to take their chances at home. During the legislature's debate on the passage of the 1903 code, the isolation section was finally defeated, owing largely to the impassioned plea from Delegate

31. *O Paiz*, November 10, 1901, 2, and August 7–12, 1902, 2; *Jornal do Brasil*, October 2, 1903, 1, and January 10, 1904, 1.

32. *Jornal do Brasil*, August 24, 1904, 3.

33. *O Paiz*, July 4, 1901, 2.

Germano Hasslocher. Hasslocher argued that forced isolation discriminated against the poor, since the wealthy were treated at home or sent to country retreats near Petropolis when they contracted a disease and since only the poor were forced into the terrible isolation centers.[34]

Another major provision of the health law allowed mosquito inspectors and public health officials to enter, condemn, and oversee the demolition of any building they deemed unsanitary. Nevertheless, it was easier to pass such a law than to carry it out. In 1903 health officials forced their way into an apartment and sprayed furniture, clothing, and eating utensils with a foul smelling disinfectant because a case of plague had been reported nearby. Outraged, practically everyone on the Rua da Ajuda turned out to shower the health officials with taunts, rocks, and "assorted debris" as the latter attempted to retreat.[35] Actually, since most residents of the downtown *cortiços* were aware that demolition teams followed closely on the heels of the health inspectors, there was nothing to be gained by letting Cruz's men enter the collective housing units. With no place to go except the notoriously unhealthy Zona Norte or the *favelas*, and with no confidence that the government would ever build low-cost housing to replace the condemned *cortiços*, tenants began to fear the health officials as much as the epidemics.[36]

Proprietors of stores who sold a wide variety of household goods and food-stuffs to inner-city residents also opposed the sanitation measures. Even if they could hold on in the face of rising property values, they stood to lose their customers when the *cortiços* were demolished in the urban renewal. Though consumers often complained that the prices for goods in these stores were high, and had targeted a number of them in some earlier demonstrations, the stores were convenient, the shopkeepers advanced consumers credit, and the owners were themselves usually from the neighborhood. In fact, the *cortiços* and the corner bar, an important social gathering place, were usually under the same ownership. Thus, the destruction of the *cortiços* and the relocation of their tenants to the northern *subúrbios* would drive a large number of downtown small shopkeepers out of business, with little chance of recouping what was owed to them. Moreover, the master plan for the "civilized" downtown sought to replace the open-air shops that sold dried beef, soap, pots and pans, and other housekeeping essentials with stores that stocked finer, imported, and more expensive goods for an elite clientele. While some of the established general stores would remain, especially on

34. *Jornal do Brasil*, November 26, 1903, 1.
35. Ibid., November 2, 1903, 1.
36. For other instances, see *O Paiz*, May 9, 1901, 1.

Alfandega Street, the stores directly dependent on the *cortiços* for their customers would not.[37]

The health codes likewise changed the way goods were sold in the city.
Pereira Passos prohibited the selling of milk directly from cows that were
lead from door to door, banished hogs and stray animals from the city
streets, refused to allow butchers to sell meat off of hooks hung in the entrance to markets, and monitored the hygiene and maintenance of food
stores and markets.[38] No matter how obviously necessary, these additions to
the health code met tremendous hostility from small-scale proprietors. On
the one hand, most of the small owners operated on a very restricted budget,
were at the mercy of larger distributors from whom they bought their goods,
and suffered during the periods of wild speculation and high inflation that
characterized market relations in the late Empire and early Republic. Most
simply could not afford to make the kind of improvements the government
required. On the other hand, better-capitalized Portuguese stores, and domestic enterprises that had obtained loans from British and American investors, already had begun to edge out the smaller shops by the turn of the
century. The added expense of the health regulations, combined with rising
rents on downtown properties, eventually would drive the less financially
stable enterprises out of business.

"Foreign interests," the shopkeepers protested, were taking over the
downtown. Historically, antiforeign agitation in Rio had been directed against
Portuguese shop owners and merchants, a group stereotyped as hardworking, tightfisted, cunning, and even marginally dishonest. Aluizio Azevedo's
chronicle of tenement life captured the truth and the exaggerations of anti-
Portuguese prejudice especially in the characters of João Romão and Miranda.[39] However, in the early stages of the sanitation campaign, shopkeepers began to shift their animus toward the tremendously powerful Rio
de Janeiro City Improvements Company. In 1901, during an earlier phase of
the renovation, the City insisted, and the municipal council agreed, that
small grocery stores, coal yards, and collective housing units install a specific
hookup to the sewer line then under construction. Also, each downtown
structure was required to erect a particular type of chimney, with materials
that could only be purchased from the City Improvements Company. At a
meeting on October 11, 1901, proprietors denounced the regulations, pro-

37. Pimentel, *Quaes os melhoramentos hygienicos*, 105–6.

38. Needell, *Tropical Belle Epoque*, 35.

39. Aluizio Azevedo, *A Brazilian Tenement,* trans. Harry W. Brown (New York: Robert M.
McBride, 1928), chap. 2.

tested the exorbitant cost of the materials, and the City's strong-arm tactics in forcing the shops to buy the required construction material. Outraged at the collusion between government authorities and the private City Improvements Company, the meeting's participants resolved to oppose all aspects of the urban renewal plan and to agitate against any further implementation of the City's "beautification" project.[40]

It was not just the downtown shopkeeper who stood to lose his business in the urban renewal; likewise the owners of the many places of entertainment in the Largo do Rossio watched as their raucous enterprises began to fall under the ax of Pereira Passos's reforms. Health inspectors attacked the dance halls, bars, beer gardens, and nightspots with near evangelical zealotry, brandishing the same authority against immorality as they did against disease. Pereira Passos took a personal interest in leveling the popular and bawdy amusements of the Largo do Rossio, bringing the Maison Moderne to court for numerous structural and hygiene code violations. Working through his own lawyers, its owner, Pascoal, obtained a court order provisionally ensuring that the amusement park could continue and granting him a specified period of time to make necessary repairs. Nonetheless, at the stroke of midnight on the day the court order expired, and without bothering to reinspect the premises, two hundred men armed with picks and shovels under the direction of the prefect himself leveled this so-called *escarro* (eyesore) in the center of the city. "When dawn broke there were no stones left standing," Vivaldo Coaracy recalled. Within a few months passersby could barely remember the park's location, except that it used to be someplace under the newly widened Rua Espírito Santo.[41]

The sanitation drive was, in the words of Coaracy, both "material and moral."[42] However, since not everyone could afford the "material" renovations or relished the "moral" outcome, a sense of inequality began to saturate the atmosphere. Day by day Rio's citizens watched as the allocation of the capital's space reflected the divisions that had always separated the population by class, by privilege, by race, and, now more than ever, by culture.

The renovation actually was helping to unify some of the hostility toward the government. In spite of the many years when customers had demonstrated against shopkeepers, or tenants against local landlords, these previously antagonistic groups found themselves in alliance against the public

---

40. Early grievances against the City Improvements Company are noted in *Jornal do Brasil*, May 13, 1892, 1. See also *O Paiz*, October 11, 1901, 2.

41. Coaracy, *Memorias da cidade*, 129.

42. Ibid.

health campaign and its attendant vaccination drive. This opposition developed from the early stages of Rio's urban renovation, intensified with each new step of the project, and eventually exploded into a violent reaction against just about everything the health department, the urban renewal contractors, the transit companies, and even the Republican government itself proposed to do in the Brazilian capital. Moreover, the popular outcry was not confined to complaints over who was to benefit from the sanitation and renewal or even who was most inconvenienced by it, but included complaints over who was to pay for it. While this issue concerned everyone in the city, it was particularly important to people whose incomes already placed them at or below the subsistence level.

During the year between November 1903 and October 1904 the debate over the many facets of the sanitation drive and the compulsory vaccination bill relegated most other issues in Rio de Janeiro to the background. Petitions, marches in the street, congressional shouting matches, vitriolic attacks on the plan in the opposition press, trade union agitation, and attacks from the Rio de Janeiro Positivists dominated the city such that, by the time the vaccination code was scheduled to take effect on November 11, everyone in the city had an opinion on the bill.

By late 1904 the sporadic resistance against what came to be known as the Yellow Fever Campaign had transformed into a more regularized and organized opposition. As Oswaldo Cruz pushed ahead with the public health plan, Rio de Janeiro's Positivists and the socialist-oriented Centro das Classes Operarias (Working Class Center), which itself was loosely affiliated with the Positivists, emerged as outspoken critics of the government. They formed the League Against Obligatory Vaccination, essentially an umbrella under which widely divergent forces clustered, and attempted initially to channel the spontaneous outburst of hatred toward the government into mass rallies and marches. Along with the well-known Positivists Senator Lauro Sodré, Barbosa Lima, and Alfredo Varela, on November 14 General Sylvestre Travassos led the cadets of the military academy in an abortive uprising against the government.

Although the political alignments and realignments, political intrigues, and petty antagonisms among the elite rarely affected the lives of the masses, sectors of the ruling strata did not hesitate to call on the laboring classes for support when the opportunity arose. In that regard, the role of the Positivists in the 1904 uprising cannot be ignored, if only because their actions, like the interminable political maneuverings during the First Republic, show the extent to which the elite engaged in power struggles over obscure ideological differences. As Robert Nachman metaphorically comments, compulsory vaccination "provided a smoke screen for more burning issues."[43]

Broadly speaking, the Positivists were a part of the radical antimonarchical Republicans who replaced the Empire and, under the leadership of Marechal Deodoro da Fonseca and especially Marechal Floriano Peixoto, fought to establish a political role for the urban protectionist domestic elite and middle sectors. Like other Republicans, the Positivists were a part of the group that opposed the traditional, rural planters, who had supported the monarchy to the last hour and remained uncomfortable with the more Republican impulses of the new government. The electoral defeat of the Florianistas, many of whom were Positivists, and their subsequent decline during the governments of Prudente de Morais (1894–98) and Campos Sales (1898–1902) have usually been considered the political demise of the most economically nationalist, urban-centered, and protectionist wing of Republicanism and the triumph of the old-guard planter aristocracy clustered around the São Paulo planters. Concerned primarily with protecting coffee exports, the Paulistas' triumph galvanized foreign investors against the few domestic competitors and paved the way for Brazil's greater reliance on foreign capital to finance national development. As concerns Rio in 1904, the Paulista Rodrigues Alves, a former minister in the last monarchical government, represented the interests of the traditional sectors, in opposition to Lauro Sodré and the other Positivists who sought to regain the presidency. The positions of each side, however, are rent with contradictions, except that they each wanted power.

Publicly the Brazilian Positivists opposed the Yellow Fever Campaign, especially the compulsory vaccination against smallpox, on the grounds that it infringed on the privacy of the individual citizen. But there was no consistency to their stance either in theory or in practice, since Positivists had called for government intervention to achieve economic progress and *social order,* what Auguste Comte saw as the last, most positive stage of human evolution. In fact, when he was governor of Pará, from 1891 to 1897, Lauro Sodré had launched a number of reforms, including improving the port, constructing new roads, overseeing state monopolies, and improving public services, all very similar to the reforms Rodrigues Alves was enacting in Rio a

43. Robert G. Nachman, "Positivism and Revolution in Brazil's First Republic: The 1904 Revolt," *The Americas* 24, no. 1 (1977): 21. Jeffrey Needell likewise argues that the Positivist officers launched the coup to remake the Republic and to win power, while the poor joined to redress their own grievances; "The *Revolta Contra Vacina* of 1904: The Revolt Against Modernization in *Belle-Epoque* Rio de Janeiro," *Hispanic American Historical Review* 67, no. 2 (1987): 233–69.

decade later. Despite his condemnation of the mandatory vaccination law in 1904, Lauro Sodré had his children vaccinated against smallpox.

Barbosa Lima, another opponent of the vaccination code, as governor of Pernambuco from 1892 to 1896, distributed Jenner's vaccine to combat an outbreak of smallpox and even sent a doctor to Paris to study at the Pasteur Institute to learn the latest in microbiological disease prevention. If it was foreign involvement in Rio's sanitation drive or even the compulsory nature of the vaccination law that he opposed, those too seem hollow objections. Barbosa Lima had as governor negotiated a plan with foreign enterprises to invest in reviving the state's lagging sugar industry, and he enforced various laws already on the books that obliged public workers to pay into pension funds. As Nachman comments, it is difficult to believe that Barbosa Lima opposed compulsory vaccination with any degree of sincerity. On the surface, it is hard to see any difference between what Rodrigues Alves was doing in Rio and what the Positivists themselves had done in their respective states. Furthermore, several of the engineers and urban planners on Pereira Passos's staff were themselves Positivists, such as Lauro Müller, the genius behind Rio's new port facilities.[44]

If the Positivists were hypocritical in their agitation against the compulsory vaccination laws and the 1903 Sanitary Code, they were nonetheless bold. Lauro Sodré, himself a former military officer, urged the army cadets of Rio's military academy to participate in a military coup against the government on November 14. As mentioned earlier, the coup failed, despite the considerable support the conspirators enjoyed among the ranks of the cadets. Schooled in Positivist doctrine, the military cadets might well have sincerely opposed the Yellow Fever Campaign because it conflicted with their understanding of the principles of individual freedom.

As is so often the case, however, the military cadets' devotion to principle was bound closely to their quest for greater autonomy and power. Here lay the essence of the Positivist opposition to the vaccination law and health campaign. First, the military Positivists opposed the conservative government of Rodrigues Alves and the foreign investors with which the government had aligned. The cadets' political future lay with the old Florianista faction, now largely marginalized since the conservatives had reclaimed the government and had established a system more heavily reliant on business and planter

44. Robert G. Nachman, "Positivism, Modernization, and the Middle Class in Brazil," *Hispanic American Historical Review* 57, no. 1 (1977): 1–23; idem, "Positivism and Revolution in Brazil," 33.

interests. Second, many in the military were drawn from the petty bourgeoisie or from recently impoverished planters of the postabolition period, who
found Positivism's doctrine of social selection an attractive alternative to the
excesses of the elite and the "rabble" of the poor. Individualism fit nicely
with the upward mobility of the military cadets, while any curbs on that upward "progress," such as Rodrigues Alves's restrictions on the participation
of the military in national political affairs, conflicted with both Positivist doctrine and with the political aspirations of the armed forces.[45]

In conclusion, Rio's Positivists agitated against the health code, denounced
Rodrigues Alves's reforms, and conspired to overthrow the government for
a number of contradictory and self-serving reasons. If anything, the events
of 1904 bring into sharper focus the absolute absence of any ideological cohesion in Positivist doctrine. When in 1904 a wing of the Positivist movement
attempted to use their philosophy as a guide to social action, they floundered, lacking as they were in any cohesive vision of class or ideological
unity. One faction of the Positivist elite could as easily join the conservative
government and its civilizing venture, under the Positivist slogans of Order
and Progress, as another faction could holler in opposition. The contradiction that was shaking down during the First Republic and was represented
in the capital city was between classes. Certainly it would have taken a philosophy far more sophisticated than Positivism to hold together these developing class antagonisms. By the end of 1904 it became clear that the Positivist bywords of "Order," "Progress," and even "Civilization" were class-
linked concepts. Thus the military and civilian Positivists who participated
in the events of 1904 did so in search of their own power and only begrudg-
ingly aligned with the working class in an attempt to stop the Yellow Fever
Campaign.

It was the socialist Centro das Classes Operarias that played an important
role in galvanizing the trade unions against the vaccination law. Organized
along loose syndicalist lines and linked, albeit remotely, to some Positivist
circles, the Centro united some of the more powerful labor unions in the city,
including the railroad workers, dockworkers, painters, machinists, carpenters, stonemasons, plasterers, and members of the maritime union. Since
many of their members lived in the downtown *cortiços* easily accessible to
the docks, quarries, and construction sites, the Centro objected to a renovation project that would turn large numbers of workers out on the streets. Its

45. Edgard Carone, *A República Velha: Instituições e classes sociais* (São Paulo: DIFEL, 1975),
166–81; idem, *A República Velha: Evolução política* (São Paulo: DIFEL, 1964), 205–6.

opposition to the vaccination law, therefore, stemmed from the same premise upon which it opposed the larger Sanitary Code: all the sanitation laws, as designed by the city elite, would only worsen the existing housing crisis for the working class.

The Centro began in July and August of 1904 to agitate among its affiliated unions against the Yellow Fever Campaign. At a rally in front of the House of Deputies the Centro presented a petition, bearing ten thousand signatures from union members, calling on the government to rescind the obligatory vaccination code and to better the miserable living conditions in the city's poor and working-class neighborhoods. While chiding the government for failing to ensure decent living conditions for the thousands of Rio's residents concentrated in the Zona Norte, the rally organizers asked what had happened to the long-standing promise to construct low-cost workers housing for the "thousands left homeless by the so-called 'beautification.'"[46]

On November 5 over two thousand opponents of the campaign packed the meeting hall of the Centro das Classes Operarias. Present were groups representative of the alliance formed to oppose the campaign. There were workers from the Central rail line, members of the maritime union, workers from the various building trade unions, machinists, and "laborers." Middle-class support came from the association of dramatic actors, possibly because the demolition of the Largo de Rossio district was leaving them homeless as well, from law students, academic clubs, students from the *polytecnica* and the law and medical faculties, members of the Brazilian Academy, students from the National Gymnásio, representatives of the navy and army academies, in addition to hundreds of individuals who simply came on their own.

The two main speakers at this event were the Positivist Lauro Sodré and Vicente de Souza, the president of the Centro. Sodré spoke first, denouncing the obligatory vaccination law for its violation of basic, individual rights guaranteed by the constitution. Sodré's prestige was well recognized because he had been secretary to Benjamin Constant, Brazil's foremost Positivist. He was a military engineer and brigade commander and, along with Barbosa Lima, was considered one of the leading Positivists of the Republic. Vicente de Souza had been influenced by Positivism years earlier, while in medical school. Moving on from medicine to journalism and eventually to the leadership of the socialist Centro, Vicente de Souza was a key link between the working class and the Positivist opponents of the vaccination law. Whether Vicente remained an adamant Positivist after his election to the presidency of the

46. *Jornal do Brasil*, July 14, 1. See also ibid., July 28, 1904, 2.

Centro is unclear, but he did grant Lauro Sodré and his comrades a podium
from which to denounce the government and to promote their views.[47]

Although Lauro Sodré chaired the meeting, Vicente de Souza's speech
was, and is, the evening's most instructive. Souza opened his comments with
the specter of a "young virgin, or wife away from her husband," forced to
bare her arms in front of an unfamiliar public health official in order to be
inoculated with the smallpox virus. The same government that required this
unthinkable action had ignored the petition of the ten thousand Centro workers, had never sided with the poor and workers in any labor dispute, and had
reneged on its twelve-year-old promise to construct low-cost housing. Now,
Souza maintained, this "government of the rich and the coffee barons" was
asking the poor and destitute to accept a law that would have them injected
with "a foreign virus." Vaccination, he continued, was only one part of the
larger renovation plan that was destroying the houses belonging to the city's
"poor and working class" and that, as he passionately concluded, the masses
had the "legitimate" right to resist.[48]

That Souza's appeal met with deafening applause broken only by frequent
denunciations of the government should come as no surprise to anyone who
has noted the years of agitation against the many parts of the sanitation laws.
Maybe as a mulatto and working-class leader Souza received more trust from
the masses; regardless, he touched a nerve. How could health officials who
stormed into houses spraying everything in sight with disinfectant or who
demolished a place of business in the middle of the night with picks and axes
be trusted with the supposedly delicate arms of wives and virgin daughters?
This government of the rich and the coffee barons, which had let foreign
railroads, trolley companies, and contractors carve up the city for their own
profits, now wanted to carve up the people, it seemed, with injections of foreign viruses. Before closing, the group formed itself into the League Against
Obligatory Vaccination and elected officers: copresidents, Lauro Sodré and
Vicente de Souza; vice-president, Barbosa Lima; secretaries, A. Suzano and
Paulino Van Ewen (one from the Positivists, one from the Centro); and treasurer, Marcos Martins de Almeida (treasurer of the Centro). The meeting

47. Nachman, "Positivism and Revolution," 24.

48. *Jornal do Brasil*, November 6, 1904, 1. Whether Souza understood and distrusted the
medical rationale for injecting the virus into a person's arm—to stimulate the formation of anti-
bodies against smallpox—is unclear. The basis of the vaccination process was known widely,
and, he knew, it was feared. He chose to say "inoculated with," *not* inoculated against," the
smallpox virus. Other information on Vicente de Souza is in Sheldon Maram, "Anarchists, Immigrants, and the Brazilian Labor Movement, 1890–1920" (Ph.D. diss., University of California,
Santa Barbara, 1972), 141.

concluded with proclamations to continue the struggle against the vaccination plan and to uphold the rights of the working class, and with vigorous "vivas" to "students, the working class, and the proletariat in general."[49]

Several aspects of the evening are striking. Sodré's role in the meeting was not as prominent as that of Vicente de Souza. Quite possibly the Positivists opted for a lower public profile and preferred for the working-class leader, Vicente de Souza, to serve as the rally's lightning rod. This added greater mass appeal to their cause, but it likewise served as a good cover for the conspiracy that was brewing against the government. Moreover, everyone who participated in the rally had a grievance larger and of longer duration than just that against vaccination. Those who argue that the November 11 riot was an "excuse by many different groups opposing President Rodrigues Alves to discredit the government" or "an exploitable issue" that subversives used to overturn the government account for the motives of the Positivists;[50] the urban poor joined the opposition for more justifiable reasons, since there was real reason to fear the vaccine, or so it was thought. During July of the year before, at the height of the legislative debate over the Sanitary Code of 1903, the *Jornal do Brasil* had carried a story with banner headlines proclaiming, "Deaths from the Vaccine!" Actually, on closer reading, only one woman had died because of complications from the vaccine, but the headline probably scared a lot of people anyway.[51]

Vicente de Souza's words resonated with the crowd because he pitted the "poor and the working class" against the "rich and the coffee barons," drawing the lines that everyone in Rio knew were at the core of the whole urban renewal and vaccination plan. In essence Souza spoke the "hidden transcript" of working-class resentment that had churned away—as James Scott notes, speaking of another place and time but similar circumstances—in the "thousands of bitter jokes, resentments, and outrage accumulated around kitchen tables, in small groups of workers, in beer halls, and among close companions."[52] The grievances of Rio's working poor against the government, the health department, and the urban renewal itself were not new. They had been raised in one form or another since the first days of the Republic.

49. *Jornal do Brasil*, November 6, 1904, 1.
50. Stepan, *Beginnings of Brazilian Science*, 89; Cooper, "Oswaldo Cruz and the Impact of Yellow Fever," 52.
51. *Jornal do Brasil*, July 10, 1903, 1.
52. James C. Scott, *Domination and the Arts of Resistance: Hidden Transcripts* (New Haven: Yale University Press, 1990), 226.

4

The Resistance

Long live the working class! Down with forced vaccination!
—Slogan from the antivaccination demonstration as
reported in the *Jornal do Brasil*, November 14, 1904

The first sporadic outbreaks of violence occurred on the evening of November 10, the day before the vaccination law was to take effect. The League Against Obligatory Vaccination called a rally in the Largo de São Francisco da Paula, in downtown Rio, which police estimated drew over three thousand people. Rally organizers called for protesters to assemble in the same location the next day and to refuse to comply with the vaccination law. Following the rally, a few gangs of youths stoned streetlights and paraded about the downtown shouting condemnations of the government and the vaccination law; otherwise the evening ended peacefully. On the morning of November 11, the city erupted in protest; marches, rallies, and riots, which continued until November 18.[1]

During the week's disturbances crowds targeted for destruction many of

1. *Jornal do Brasil*, November 11–12, 14–19, 1904, 1–2.

the public works improvements installed as a part of the urban beautification plan. They overturned and vandalized streetcars, broke gas and electric streetlights, erected barricades to cut off access to streets, and vandalized train stations on lines out to the *subúrbios*. Police infantry and cavalry units were pelted with rocks when they attempted to break up crowds of demonstrators, and on more than one occasion demonstrators armed with handguns and rifles defended their barricades against police and army units. The protests, ranging from street rallies and marches to the exchange of gunfire, were accompanied by shouts of "Death to the police!" "Long live the working class!" "Down with forced vaccination!" and, occasionally, "Long live the Republic!"[2]

Possibly the most remarkable feature of the riot was what was not attacked. With the exception of a barrage of cries against the vaccination law, little hostility was directed toward the public health department, its buildings, or its crews of inspectors. On two separate occasions health department personnel and property came under attack, and in both cases it is unclear whether the health agents were targeted or were simply caught in the wrong place at the wrong time. In the first incident a health inspector, caught in the midst of a melee between demonstrators and police, became the object of the crowd's wrath. They pelted him with rocks and sent him running off slightly wounded.[3] At another time a wagon belonging to the health department was overturned and set ablaze, along with several other cars.[4] These were, however, isolated incidents, and even if there were a few others that were overlooked in the press reports on the riot, the point remains that demonstrators were not focusing on the health department property and personnel. Considering that passage of the vaccination law was the reason for calling the demonstrations in the first place, this was remarkable.

Whether the intent of the league organizers or not, clearly the crowds' anger was directed primarily toward the changes wrought by the renovation and beautification of the downtown. Wrath that one might have expected to be focused on the public health department was instead unleashed on the urban renewal contractors. The targets of the riot were construction sites, streetcars, gas and electric generator stations, and streetlights, along with the sites of the newly "civilized" showplace of trade and commerce. A few examples from the rioting demonstrate that the Rio crowds did not consider compulsory vaccination an issue unconnected to the downtown renovation

2. Ibid.
3. Ibid., November 16, 1904, 1.
4. Ibid., November 13, 1904, 1.

and beautification project. On the afternoon of November 13 crowds gathered on the Avenida Passos, where a major streetcar line was located. They built barricades with the lumber from several construction sites located on that and adjoining streets. The barricades, placed next to four streetcars wheeled together on the tracks, were ignited. The four streetcars, also splashed with kerosene, were likewise set ablaze, to the cheers of the crowd. Three of the cars belonged to the by-now-infamous Companhia São Cristóvão, one to the Companhia Carris Urbanas of the sanitation department.[5]

Attacks on streetcars reached such an intensity that by the morning of November 15 the Companhia São Cristóvão suspended operation of all of its lines until "calm [could] be restored throughout the city."[6] The Companhia Jardim Botânico stopped operating as well. By the morning of November 16 all municipal transportation from downtown Rio to the *subúrbios* had come to a halt because of repeated attacks on the cars, barricades on the tracks, and even assaults on drivers who attempted to maintain service in the face of the demonstrations.[7] As they were destroying streetcars and tracks, masses of people descended on the rail stations of lines that connected the downtown with the outlying *subúrbios*. On November 15 fifty people invaded the Encantado train station, serving the Central, stoned the station agent when he attempted to prevent their entry, broke into the station offices, and destroyed what authorities described as "important documents."[8]

By November 14 streetlights were smashed on all downtown streets and in some of the *suúrbios*. In the center city lights were out in Ouvidor, Quitanda, Gonçalves Dias, Uruguaiana, Carioca, and Sete de Setembro Streets. Hundreds of demonstrators converged in groups on the downtown area near the Frei Caneca Gazometro, Rio's central gas generator station, and attempted an assault on the utility works but were repelled by cavalry units.[9] Not confined to the downtown business district alone, protesters cut telephone wires, vandalized and set ablaze streetcars, and broke streetlamps in Catete, Botafogo, and Gávea, zones bordering the center city on the south.[10]

Reportedly, shopkeepers in the downtown business district provided roaming crowds with cans of kerosene for setting streetcars and construction sites ablaze. More-committed shopkeepers arranged for a network of "kerosene couriers" to transport the fuel to awaiting crowds in front of con-

5. Ibid., November 14, 1904, 1.
6. Ibid., November 16, 1904, 1.
7. Ibid., November 17, 1904, 2.
8. Ibid., November 16, 1904, 1.
9. Ibid.
10. Ibid., November 15, 1904, 1.

struction sites and streetcar terminals in distant reaches of the city.[11] Shopkeepers were in this way able to support the rioting while standing guard
over their own businesses and preventing any attack from roaming bands. At
the same time, a store owner known for supplying kerosene to the crowds
might have stood the best chance of holding his own business intact.

Fierce fighting broke out between crowds of protesters and the police in
the central business district; an especially long battle raged on November 14
and 15. Protesters held off a police attack against them in the several-square-
block area bordered by Alfandega, General Camara, Hospício, and São Pedro
Streets, the Avenida Passos, and the Largo de Capim. The two-day siege of
the area and considerable vandalism toward construction sites and businesses within the perimeters of the barricades constituted one of the longest
and most violent battles of the entire demonstration, made possible by the
protesters' fortuitous capture of an arms cache intended for the police.[12] At
the same time, another long and violent battle was taking place in (ironically)
Saúde, a district where most of the stevedores and port workers lived. A
large band of protesters held out against artillery barrages in a trench they
named Port Arthur, after a fortress that had been made famous for its resistance to a Japanese attack in the recent Russo-Japanese War. When a cavalry
assault was finally launched, the demonstrators abandoned their post, leaving behind five people too wounded to flee and the body of a demonstrator
killed during the fighting.[13]

Some accounts of the riot have attempted to discredit the demonstrators
by emphasizing that streetlamps were broken to provide the cover of dark-
ness to bands of looters and vandals.[14] Looking at the demonstration as a
whole, however, there is no indication that violence escalated at night, nor
does the nighttime violence seem to be of a different nature from that during
the day. The press reported only one assault on an individual and very few
cases of looting and vandalism against the property of individuals, as opposed to that against the renovations and the property of the urban renewal
contractors. In fact, most of the major demonstrations, with the exception of
some evening disturbances in Catete, Botafogo, and Gávea, occurred in the
daytime. Rioting was a day-and-night activity, particularly from November 14
through 16, and was most intense during the daytime.[15]

11. *Jornal do Commercio*, November 13, 1904, 1.
12. *Jornal do Brasil*, November 16, 1904, 2.
13. Ibid., November 17, 1904, 2.
14. José Maria Bello, *A History of Modern Brazil, 1889–1964*, trans. James L. Taylor (Stanford: Stanford University Press, 1966), 182.
15. *Jornal do Brasil*, November 16–17, 1904, 1.

No single record on the number of protesters involved in the riot exists, but the number was clearly in the tens of thousands. At least three thousand gathered in the Largo de São Francisco da Paula on November 10, filling the square so that it was impossible to walk from one side to the other. On the following day, crowds again gathered in the same plaza and, while awaiting the speakers, were attacked by saber-brandishing cavalry units. The *Jornal do Brasil* estimated that a single group split off from the main assembly numbered more than a thousand. The main gathering they estimated at three times that size.[16] During the week's disturbances, police consistently counted between thirty and fifty young men in any one of the bands of protesters that roamed the city, and there were hundreds of these gangs. A conservative estimate of the number involved would be five thousand, but more likely the number reached closer to ten thousand at the height of the riot on November 14 and 15. Considering that the center-city region had a population of about 300,000 people and that the whole city had a population of around 800,000, between 1 and 3 percent of the city's residents were engaged in the demonstrations at one point or another.[17]

Those participating in the riot included workers as individuals, as well as working-class organizations. In addition to the pivotal role of the Centro das Classes Operarias, various unions lent their support to the demonstrations or published statements calling for an end to forced vaccination and police brutality against the protesters. The anarcho-syndicalist Federação das Associações de Classe (Federation of Class Associations) sent to the legislature on November 12 a statement listing the painters, hatmakers, firefighters, cigarmakers, carpenters, stonemasons, and plasterers unions in support of the protest.[18] In a separate solidarity statement published concurrently with that from the Federação, the maritime workers union declared that it "cannot fail to protest against an illegal act decreed by the government of a republic that calls itself civilized."[19]

Nonetheless, the working class was not united in its support of the protest. Several unions refused to work during the disturbances, but they claimed that the chaos that reigned throughout the city made their jobs unsafe. Lest employers might seek reprisals, unions issued emphatic statements enumerating their members' reasons for failing to report to work. In a letter to man-

16. Ibid., November 12, 1904, 1.
17. Ibid., November 16–17, 1904, 1; *Jornal do Commercio*, November 14, 1904, 1.
18. John W. F. Dulles, *Anarchists and Communists in Brazil, 1900–1935* (Austin: University of Texas Press, 1973), 544; Boris Fausto, *Trabalho urbano e conflito social* (São Paulo: DIFEL, 1976), 120.
19. *Jornal do Brasil*, November 12, 1904, 2.

agement published in the newspaper, the president of the stevedores union declared that "despite intimidation and harassment from management, the União dos Operarios Estivadores will stay off work until such time as adequate guarantees for their safety" can be provided. The papers carried similar messages from groups of municipal garbage collectors, streetcar conductors, and machinists.[20]

The safety question was not an abstract concern. The union members were working on the urban renovation projects—docks, streetcars, railroads, garbage collection wagons, and so forth—all of which were targeted by demonstrators who were angry with the priorities of the sanitation and renovation plan. No doubt these were, during the riot, the most dangerous workplaces in the city. Nonetheless, it is impossible to say whether union members who were refusing to work were "reporting for duty" at barricades instead of job sites. Many workers in these occupations lived in the *cortiços*, close to the downtown workplaces, and were angered at the loss of their living quarters and their relocation to the *subúrbios*. Pleading hazardous working conditions protected the union from reprisals and accusations of lending support to the riot.

Arrest and hospitalization records carried in the city newspapers bear out this conclusion, showing the majority of riot participants to have been young working men, and counter to police claims at the time, most were Brazilian, not foreign-born. Though police documents are sparse, hospital admission statistics, carried in the press, identified detainees brought in by the police for medical treatment. The majority listed their occupations as "worker." One more-specific roster listed the following detainees: porter, shoemaker, coachman, cook, sailor, and streetcar conductor.[21] Police reports carried in city newspapers show that of fifty-two protesters apprehended on November 15, five were foreigners: one Arab (Sirio), one Spaniard, two Portuguese, and one Italian. The youngest of this group was thirteen, the oldest forty.[22] In the taking of Port Arthur, the holdout of protesters in Saúde, five young men were injured and one killed. All of these were listed as "workers" by the police in their report carried the following day in the major city newspapers. One of those injured was Portuguese; the rest were Brazilian. Killed in the assault was a twenty-eight-year-old Brazilian (listed as "Negro"); nineteen demonstrators were arrested.[23]

Positivist cadets at the Escola Militar, led by General Sylvestre Travassos,

20. Ibid., November 17, 1904, 1.
21. Ibid.
22. Ibid., November 16, 1904, 2.
23. Ibid., November 17, 1904, 1.

revolted on November 14. Despite the participation of Lauro Sodré and support from Barbosa Lima, the revolt was of short duration, and Travassos and the cadets were quickly arrested. Since the military revolt focused attention on the leadership of the League Against Obligatory Vaccination, Souza, Sodré, and other leaders were arrested and detained pending charges.[24]

Although apprehended with the other military conspirators, no clear link connected Vicente de Souza and others from the Centro with the aborted military revolt, particularly since the revolt appears to have been designed to show the discontent of the young officers with the policies of the Republican government. Though Sodré shared leadership of the league with Souza, the military never entered into a principled partnership with the labor organization. Sodré and the officers called press conferences separately from the Centro and generally surrounded their actions with intrigue and secrecy. In effect, the military joined the movement in action, not just words, only after the street demonstrations had reached their height.[25]

Calm returned to the capital on November 18, though the demonstrations had died back considerably by the afternoon of the day before. On November 17 the government rescinded the compulsory aspect of the vaccination code, which no doubt contributed to the quiet that overtook the city. By November 19 the press reported, "[The] streets are almost clear of the mountains of garbage and destruction that during the last days have made them almost impassable; public lighting is reestablished; and the transit of streetcars on all lines is completely restored."[26] In rather remarkable fashion the riot appears to have simply come to an end. There were no victory celebrations, despite the announcement that compulsory vaccination had been rescinded.

Apart from what they accomplished, what were the crowds' actions saying? Why, when they had ostensibly taken to the streets to protest a vaccination law, did people break streetlights, vandalize gas and electric generator stations, and burn construction sites? If the cause for the riot was a public health law, why were crowds attacking streetcars and train stations? As with most street disorders, there remains little concrete evidence regarding the crowds' specific motives; however, some evidence fits with patterns of previous riots.

In the first place, it is clear that hostility toward the transportation compa-

24. Ibid., November 16, 1904, 1; Edgard Carone, *A República Velha: Evolução política* (São Paulo: DIFEL, 1964), 205–6.

25. *Jornal do Brasil*, November 16–17, 1904, 1–2.

26. Ibid., November 19, 1904, 1. No doubt the restoration to which the paper referred was complete in the downtown district of the city only.

nies was long-standing, both because of their ruthless price-gouging and because of their role in the urban renewal. Second, the protesters realized the
full implications of the "sanitation" laws, of which compulsory vaccination
was one part. Sanitation and beautification were code words for declaring
the downtown off limits to the "uncivilized" working class. Not surprisingly,
protesters hit hard at the amenities "civilization" provided to the rich and
denied to the poor. In this regard, the housing crisis was primary: as rapidly
as the wealthy were improving their residences, the poor were losing theirs.
The correlation was not lost on many of the working poor.

Their rhetoric about public health aside, the civilization-minded ruling
elites were anxious to push their health problem out to the *subúrbios*. Moreover, protesters were aware that the municipal transportation lines were not
playing a neutral role in the renovation/beautification. Adequate transportation service that would bring the working class in from the *subúrbios* to workplaces on the docks, in the quarries, or in the homes of the wealthy was
essential once the *cortiços* were demolished. Since "civilization's" victims
were well aware that even if they worked downtown, they were not going to
live there, they logically attacked the transportation service that was making
this relocation a reality.

Was the riot fomented by groups interested in overthrowing the Rodrigues
Alves's government? The answer is complex. Primarily, it is worth noting
that the uprising was planned for the anniversary week of the declaration of
the Republic, which, while coincidental with the vaccination deadline, was
certainly a date that promised to build on existing and fairly widespread
disillusionment with the Republican administration. On the other hand, the
uprising seems to have exploded far beyond the boundaries set by the
conspirators.

Following its prominent role in organizing the early rallies, the League
Against Obligatory Vaccination lost control of the protest. Since the leadership of the Positivists and socialists did not derive from a fusion of their respective ideological convictions with the ongoing mass struggle, they were
unable to control and direct the protest. While Vicente de Souza's speech at
the November 5 rally pointed to the housing crisis and government duplicity
as reasons for the misery of the working class, he was probably echoing a
widespread view. Neither the Centro das Classes Operarias nor their allies,
the Positivists, grew in influence as a result of the riot. In the months after
the riot the Centro disappeared from the scene of Rio's labor organizations,
possibly because the failed military coup cast the socialist leader in a bad
light. He seemed too close to the Positivists and too involved in their in-

trigues at the expense of the workers' cause.[27] Moreover, the controversy over the Yellow Fever Campaign had already split the Positivists, and thus their role in the league was weakened from the beginning. In addition, the military cadets' coup attempt turned into a debacle, further reducing the influence of Positivist ideology among the young officers, as well as discrediting the Positivists among the working class. In spite of the league's weak role in directing the protest, petty bourgeois shopkeepers and working-class protesters had formed a cross-class alliance on their own and had managed to damage, and in many cases destroy, the sites of the renovation/sanitation project.

In addition, it was no accident that the riot broke out on the day the vaccination was to take effect. The catalyst for the riot, compulsory vaccination, provided the backdrop against which broader issues raised by the Yellow Fever Campaign were angrily brought to center stage. Two striking aspects of the riot lend support to this contention: (1) the public health department was not targeted as were urban renewal and transportation companies; and (2) no victory celebration greeted the November 17 rescission of the compulsory vaccination law, since the larger issues that had provoked the disturbance remained unresolved. Nevertheless, it would be an error to dismiss the importance of the vaccination issue itself, even if it was only the springboard from which other complaints arose. People were genuinely afraid of vaccination, either instinctively or because of the hysterical accusations that surrounded the vaccination law. Viewed in this light, the riot combined genuine premodern suspicion of public health codes with modern resistance to an urban renewal plan that discriminated against the lower class. The riot illustrated what Eric Hobsbawm referred to when he noted that "most prepolitical movements of political importance are today mixtures and combinations of the old and the new . . . most pre-political movements are combined with, or come to terms with, some sort of modern one, whether by imbuing them with their content, by selecting between them, or in other ways."[28] This explanation is far more satisfactory than accounts that attribute the riot entirely to ignorance and superstition, seeing the riot as an example of the "rabble's" hostility toward modern science. Certainly the Rio masses had been given little reason to trust the motives and actions of the Republican government. And in a case of cruel irony, the aspect of the campaign that

27. Sheldon Maram, "Anarchists, Immigrants, and the Brazilian Labor Movement, 1890–1920" (Ph.D. diss., University of California, Santa Barbara, 1972), 141.

28. Eric Hobsbawm, "Pre-political Movements in Peripheral Areas" (paper presented at the Conferencia sobre História e Ciencias Sociais, Campinas, Brazil, May 26–30, 1975), 11.

was most beneficial to the lower classes was rescinded as a result of the riot. Considered in this way, the riot did not bring positive changes to the lives of those who opposed the campaign.

Finally, the riot unfolded as a cross-class alliance of the urban poor, working class, and petty bourgeoisie against the plans forged by the Brazilian bourgeoisie and British imperialists. Not only did the popular classes live in close proximity and thus tend to hold the same grievances against the city's administration and the plans of the renovation contractors, but they also shared many of the same problems. The interclass character of the urban crisis defined in turn the popular mobilization against vaccination and the renovation. Propertied shopkeepers, military Positivists, the working class, and the marginalized poor together opposed the government in a way that seldom reoccurred in later years. Seen from this perspective, the riot of 1904 was probably the best example of a "classic urban riot" in Rio's history. Characteristically, "classic" uprisings are those that occur in societies where the rich and the poor reside in close proximity, intermingling in the centers of power; where groups are "ideologically unified," which grants the insurgents, as well as the suppressors, legitimacy; in societies undergoing wide fluctuations in the cost of living; and, finally, where mechanisms for redress of grievances in ways other than direct action are rare.[29] Although these conditions were constant in Rio for generations and the city was frequently the scene of disturbances, the pot boiled over in 1904. The crisis broke out because of the virtual absence of mechanisms to resolve the drastic problems facing the mass of Rio's residents; nevertheless, the Yellow Fever Campaign, and the vaccination issue in particular, provided the ideological glue to unify disparate groups across class, race, and gender lines into a common front.

Despite the riot, President Rodrigues Alves, Public Health Minister Oswaldo Cruz, Mayor Pereira Passos, and others pushed ahead with the beautification and sanitation program. The major success of the project was the elimination of mosquito breeding grounds in downtown Rio and a drastic reduction in yellow fever epidemics. By 1906 Oswaldo Cruz was able to report to the president of the Republic and to Congress that the city had only a handful of yellow fever outbreaks, and by 1909, that the disease was entirely eliminated. Even so, smallpox again struck Rio in 1908, leaving nine thousand dead in the capital's worst epidemic.[30] When the epidemic ended

29. Ibid., 16; Manuel Castells, "Urban Social Movements and the Struggle for Democracy: The Citizens' Movement in Madrid," *International Journal of Urban and Regional Research* 2 (March 1978): 135.

30. Nancy Stepan, *Beginnings of Brazilian Science: Oswaldo Cruz, Medical Research and Policy, 1890–1920* (New York: Science History Publications, 1976), 90.

in 1909, the public health authorities moved quietly to vaccinate the population and met little resistance. Within a few years, smallpox epidemics ceased to claim the huge numbers as in the prevaccination days, though it was by no means eliminated from the poorest districts of the city.[31]

Several factors account for the 1909 change in the public's attitude, a change that allowed vaccination to proceed without incident. Primarily, by that time much of the urban renewal was completed or well underway; thus vaccination no longer linked the Yellow Fever Campaign and the urban renewal project. To be sure, discontent among former occupants of the downtown *cortiços* continued, but gone was a single issue, such as the vaccination law, around which the many affected forces could rally. In addition, Cruz's success in eradicating yellow fever convinced skeptics among the medical and political community of the validity of his theories on both mosquito control and vaccination. Although critics from professional and political circles had not participated in the riot, or at least in very large numbers, they had written letters to newspapers and otherwise fueled the opposition to the campaign, especially among the middle-class Positivists. The riot, however, horrified these more affluent critics and overshadowed their doubts about Oswaldo Cruz and his public health drive. Faced with the uprising of the lower classes, the city's ruling class closed ranks, effectively stifling the opposition from wealthier residents and professional groups.[32]

When the disturbances died down in late November, the government, with the full support of the press, the commercial groups, and the major political factions, moved to eliminate the possibility of a reoccurrence. The civilizers responded to the issues raised in the protest in the same way they greeted most complaints from the lower classes: they ignored them. In early 1905 J. J. Seabra, minister of justice, presented his summation on the causes of the riot to President Rodrigues Alves. He blamed it on "foreigners, vagabonds, and prostitutes," completely overlooking evidence indicating that protesters came from diverse working backgrounds. Speaking of "pernicious elements" that have blended into and influence the people of Brazil, the minister attributed the "constant ferment" to foreigners and vagabonds who "take advantage of the gullibility of the people and the vulnerable sensibilities" of this young country. According to Seabra, these "foreign anarchists," who "influence, agitate, exploit the humble [people], and bring in bad elements to tear apart society," were responsible for the November riot. More-

31. Directoria Geral de Saúde Pública, Placido Barbosa e Cassio Barbosa de Rezende, *Os serviços de saúde pública no Brazil especialmente na cidade do Rio de Janeiro de 1808 a 1907* (Rio de Janeiro: Imprensa Nacional, 1909), 2:890–901.
32. Stepan, *Beginnings of Brazilian Science*, 99–100.

over, the minister claimed that the "principal authors of the destruction were the unemployed, who have infested Rio de Janeiro" and against whom the police have not been "sufficiently repressive." Added to these "unemployed anarchists" were pimps and prostitutes, who Seabra claimed were responsible for the widespread damage to the downtown district.[33] No doubt the minister drew his conclusion that pimps and prostitutes were involved, because *cortiço* residents took part in the disturbances and these dwellings were notorious among ruling circles as "havens of vice."

Armed with his sociological profile of the rioter as an unemployed anarchist prostitute, pimp, or vagabond (wrapped into one or not he left unclear), Seabra called for a massive mop-up, whose object was the elimination of these so-called pernicious elements from Rio society.[34] Foreigners, labor activists, and people from the poorest rung of Rio society were arrested, detained briefly at the Ilha das Cobras (Isle of the Snakes) correctional facility, and then deported from Brazil or shipped to Acre in the Amazon region.[35]

Claiming that the Centro das Classes Operarias had been overtaken by "bad elements," the justice department closed it down, and officials suggested that "foreign anarchists" be banned from joining any working-class associations.[36] Although most likely unenforceable, the demand indicates the elites' xenophobic reaction to the upheaval and their refusal even to consider the cause of the demonstrators legitimate. Blaming the riot on "foreign anarchists," vagabonds, prostitutes, or pimps provided officials with scapegoats while reinforcing the civilizers' prejudice toward the lower class. More than that, it was hardly an original idea. The Republican elite had succeeded in attributing any conflict in Brazilian society, from backlands peasant uprisings to urban labor disputes and peaceful marches, to foreigners, anarchists, vagabonds, or "pernicious elements" of one sort or another. Needless to say, this explanation coincided with the civilizers' drive to combat encroaching barbarism by cleaning up downtown Rio de Janeiro. Deportation and relocation to Acre of large numbers from the community that just happened to reside in the unsightly *cortiços* was simply one more addition to the original urban renewal project.

Furthermore, seeing the riot as the work of a few malcontents allowed

33. Ministerio da Justiça e Negocios Interiores, *Relatório apresentado ao Presidente da República pelo Dr. J. J. Seabra, Ministro da Justiça e Negocios Interiores* (Rio de Janeiro: Imprensa Nacional, 1905), vol. 1, app. G, 3–5.

34. Ibid.

35. The constitution of the Republic had granted to the government the right to deport "undesirables" to "other areas of the national territory." Directoria da Justiça, Article 80 (Rio de Janeiro: Imprensa Nacional, 1891).

36. Ministerio da Justiça e Negocios Interiores, *Relatório* (1905), 5.

Rio's authorities to turn their backs on the social problems at the root of the popular classes' discontent. Just as the city elites had charged in 1891 that the downtown streets were filled with "deprived and unstable" people, fourteen years later they blamed this same group for the riot. In so doing, and in keeping with the social theories that gained popularity in the late nineteenth century, Rio's civilizers enshrouded their explanations of civil unrest in the scientific thought of the day—a system of principles in which human life was increasingly interpreted as the result of "natural biological laws."[37] As a result, science, as well as what passed as scientific explanation at the time, was integral not only to the government's health campaign but to the far-reaching social and cultural rationale used to bolster the urban renewal plan. And that science, since discredited as "pseudo science," was eugenics.[38]

Eventually eugenics, the science of engineering heredity as a way of eliminating disease, poverty, and vice, amassed an enthusiastic following among Brazilian scientists, government officials, legal experts, and mental hygienists. As Nancy Stepan shows, the eugenics movement in Brazil was a complex and flexible set of scientific interpretations at whose core was the notion of racial improvement. Leaving aside a comprehensive discussion of the various and often contradictory racial theories that formed the basis of turn of the-century eugenics discourse, it is nonetheless important to recognize that a belief in Anglo-European racial superiority was sanctioned as "science." In turn, science bound the ruling group's concept of civilization to the health campaign, since the supposed indisputability of scientific experimentation legitimized the public health program as well as the whole concept of civilization. Conveniently, the public health project paved the way both economically, through the firms that sponsored and financed the program, and culturally, through the conception of science as the standard-bearer of civilization, for deeper penetration of Franco-British influence into Rio during the opening years of the twentieth century.

Not only did the elite rely on scientific arguments to justify the sanitation and renewal of Rio de Janeiro, but ultimately they extended their argument to rationalize the removal of the unsightly poor, along with their attendant vices, from the downtown as well. Conversely, the more the elite were able to wrap their cause in the legitimacy of science, the easier it was to discredit the opposition, labeling it, as they did, the recalcitrance of superstitious, ignorant, and backward poor people unable to comprehend the necessity

37. Nancy Leys Stepan, *"The Hour of Eugenics": Race, Gender, and Nation in Latin America* (Ithaca: Cornell University Press, 1991), 21.

38. Ibid. Stepan makes the crucial point that there was nothing really "pseudo" about eugenics; it was the science of its day.

of health and sanitation. No matter that the protesters had included military cadets, students and intellectuals, the poor as well as the not so poor. Reduced in the official record to a "deprived and unstable" mob of "pernicious elements," the protesters could be dismissed as an innately, even biologically, inferior and hopeless mass of humanity whose miserable state stemmed from nature rather than from any real social or economic factors.

The extent to which the elite sought to back up social policy with scientific authority was not unique to Brazil. The late nineteenth and early twentieth centuries saw a proliferation of urban development and sanitation projects funded and administered by British companies throughout the formal and informal empire. Hong Kong, Johannesburg, Kingston, Freetown, and Buenos Aires were sites of similar public health campaigns and accompanying urban renewal projects that closely resembled the one in Rio. In Freetown, Sierra Leone, British colonial authorities in the late nineteenth century directed an extensive sanitation project against the malaria and yellow fever that frequented the port city and impeded the flow of imperial trade. However, the end result did more than simply eliminate disease. It established a color bar separating black and mixed-race Africans from the growing white settler population.[39]

Brazil's neighbor, Argentina, also underwent an urban renewal project following the 1871 yellow fever epidemic in Buenos Aires. At that time the Porteñõ elite, or, the term they preferred for themselves, the *gente decente*, became increasingly hostile toward the European immigrants filling the downtown district where they lived, as in Rio, in notoriously unsanitary tenements. The so-called decent people of Buenos Aires embarked on a health and renovation project that transformed the city into a model of Parisian architecture and cultural refinement while simultaneously eliminating the yellow fever scourge. The rising property values in the Plaza district forced low-income residents out to squalid suburbs or into already horrendously crowded tenements in the largely Italian immigrant district of La Boca, from

39. Leo Spitzer, "The Mosquito and Segregation in Sierra Leone," *Canadian Journal of African Studies* 2, no. 1 (1968): 49–61. On other urban renewal projects, see Charles Van Onselen, *Studies in the Social and Economic History of Witwatersrand, 1886–1914*, 2 vols. (New York: Longman, 1982); Greer Williams, *The Plague Killers* (New York: Charles Scribner's Sons, 1969); Colin G. Clarke, *Kingston, Jamaica: Urban Development and Social Change, 1692–1962* (Berkeley and Los Angeles: University of California Press, 1975). See the following articles in A. Lafuente, A. Elena, and M. L. Ortega, eds., *Mundialización de la ciencia y cultura nacional: Actas del congreso internacional "Ciencia, descubrimiento y mundo colonial"* (Madrid: Ediciones Doce Calles, 1993): Molly Sutphen, "Plague, Race, and Segregation: British Colonial Response to Contamination in Cape Town"; Ann F. La Berge, "The Conquest of Algeria and the Discourse on Public Health in France"; Eduardo A. Zimmermann, "Raza, Medicina y Reforma Social en la Argentina, 1890–1920"; Diego Armus, "La Ciudad Higiénica entre Europa y Latinoamérica."

which they traveled to work on streetcar and rail lines installed, as in Rio, with British money and expertise.[40]

In each of these three cases, Rio de Janeiro, Freetown, and Buenos Aires, measures such as stopping disease, enforcing sanitation regulations, improving or installing transportation and communication networks, and building new cultural and mercantile centers ultimately enhanced the city's trading potential and transformed these colonial and neocolonial outposts into attractive metropoles for the experts and entrepreneurs who staffed foreign firms abroad. Thus, in addition to making the city safe for imperialist trade and for its agents, these projects introduced the "expert" and the concept of "expertise" as the ideological and cultural property of the emerging imperialist world order. Furthermore, the scientist came onto the world stage as the foremost expert in this modernizing society, an expertise, as Stepan remarks, "based on its claim to facticity, neutrality, and universality."[41]

In Rio, and in general, science and scientific professionals played a pivotal role in determining and enforcing the standards of acceptable behavior within the modern capitalist culture. In general, professionals in the health field helped to define standards of sickness and health, both physical and mental, and the means through which society's health was both regulated and maintained. Moreover, health experts, wittingly or not, established the criteria of a society's social ills, or, in Terry Johnson's words, its "criminality, deviancy, poverty."[42] Ultimately, a society could be cured through the elimination of poverty and its accompanying vice and sickness. Short of a cure—and most societies have fallen woefully short—the problem and the bearers of the problem, the poor, could simply be pushed aside, out of sight of those drawing up the judgment. In Rio de Janeiro, as in Freetown or Buenos Aires, following the examples of Paris and London, the experts determined that neither science nor regulation could fully eliminate the root causes of physical and social disease, or they were unwilling to undertake the social cost such a remedy would have entailed. Instead, they used science and their own particular variant of scientific explanation to justify their motives, to remove, at least from the most visible locales, those most susceptible to disease.

The case of Rio de Janeiro is an interesting example of the various and often subtle methods through which capitalist culture and its standards of behavior penetrate a society. Rather than impose a "monolithic, all-

40. James R. Scobie, *Buenos Aires: From Plaza to Suburb, 1870–1910* (New York: Oxford University Press, 1974), 122–24, 160–207.

41. Stepan, *"The Hour of Eugenics,"* 11.

42. Terry Johnson, "What Is to Be Known? The Structural Determination of Social Class," *Economy and Society* 6, no. 2 (1977): 220–28.

devouring system of political domination and cohesion," the state regulates society through a variety of means, one of which, as Johnson argues, is colleague control.[43] The primary method through which professionals and experts regulate themselves, colleague control implies expertise and functions through a body of individuals and institutions deemed capable, because of education, training, and practical experimentation, of determining society's values. The concept of colleague control, therefore, occupies a middle ground between the iron conformity that might be enforced by the state and the rather amorphous sense of "consciousness" that might pertain apart from structural determinants. In essence it removes from the state the necessity to intervene in the direct determination of acceptable standards for social behavior. Nevertheless, the "'objective expert' comes to his work as prejudiced as the next person," or even more so, limited as he is by the technical "climate," cultural habits, career considerations within a restricted line of work usually for a specific company, and the popularity of recent intellectual trends.[44]

In Brazil, developing as it did under the heavy influence of a foreign power and importing both its experts and its standard of expertise from abroad, this process of self-regulation, or colleague control, among professionals proceeded somewhat differently from the pattern in England and the United States that Johnson described. Primarily, whatever existed as an apparatus of domestically controlled "colleagues" within Brazil was extremely tenuous. Although it was during the First Republic that an urban and educated elite became better known, clustered around the polytechnic and Oswaldo Cruz's Manguinhos Institute in Rio de Janeiro, the School of Mines in Ouro Preto, and Butantã in São Paulo, these institutions were young.[45] Brazilians continued to look to France, Germany, and England for scientific and technological leadership, sent students to the great institutions of Europe for training, and generally adopted wholesale the standards of expertise from the European models. As a result, Brazil's notion of expertise, as well as what constituted expert or professional conduct, was defined abroad and according to a foreign standard. Brazilian doctors, sanitation engineers, and city planners adapted to the cultural standards of the Franco-British experts, just as the ruling elite adopted the Franco-British definition of civilization.

43. Ibid., 221.
44. David F. Noble, *Forces of Production: A Social History of Industrial Automation* (New York: Alfred A. Knopf, 1984), 145.
45. José Murilo de Carvalho, "Brazil, 1870–1914: The Force of Tradition," *Journal of Latin American Studies* (Quincentenary Supplement, 1992), 147.

Tying science and scientific investigation to often arbitrary sets of cultural and political ideals, biases, and constructs is anathema to the view of "objective" or Darwinian science and technological development that has enjoyed currency among social scientists. David Noble effectively disputes the notion that science selects out the most technologically sound solutions, accepts the most economically viable and, through the mechanism of the marketplace, allows only the best innovations to survive. As he shows, alternatives that contradict the class and cultural prejudices of a society have never been seriously considered. Trolley lines to Ipanema, with its ninety-six buildings and sparse population, rather than to Inhaúma, Campo Grande, or Santa Cruz, with over 100,000 people; lighting for downtown streets, which were mostly used during the daytime, instead of for districts where people lived at night; and sanitation and improvements for the downtown, where 37 percent of the population resided, but nothing for the districts where the other 60 percent lived—these are vivid historical illustrations of Noble's point that "economic viability" and "technical viability" are not really economic or technical categories at all, but are instead cultural and political ones.[46] In addition, there is no evidence that the works of the English engineers—the waterworks, drainage systems, retaining walls, and pumps installed by the City Improvements Company—were the most effective means for sanitizing the city. All that is known is that they were installed, that they were very costly, and that they worked for a while. Furthermore, there is no evidence, and quite a lot to the contrary, that the transportation networks, trolley lines, and trains put in place by the various monopolies were the most efficient means for moving goods, services, or people.[47]

At the turn of the century, expert planners, engineers, health officials, doctors, and countless medical personnel worked in Rio at the behest of a supposedly impartial scientific inquiry and experimentation. In so doing, they used science as a powerful tool in the interest of cultural imperialism; they embodied, as does science, the image of truth, of legitimacy, most of all, of neutrality, enforced by seemingly honest and impartial experts. However, very little in the history of science is impartial and disinterested. Without discounting the benefits of public health, essential to the well-being of society, one cannot deny that otherwise impartial, even well-meaning, doctors of tropical medicine or railway engineers, who in no way saw themselves as agents of imperialism, carried out an activity whose ulti-

---

46. Noble, *Forces of Production*, 145.
47. José Alvaro Moisés and Verena Martinez-Alier Stolcke, "Urban Transport and Popular Violence: The Case of Brazil," *Past and Present* 86 (February 1980): 86.

mate goal was to ensure that peripheral territory was secure for metropolitan investment.[48]

In Rio de Janeiro the urban renewal plan and public health campaign created for the foreign and domestic ruling elite *a cidade marvilhosa* (the marvelous city), acclaimed throughout the world for its beauty. Of course, few of the city's elite or its foreign merchants and tourists bothered then, as now, to venture far from the wide avenues and beaux arts monuments in the center city, or from the beaches of Copacabana and Ipanema in the renowned Zona Sul, to the sprawling and disease-infested shantytowns and suburbs, where the poor and working class resided and where they were left to wage their struggles alone.

Within this context, the riot and the overall opposition to the renovation of the city loom larger and are more ideologically weighted than a local disturbance would imply. Similar to their counterparts in other countries and at other times, the Carioca crowds were motivated by more complex issues than simply superstition, and their protest represented far more than a case of misdirected mob action. Different from crowd activities in Europe and the United States, the Rio de Janeiro conflict exhibited characteristics that have since become near constant features of struggles in developing cities of the periphery during the modern period. Since the drive to civilize Rio de Janeiro through the Yellow Fever Campaign and its attendant urban renewal plan was an effort to create a city in keeping with the interests of an export-oriented economy, dependent on foreign investment, the opponents to this drive were spontaneously, and for the most part unknowingly, reacting against what that type of development, or, better, that type of civilization, portended in their lives.

For their part, the Republican liberal elite, convinced of the righteousness of their struggle against barbarism, reacted against any opposition to the priorities of their civilization drive. The repression that greeted the November 1904 riot became a common feature of political administration during the Old Republic, as the Republican liberals further retreated from any earlier democratic-reformist impulses and opted for authoritarian solutions to the problems of urban society. Nevertheless, the problems remained. Government inattention to food and housing shortages, poor transportation service, and deplorable sanitary conditions provoked rioting in Rio's working-class neighborhoods and *subúrbios* in succeeding decades.

48. Lewis Pyenson, "The Limits of Scientific Condominium: Geophysics in Western Samoa, 1914–1940," in *Scientific Colonialism: A Cross-Cultural Comparison,* ed. Nathan Reingold and Marc Rothenberg (Washington, D.C.: Smithsonian Institution Press, 1987), 251.

5

Living and Working Conditions

> I don't very much believe in these houses, that is, that they
> will ever be built.
> —Comment from a worker, reported in the
> *Jornal do Brasil*, April 6, 1906

In the wake of Rio's urban renewal project, and as a result of changes in the geographic distribution of social classes, in its demographic makeup, and in the social structure of the city, new forms of collective action and popular protests appeared. The most obvious difference was that protests in the post–urban renewal period less often reached the downtown government and commercial offices and thus posed a less immediate threat to the stability of commerce and state functions. Another change was that the relocation of the lower classes away from the downtown, combined with the sanitation of the Old City, had appeased those property owners who were previously discontent with the manner in which the city government had been handling the sanitation and housing dilemma. Rio in 1906 was emerging as a different metropolitan area, one in which the urban space was reallocated in a dramatically new fashion. As a result of the Yellow Fever Campaign, problems of health care and sanitation were no longer the fear of the wealthiest Cariocas; rather, they had become the concern of the *suburba-nos*—the urban poor and working class amassing in the settlements on the outskirts of the downtown.

Nonetheless, the renovations never resolved the issue of social control entirely; instead, they merely introduced a new set of antagonisms and changed the contours of the struggle between those who were benefiting from the new Rio and those who were not. In the years following the urban renewal, the more prosperous of the residents in the Zona Norte and the suburbs, or those with enough money to take the streetcars and enough education to write complaints to city authorities over its terrible service, loudly protested living conditions and services in their neighborhoods. Driven from the Old City by higher property values and attracted to the better air and wider spaces of the outlying regions, many government and commercial workers moved to the Zona Norte, while the most affluent were able to settle in the Zona Sul. Those who went north found the most inadequate public services. Just as industrial workers in the mills were calling for shorter hours and higher pay, residents of the fast-growing suburban towns were asking for better city services.

These changing contours of urban protest extend the boundaries of James Scott's concept of the "hidden transcript."[1] While some of the masses' day-to-day disgruntlement remained sublimated, more often their discontent was quite apparent. What was in this case hidden, at least from the intellectual leadership of the workers' movement, was the need to correlate the "transcript" of consumer rebellion with the militant "transcript" of the shop floor. On those few occasions when the transcripts fused, their collective strength was formidable.

Conditions in the outlying areas worsened in the years following the Yellow Fever Campaign, while the settlement pattern that had begun decades earlier became more entrenched. The most affluent residents settled in the Zona Sul (Catete, Flamengo, Botafogo, Laranjeiras, Jardim Botânico, Copacabana, and eventually Ipanema), while the working class settled in the Zona Norte (São Cristóvão, Catumbí, Rio Comprido, Andaraí, Vila Isabel, and Tijuca) and in the *subúrbios* extending out from the North Zone. After 1905 more people moved into unhealthy areas with fewer public services and less access to water and power lines. Whereas the population in the seven center-city districts—Sacramento, Candelária, São José, Santa Rita, Sant'Anna, Gló-

1. James C. Scott, *Domination and the Arts of Resistance: Hidden Transcripts* (New Haven: Yale University Press, 1990), esp. chap. 7.

ria, and Santo Antonio, in which the health and renewal program had concentrated—had increased by 62 percent from 1872 to 1890, the rate of growth dropped to 12 percent during the period from 1890 to 1906 as the urban renewal got underway. During the years following the urban renewal, when the Federal District as a whole grew by 39 percent, population growth in the downtown was a mere 4 percent. The destruction of the *cortiços* caused thousands of inner-city residents to abandon the center city and join the multitudes of European immigrants and migrants from Brazil's countryside in the miserably poor zones to the north of the downtown or cropping up on the outskirts of the city. Thus an important aspect of the downtown renovation had been to move more and more people into areas already notorious for inadequate sanitation and public services.[2]

More striking, however, are the comparisons between population increases in the downtown with those in the developing industrial areas and, in particular, the *subúrbios*. From 1890 to 1906, when the population in the seven center-city boroughs increased by 12 percent, that of the developing industrial zones grew by 118 percent, and the *subúrbios* by 106 percent. Moreover, in the years from 1906 through 1920, after the completion of the urban renewal, the population grew by 4 percent in the areas with the most extensive renovations, while in the other areas of the Federal District, where few or none of these improvements had taken place, the population increased by 61 percent. It was the *subúrbios* that registered the most astounding increase during these years, as European immigrants and migrants from the Brazilian countryside pushed the growth rate in Irajá, Jacarepaguá, Inhaúma, Guaratiba, Campo Grande, and Santa Cruz up by 96 percent.[3]

In fact, the single most important source of popular protest in the post–urban renewal period was the fact that only 28 percent of Rio's residents enjoyed the benefits of living in a healthy and beautified city, while nearly twice that number lived in districts lacking basic health, transportation, communication, and other public services. The social movement that arose, combining the demands of consumers with those of industrial workers, reflected what Ira Katznelson and others have shown to be the "structural properties"

---

2. Directoria Geral de Estatística, *Recenseamento Geral da República dos Estados Unidos do Brazil en 31 de Dezembro de 1890, Districto Federal* (Rio de Janeiro: Imprensa Nacional, 1895), lxxiii; idem, *Recenseamento do Rio de Janeiro Realisado em 20 de Setembro de 1906* (Rio de Janeiro: Imprensa Nacional, 1907), 180–265; idem, *Recenseamento do Brazil Realisado em 1 de Setembro de 1920, População do Rio de Janeiro (Districto Federal)* (Rio de Janeiro: Imprensa Nacional, 1923), 2:xxvi.

3. These figures are the recalculation of the combined increases of the developing industrial, *subúrbios,* and other areas from previous tables. See Table 3.

Table 3. Population Percentage by Area, 1872–1920

	1872	1890	1906	1920
Center city [Renewal area]	63.2%	52.7%	37.2%	27.8%
North Zone [Poor/working-class area]	15.0	22.8	32.1	33.6
Subúrbios	15.1	16.6	22.0	30.9
Other areas	6.5	7.7	8.5	7.5

of capitalism that always accompany urban growth. As Katznelson argues, not only have urban protests been a major feature of political life for the past quarter century, they also form a "family of cases . . . organized at the place of residence, not at work." Although describing the United States and Europe, Katznelson's comments are equally applicable to Rio de Janeiro when he notes that the themes of urban protest have concerned "the delivery of collective services by government and the impact of housing, transportation, and social services on the built form of the city and on the quality of city life."[4]

Afonso Henriques Lima Barreto described the *subúrbio* as a long strip of land that extended from the Rocha and São Francisco Xavier to Saporemba, bordering on the Central rail line, where one could find every conceivable model of dwelling from houses to huts to makeshift stalls once built for animals but subsequently converted to shelters for people. The new arrivals cobbled together structures in a few hours or overnight, consisting of no more than four posts topped by wood beams held together with a webbing of bamboo slathered with lath and plaster. The more fortunate were able to side their houses with sheets of zinc, but many others simply draped scavenged rags and blankets down from bamboo poles for walls. They were motley conglomerations of buildings housing an equally motley assortment of poor and working-class residents, including the regularly and casually employed, whose interests coalesced around their common need to have access to the rail line. Other settlements sprang up around the textile mills, in company towns the factory owners provided for their workers at extortion-

---

4. Ira Katznelson, *City Trenches: Urban Politics and the Patterning of Class in the United States* (Chicago: University of Chicago Press, 1981), 210.

ate rents. Population clustered around these two institutions—the factory and the rail line—since there was really no other raison d'être for the neighborhoods.[5]

Settlements that sprang up near the existing routes, and lines were quickly extended to connect with rapidly growing districts adjacent to factories. Neighborhoods of makeshift housing lined railroad and trolley tracks, settlers grouping in these areas because of the access they afforded to their places of work. In addition, small shops sprang up that sold food, liquor, and household items to the residents of the mushrooming population centers. With the basic settlement pattern determined by the location of a rail or trolley line, the influence of the transportation companies was clearly enormous. A fare increase, delay in service, or termination of a line had a disastrous impact on hundreds, even thousands, of people who were more or less held captive by the whims of the transportation companies.

Despite the 1904 riot and the continual demands from labor and community groups, the city government built only a few units of low-income housing to replace the *cortiços* and to alleviate the city's drastic housing shortage.[6] A plaintive comment in an anarchist newspaper in 1906 summed up the effect of the destruction of the *cortiços*: "With each stone that falls, with each roof that comes down, also fall the tears of those who tomorrow will be left without even a miserable cubicle where they can rest their limbs, fatigued from a day of badly paid labor."[7] When questioned by a reporter from the *Jornal do Brasil* about the government's long-promised housing projects, a worker replied: "I don't very much believe in these houses, that is, that they will ever be built." According to the inquiring reporter, the worker responded with the "cynicism of his class" toward the government's many unfulfilled promises.[8]

Was it cynicism or realism? Oswaldo Cruz had declared Rio free from yellow fever in 1909 and, after the smallpox vaccination campaign that year, stated that all other *major* epidemics had been eliminated. In response, An-

5. Afonso Henriques Lima Barreto, *Clara dos anjos* (Rio de Janeiro: Mérito, 1949), 111.

6. Ministerio da Justiça e Negocios Interiores, *Relatório ao Presidente da República pelo Dr. J. J. Seabra, Ministro da Justiça e Negocios Interiores* (Rio de Janeiro: Imprensa Nacional, 1906), 2:300–31. Evarardo Backheuser, an architect and engineer, presented his plans for workers' housing to Seabra in 1906. The study, "Habitações Populares," is appended to the above *Relatório*, 13–126. See also Rubens d'Almeida H. de Porto, *O problema das casas operarias e os institutos e caixas de pensões* (Rio de Janeiro: Imprensa Nacional, 1938), 79–81, for a summary of housing units that were planned but never completed.

7. *Novo Rumo*, July 20, 1906, 1.

8. *Jornal do Brasil*, April 6, 1906, 1. Eight years later workers were still reporting that nothing had been done to meet their desperate housing needs; *Voz do Trabalhador*, January 1, 1914, 1.

tonio Evaristo de Moraes, a founding member of the Brazilian Socialist Party, delivered a devastating critique in the party journal, *Clarté*, denouncing the members of the medical establishment who celebrated the "hygienic state" of the city, the developers ("truly hired killers of the masses") who had ruined the downtown avenues, and all of the elite who routinely partook of festivities in the city commemorating the Red Cross, the League Against Tuberculosis, and the St. Vincent's Paternity. In the face of these celebrations marking the accomplishments of the public health drive, the socialist critic noted that the government's own statistics showed that from 1903 to 1920 the combined total of deaths from epidemics of yellow fever, plague, whooping cough, scarlet fever, diphtheria, and smallpox numbered 64,741, while a total of 68,985 city residents had died of tuberculosis alone during the same period.[9] Little had changed in the years after the health drive; as one observer summarized: "There are no houses for the poor, meat is a food they can rarely touch, tuberculosis chooses them as its preferred victims, anemia paralyzes them, and maladies of the digestive tract decimate and annihilate them."[10]

In some parts of the city tuberculosis, the killer most linked to unsanitary living conditions, swept through the dilapidated housing units into which crowded even more bodies than before the public health drive. A commentary from Dr. Alfredo Leal de Sá Pereira that appeared in the *Jornal do Commercio* in 1910 was widely quoted in the socialist and anarchist press and eventually found its way into Rui Barbosa's *Questão Social e Política* (The social and political question) in 1919. Notably, the doctor's description of the housing available to most of the city's laboring poor differed hardly at all from the outcries voiced before 1904 : "They are habitations without air or light, where adults and children live in the most sordid promiscuity; where the most modest, when obeying the laws of perpetuating the species, cover themselves behind a semitransparent red curtain; where at night in the closed environment the room contains air for only one-third as many people as crowd into it; where the daily provisions, hanging from the walls, add their perfume to the foul-smelling atmosphere; where coal or kerosene stoves blacken the walls, [leaving occupants] asphyxiated and sickened; where [those afflicted] with tuberculosis are spitting everywhere, as if distributing their 'unwanted gifts' to all around them; where filthy and stunted children play in dark corridors; where clothing is washed in basins inside rooms and

9. Evaristo de Moraes, "O problema da tuberculose e o problema da habitação das classes pobres," *Clarté* 1, no. 6 (1921): 167–70.
10. *Jornal do Brasil*, June 28, 1905, 1.

left to dry by whatever air enters through the windows."[11] Barbosa cited statistics that recorded 247 people crowded into 69 rooms with one bathroom, or even no bathroom at all, a tenement of 15 rooms housing 40 people and another with 39 units and 193 inhabitants and neither with bathrooms.[12]

Cynical toward the government's many unfilled promises, relegated to the least serviced sections of the city, and continually frustrated by employers who raised prices but seldom wages, consumers and workers continued to protest against their living conditions. Demands usually considered "premodern" in advanced capitalist countries were showing themselves, in Brazil, in the strikes of the "modern" trade union movement, as well as in consumer protests. These consumer, community-based struggles eventually received their direction from the most politically conscious sector of the Rio de Janeiro workers' movement: the anarchists.[13] In fact, the anarchists registered some of their greatest gains, namely, the general strike of 1917, when they fused the demands of the community struggles with those raised on the shop floor. This may have occurred because of the symbiosis between the grievances of the laboring poor as both consumers and producers, a particularly strong characteristic of Rio's working class, given the transience of jobs. Of the strikes between 1905 and 1914 the majority were in civil construction, on the docks by stevedores, firemen, and laborers, in municipal services by drivers and coachmen, firemen, and commercial maritime workers, and among skilled trades, especially shoemakers, stonemasons, and construction workers. Fewer job actions and work stoppages affected basic manufacturing: a 1906 "general strike" of shoemakers, one among textile workers in solidarity with a walkout at the Fabrica de Tecidos Carioca in São Paulo, and another in 1910 in several textile mills were the exceptions.[14]

11. Moraes, "O problema da tuberculose," 123.
12. Rui Barbosa, "A questão social e política no Brasil," in *Escritos e discursos selectos* (Rio de Janeiro: Editora José Aguilar, 1960), 430–38.
13. Contrary to what Sheldon Maram contended in his pathbreaking studies of the Left and Brazil's labor movement, the prevalence of anarcho-syndicalism among the working class did not necessarily impede a militant response to oppression; "Labor and the Left in Brazil, 1890–1921: A Movement Aborted," *Hispanic American Historical Review* 57, no. 2 (1977): 294.
14. Strikes in 1905 included civil construction workers, dockworkers, stevedores, and firemen; *Jornal do Brasil,* May 30, June 18–21, July 31, 1905. In 1906 strikes involved textile workers, warehouse and coffee workers, stevedores, shoemakers, drivers and coachmen, and commercial maritime workers; *Jornal do Brasil,* May 26–30, June 2, August 21–31, December 18–23, 1906. There was little activity in 1907 and 1908 except for an April 11, 1908, strike of workers at the Companhia da Gaz; 1910 was the year of the most activity in basic manufacturing, with a militant strike at the Fabrica São João textile mill throughout February and a walkout by semi-skilled shoemakers the same month; *Gazeta de Notícias,* February 3–5, 16, 24, 1910. Construction workers struck in October 1912, and stevedores in January 1914; *Jornal do Brasil,* October 8, 1912, and January 19, 1914.

The 1906 shoemakers' strike is one of the most well known of this era, possibly because the shoemakers were the sector of the Rio working class with the longest-running union affiliations, having formed one of the earliest artisan mutual-aid societies, Sociedade de Soccorros Mutuos Protectora dos Artistas Sapateiros e Classes Correlativas, in the 1870s. Formed into local and broader regional unions and societies from the 1870s on, by the first decade of the twentieth century they were mainly concentrated in the Liga dos Operários em Calçado and the União dos Cortadores de Calçado. Shoemakers were one of the few sectors of the working class that had made the transition from small artisanal shops to larger factories but had consistently opposed mechanization of the labor process and the resultant layoffs and, eventually, had struck for the eight-hour day, higher pay, and better working conditions. They struck in 1902 and 1903, carried out a short "general strike" of shoemakers in 1906, went out again in 1909 and 1911, and supported the citywide general strikes of 1917 and 1918.[15]

With the exception of the militancy among shoemakers, who were often protesting the routinization, mechanization, and subsequent proletarianization of the labor process, and individual strikes in textile mills, job actions between 1890 and 1910 mainly centered on municipal services. In that regard the workers were raising issues reflective of the broader social protests in the city. In fact, on those occasions when the anarchist organizers looked beyond the factory gates, into the neighborhoods and onto the trains, they saw a disputatious mass, voicing its anger as both the producer and the recipient of city services.[16]

Protests in this second period, from 1905 through 1915, were directed at the transportation companies, many of whom had been involved in the urban renewal plan. Although, as noted earlier, popular outcries against fare increases were not uncommon in the years before the urban renewal, after 1905 commuters zeroed in on the fine points of company policy and services: the decision to reroute a line, irregular and erratically kept schedules, or the failure to extend a line to a specific neighborhood. The renovations had brought with them a consolidation of transit companies into three major streetcar lines—Jardim Botânico, Carris Urbanos, and Vila Isabel—which in 1905, along with the auxiliary Carioca and Jacarepaguá lines, carried

15. Eileen Keremitsis, "The Early Industrial Worker in Rio de Janeiro, 1870–1930" (Ph.D. diss., Columbia University, 1982), chap. 5; Maria Cecília Baeta Neves, "Greve dos Sapateiros de 1906 no Rio de Janeiro: Notas de pesquisa," *Revista de Administração de Empresas* (Fundação Getúlio Vargas), June 2, 1973, 49–68.
16. Timothy Harding, "The Political History of Organized Labor in Brazil" (Ph.D. diss., Stanford University, 1973), 2, 8, 33n.

110,570,927 passengers. The next year, the Central alone carried 19,239,236 riders.[17] The recipe for trouble was apparent in the huge number of riders dependent on a few inadequate, poorly maintained lines run by a handful of owners.

Other protests arose over the government's refusal to provide public services—including sanitation, road construction, disease control, lighting, and housing—to the working-class zones. Community protests over these two sets of issues, transportation and public services, revealed both the shortcomings of the urban renewal and the government's lack of concern for the needs of large numbers of the Carioca citizens residing far from the newly refurbished downtown. Additionally, protests broke out over price increases and shortages, which, as in the years before 1905, followed national government policies. Simply stated, during the years from 1905 through 1915 hostility toward the government, and toward the elite and foreign investors it served, mounted as the popular classes became increasingly aware that they were getting less and less while paying more and more.

Fluctuations in transportation costs most affected government and commercial workers and skilled and stably employed factory workers, who used the public transportation lines to travel to downtown workplaces and who were better off than the casual and day laborers, who often walked. Many of the salaried workers were not necessarily middle-class in the traditional sense; rather, they were a sector of workers with enough money to afford a streetcar ride, something prohibitively expensive to industrial workers. Arguing that streetcar fares were exorbitantly high, the *Jornal do Brasil* published the results of its own survey, which found that it cost more than the average worker's monthly wage to pay the streetcar fare for himself and three other adults, round-trip, first-class, from the *subúrbios* to the downtown in order to attend the theater. In fact, the theater tickets alone cost far more than a month's wages, clearly indicating that a working-class family's budget would never accommodate a theater performance. Pointing to the importance of the national theater as a means of cultural enrichment for the working class, the newspaper called on the government to institute reforms to lower the price of streetcar rides and theater tickets so that lower income families could attend performances downtown.[18] Another article in this same series examined the cost for a working-class family of six to take a Sunday outing from the *subúrbios* to a beach at Leme or Ipanema. The cost for the

17. Sylvia F. Padilha, "Da 'Cidade Velha' a periferia," *Revista Rio de Janeiro* 1, no. 1 (1985): 19–22.
18. *Jornal do Brasil*, July 4, 1905, 1.

trip—the fare, one drink for each family member (but no food)—came to 10 milreis, more than many textile workers' monthly wage. Arguing that "man does not live by bread alone," the *Jornal do Brasil* called on the streetcar companies to add an additional service on Sundays designated specifically to serve low-income passengers on an afternoon outing to "points of interest in the city."[19]

The *Jornal do Brasil*'s concern that *suburbanos* were unable to attend the theater or go to the beach appears ludicrous when juxtaposed to commuters' demands for lower streetcar fares so they could get to and from work and thus maintain a livelihood. More interesting is the fact that the *Jornal do Brasil*, aware that passengers from time to time rioted against the fares and services the streetcar companies provided, apparently ignored the desperation that led to the riots. Clearly passengers wanted to use streetcars for diversion as well as to get to work, but the *Jornal do Brasil* chose to focus on diversion. No riots had been instigated by irate commuters unable to reach the theater or the beach on the weekend, since, no matter how lovely an idea, *suburbanos* were angry that faulty transportation systems denied them access to work. As Gareth Stedman Jones argues in his critique of studies that look only at leisure-time activities as means of isolating and controlling the working class, "[T]he greatest 'social control'—if one wants to use the word—available to capitalism is the wage relationship itself—the fact that, in order to live and reproduce, the worker must perpetually resell his or her labour power."[20] It was the circumstances surrounding the sale of their labor that most angered Rio's masses.

On the other hand, the *Jornal do Brasil* implicitly, if not explicitly, exposed the fact that the downtown renovations were never intended to serve anyone but the most elite of the city's residents. Obviously the cost of theater or opera tickets, and even the streetcar fare to get from the outlying districts to the downtown, placed these "civilized" diversions beyond the reach of all but Rio's elite. One recalls the British traveler Alured Bell's approving comment that the smart new promenade along the Beira Mar would serve the "Rio of the future."[21] The majority of Rio in the present (and in the future, if the renovation worked) were never going to stroll the scenic promenade. Finally, the *Jornal do Brasil*'s findings suggest that although many industrial workers and sometimes the urban poor used the new transportation system,

19. Ibid., July 1, 1905, 1. At this time 400 reis would have bought one kilogram of rice.
20. Gareth Stedman Jones, "Class Expression Versus Social Control: A Critique of Recent Trends in the Social History of 'Leisure,'" *History Workshop* 4 (Autumn 1977): 169.
21. Alured Grey Bell, *The Beautiful Rio de Janeiro* (London: William Heinemann, 1914), 14.

most of the city's poorest residents could seldom afford it. They walked to work.[22]

Riders had ample cause for discontent. The transportation and utility companies enjoyed a great deal of freedom in their operation and influence over the weak central government. The British-controlled and -owned transportation companies that had helped finance the urban renewal enjoyed complete freedom from government supervision in the years following it. On the other hand, Brazilian government officials satisfied with the comfort and hygiene of the newly beautified downtown little heeded the complaints of the *suburbanos* against the streetcar and railroad companies. In the absence of strict official regulation and oversight, the transportation companies raised fares and passed on tax increases to passengers, as well as terminated and extended lines when they chose. These private companies were highly influential in determining the settlement pattern of the city, one in which railroad lines extended to the *subúrbios* and connected these districts with the industrial areas of Vila Isabel, São Cristóvão, Meier, and others, while streetcar lines traversed the downtown and extended out to the developing industrial zones.[23]

As the government showed itself unwilling to regulate or even pay attention to commuters' grievances against the transportation companies, crowds more and more resorted to direct action. In August 1908 passengers rioted after hearing that the Companhia Estrada de Ferro Leopoldina was raising its fares. The Leopoldina, which had formed in 1897, connected São Francisco Xavier with Bonsucesso, Penha, and Meriti. It had grown in importance along with the population centers it serviced, climbing from 582,860 riders in 1900 to 1,163,681 in 1906. The company had not improved its service or updated its schedules in line with the increase in passengers, however, and hit with a fare hike in 1908, the latter rebelled. Beginning in Campos, far to the outskirts of the city, and continuing in neighboring communities along the route, commuters attacked the trains and tore up sections of the tracks in protest over the projected fare increase. The riot raged for three days, in the course of which protesters overturned and set ablaze three railcars and

22. Similarly, James Scobie argues that the working class and urban poor of Buenos Aires did not ride the newly installed transportation lines. There, also, the fares were too high for industrial workers, most of whom lived on the outskirts of the factory zone and walked several miles to work. James R. Scobie, *Buenos Aires: From Plaza to Suburb, 1870–1910* (New York: Oxford University Press, 1974), 165–68.

23. Francisco Ferreira da Rosa, *Rio de Janeiro* (Rio de Janeiro: Edição Official da Prefeitura, 1905), 248–59; *Jornal do Brasil*, June 15, 1903, 1, and March 14, 1903, 1; *Gazeta de Notícias*, February 12, 1910, 2–3, and February 21, 1910, 2–3.

vandalized at least one station. In the end mounted police intervened to prevent the crowds from reaching the tracks, cordoned off the stations, and
brought the disturbance to a close.[24]

In the course of the riot, commuters raised long-standing grievances
against the Leopoldina line: service was terrible, trains were frequently late,
sometimes delayed for half a day, and the fare was always going up. They
complained that the Leopoldina's undependable schedule made them late to
work or unable to get there at all, and often caused them to lose jobs.[25] Despite the vehemence of the protest, the Leopoldina company held firm and
instituted the higher fare, paying little attention to the many grievances
raised by passengers during the riot. The protest ended when riders with no
other way to get to work or to stores, to visit relatives, or even to see the rest
of the city were forced to accept the increase.[26]

While protesters may seldom have successfully changed a transit policy
or decision, rioting was at least as effective as more legitimate methods. For
instance, a riot broke out in 1909 when the Canadian-owned Companhia de
Light e Power, owner of the main trolley service as well as the city's lighting
system, attempted to reroute a trolley line. Angry with a change that would
leave them with no transportation at all, protesters set upon cars and barricaded the tracks. Fifteen people were arrested when police intervened. In
the end, the Companhia de Light e Power changed its plans to cancel the
route.[27]

By contrast, a similar incident the following year, involving the same company but a different line, resulted in the opposite outcome. When the *companhia* announced plans to terminate trolley service to Jacarepaguá and to
install a line to Cascaduro, residents of Meier directly serviced by the Jacarepaguá service protested the change. They called a meeting and drew up a

24. *Voz do Trabalhador*, August 16, 1908, 1. This newspaper was the organ of the Confederação Operaria Brasileira, formed in March 1908 in Rio, a group that represented abut fifty labor
associations in various cities of Brazil, fourteen in the Federal District through the Federação
Operaria do Rio de Janeiro. John W. F. Dulles, *Anarchists and Communists in Brazil, 1900–1935*
(Austin: University of Texas Press, 1973), 23; Gerald Michael Greenfield and Sheldon L. Maram,
eds., *Latin American Labor Organizations* (Westport, Conn.: Greenwood Press, 1987), 88–89.

25. The Leopoldina paid its highest dividend in 1907, after a decade of tenuous debt-servicing
to its British creditors. From 1907 through 1912 the line reaped its best profits. Richard Graham,
Britain and the Onset of Modernization in Brazil, 1850–1914 (Cambridge: Cambridge University Press, 1968), 57.

26. *Voz do Trabalhador*, August 16, 1908, 1.

27. Ibid., July 8, 1909, 3. The Companhia de Light e Power, or Light and Power Company (Rio
de Janeiro) was also a part of Rio de Janeiro Tramway, Light, and Power Company, Limited, a
subsidiary of the Brazilian Traction, Light, and Power Company (Canadian). Dulles, *Anarchists
and Communists,* 546.

letter of protest, detailing their opposition to the company's projected change. The complaint, sent to both the Companhia de Light e Power and to the newspapers, noted that the change would leave a large number of Meier residents stranded without service or forced to walk long distances to another station. The *companhia* ignored the Meier commuters' petition, issued no reply, and promptly terminated the Jacarepaguá line as planned.[28]

In two other incidents, transportation companies proved at least as willing to listen to the demands of rioters as those of peaceful petitioners. In February 1910 residents of Rio dos Pedras sent a letter to Paulo de Frontin, director of the government-owned EFCB ("Central"), asking that he authorize a train stop in the rapidly growing *subúrbio*. The letter enumerated the problems Rio dos Pedras's residents faced: they had to walk long distances to the closest train station, and young men desperate to reach work were forced to hop the train as it sped by. Noting the danger and discomfort endured by the district's residents and pointing to the obvious need for a new stop, the letter respectfully asked that the railroad director look into their complaint. The residents also sent their letter to the *Gazeta de Noticias* with an additional note calling on city authorities to place pressure on the Central to install a stop in the district and generally improve the service. Neither the Central nor the city officials even responded to the commuters' complaint.[29]

Not surprisingly, a riot involving commuters from Rio das Pedras broke out in March and April of the following year. No doubt convinced that neither the government nor the private transportation companies were going to improve service, frustrated commuters attacked streetcars belonging to the Companhia São Cristovão and Companhia Vila Isabel. Apparently precipitated by late trains and streetcars on the morning of March 21, hundreds of demonstrators mounted the cars when they finally arrived, overturned several, and chased off the drivers. The passengers rallied along the tracks for a week, demanding an end to the long hours of delay in the streetcar service and that the government investigate the insufficient transportation system serving this large *subúrbio* and place a ceiling on ticket prices. While not totally successful, the riot forced the São Cristovão and Vila Isabel companies to restore fares to their preriot level and to issue a promise to investigate complaints over the schedules.[30] Although protests in later years would indicate that the company reneged on some of its promises, at least commuters directed the government's attention to their plight and won a short-term re-

28. *Gazeta de Notícias*, February 9, 1910, 2.
29. Ibid., February 28, 1910, 6.
30. Ibid., March 21–23, 1911, 1–2, and April 1, 1911, 1–2.

prieve from company policy, which was a response equal to, if not better than, what they got from their polite, respectful letters. Actually, the government's inattention to petitions and letters was teaching *suburbanos* to resort to collective violence instead.

If bad service on streetcar and railroad lines had been the only problems facing the newly relocated *suburbanos*, their complaints could have been weighed against the benefits of the Yellow Fever Campaign, namely, the eradication of disease. Transportation problems, however, were only one of many hardships confronting those who were forced to live on the outskirts of the central district, now called the Old City. Poorer districts lacked sanitation, disease control, gas or electric streetlights, water, police protection, and schools.[31] In June 1908 the *Jornal do Brasil* noted that its offices were swamped with letters from the *suburbanos*, complaining of deplorable living conditions, including no water or sewage treatment facilities, no mail delivery, unpaved streets, and continual outbreaks of malaria, smallpox, and other diseases. Under the title *Vida e Miseria* (Life and misery) from 1908 through 1912 the *Jornal do Brasil* and *Gazeta de Noticias* ran columns documenting horrendous living conditions in the poorest districts of Rio de Janeiro and the surrounding *subúrbios*.[32]

In July 1908 a reporter observed that there was not a single accredited school in the entire area stretching from Engenho de Dentro through Encantado and Piedade. An accompanying editorial accused the Republican government of ignoring the "minds of the young" in the suburban districts.[33] Other critics linked the absence of schools to the constancy of assaults by gangs of youngsters who roamed the streets day in and day out, either abandoned permanently or simply left alone by working parents. A resident of Vila Isabel complained in 1910 that in the district where he lived, "a very large zone, bordering Engenho Novo, Conde de Bonfim, Andaraí, and Tijuca," gangs of children roamed the streets day and night, stoning streetcars, robbing houses and stores, and generally constituting a nuisance to the area.[34] In 1911 Rivadavia da Cunha Correa, minister of justice and internal affairs, wrote up a report documenting the extreme problem of abandoned and delinquent children in the Federal District, saying that there were not nearly enough orphanages, schools, or reformatories to contain those

31. Directoria Geral de Saúde Pública, *Relatório apresentado ao Dr. Cruz pelo Dr. Theophilo Torres, Inspector Geral Districto 8 Sanitário*, vol. 5, app. 10 (Rio de Janeiro: Imprensa Nacional, 1906), 5–6; *O Paiz*, July 21, 1906, 4, and August 26, 1906, 2; *Jornal do Brasil*, May 30, 1908, 1.
32. *Jornal do Brasil*, June 15, 1908, 1.
33. Ibid., July 20, 1908, 1.
34. *Gazeta de Notícias*, February 19, 1910, 8.

youths who roamed the streets, engaging in crimes and making a nuisance of themselves throughout the city. The minister argued that the best solution for Rio's crisis of abandoned children was to create a network of reform schools that would house the youths for a number of years before they could be apprenticed to industry and onto ships—a system similar to the work-houses of England and the United States. But the government was unable to establish the proper jurisdiction over the youths, and the entire system simply fell to the police, who were unable to manage it.[35]

Others complained that there was neither a market nor a cemetery in the entire Vila Isabel district, that the streets were never cleaned, that stray dogs roamed the alleys and roads and were a public health hazard. Calling on the mayor's office to attend to the many problems in their district, their letter ended with the admonition that the "honorable people" of Vila Isabel deserved better treatment from the municipal authorities.[36]

Striking among the complaints from the city's residential districts was the absence of any government-sponsored improvement program. Two years later, after the Vila Isabel residents had lodged their complaints, letters and petitions were still pouring in from other areas, indicating that little or nothing was being done in response to this continual stream of complaints, even if they were from "honorable" people. On January 11, 1910, residents of Tijuca, whose neighborhood was bordered by Campos Sales and Gonçalves Crespo Streets, complained that when it rained, people were unable to leave their houses for fear of drowning in the rushing water in the streets. "As for hygiene," their letter stated, "the sanitation authorities allege that mosquitoes are a vehicle for carrying dangerous fevers. Well, the residents of these streets (in Tijuca) are unable to sleep at night because of the enormous swarms of mosquitoes that pass through our area."[37]

Whereas streetlights lined the avenues of Rio's newly beautified downtown, electricity was not extended to the *subúrbios* and poorer neighbor-

35. Directoria do Interior, *Relatório apresentado ao Presidente da República dos Estados Unidos do Brasil pelo Ministro de Estado da Justiça e Negocios Interiores, Dr. Rivadavia da Cunha Correa* (Rio de Janeiro: Imprensa Nacional, 1911), 77–78. For a summary of the abandoned children problem, see also Ministerio da Justiça e Negocios Interiores, *Relatório apresentado ao Presidente da República pelo Dr. J. J. Seabra, Ministro da Justiça e Negocios Interiores* (Rio de Janeiro: Imprensa Nacional, 1905); Directoria do Interior, "O Abándono Material" and "O Abándono Moral," pts. 1 and 2 of *Relatórios apresentado ao Ministro da Justiça pela Commissão Inspectora dos estabelecimentos de alienados, públicos e particulares, no Districto Federal, e pelos membros das respectivas Commissões Inspectoras nos Estados de Minas Geraes e Rio Grande do Sul* (Rio de Janeiro: Imprensa Nacional, 1905), 3–53.

36. *Gazeta de Notícias*, February 19, 1910, 8.

37. Ibid., January 12, 1910, 4.

hoods, where, possibly as a consequence, nighttime assaults were frequent. Police did nothing for these districts except disperse the crowds and quell riots when people protested, leaving residents to their own devices to fend off assaults and robberies as best they could. In Tomás Coelho, a district near the furthest end of the Central line, people complained that they could barely sleep because of the continual noise in the streets, including frequent brawls and gun battles.[38] Similarly, a letter, again from self-proclaimed "decent families" in Todos os Santos, called on the city government to provide police protection to this district, on the public works department to install streetlights, and on the appropriate officials to prevent abandoned youngsters from roaming the streets and creating chaos throughout the district. As with the complaint from Tomás Coelho, the letter noted that the streets were too dangerous to travel after ten o'clock in the evening and that noise from gun battles and fights kept residents awake all night.[39]

The obvious discrepancy between services in Rio's downtown and those in the working-class neighborhoods did not pass unnoticed. Writing in a labor newspaper in 1911, a number of textile workers pointed to the hypocrisy of a recent announcement from the public health department extolling the city's health campaign as a "great benefit to humanity." In response, the workers pointed out that if the "public health (department) thought that workers also make up a part of humanity," it would be attempting to improve conditions in workers' neighborhoods. Instead, the letter claimed, the entire public health project had "only served the bourgeoisie."[40] The letter listed deplorable conditions in the outlying districts, especially in Saporemba, where neither the textile mills nor adjacent neighborhoods had access to clean drinking water.

Textile mills were located in the Zona Norte and the developing *subúrbios,* where conditions both inside the mills and in the surrounding areas were known to be terrible. Factory workers, a portion of whom were women and children, worked from six in the morning to past seven or eight in the evening, with one hour for lunch, usually taken standing or crouching at the door of the factory. Whereas women were concentrated in the unskilled positions on the factory floor, men held jobs ranging from supervisors to mechanics, cutters, technicians, as well as unskilled laborers. Children, including boys as young as eight years old, ran the length of the factories, pulling thread, cleaning, running errands, and tending the machines. The harsh

38. Ibid., February 28, 1910, 6.
39. Ibid., March 5, 1910, 4.
40. *A Vanguarda,* May 13, 1911, 3.

Fig. 7.   Men and boys working in a mill in the first decades of the twentieth century. Jennings Hoffenberg Collection.

working conditions in the mills—including dust-filled air, poor ventilation, dangerous, loud, and unprotected machinery—and long hours took years off the lives of adults and turned children into old men and women while still young in years. The deprivations that workers suffered in the mills and factories were probably common knowledge then and have been cited in most studies of Brazil's working class since. Timothy Harding notes that legislation to alleviate the horrendous conditions or afford labor any recognition was all but nonexistent early in the century. "Accident protection legislation was slow in developing in Brazil, as compared to Uruguay and Argentina," and labor-protection laws that were presented in Congress were defeated until 1919.[41]

By August 1911 *suburbanos* had turned from complaining to organizing against their conditions. Residents of Engenho Dentro, Tijuca, and São Cristóvão met to discuss the problems in their neighborhoods and what could be

41. Harding, "Political History of Organized Labor," 36–38; *Jornal do Brasil*, April 4, 1903, 1.

Fig. 8.   Rudolpho Crespi textile mill at the turn of the century. Miriam and Ira D.
Wallach Photography Collection, New York Public Library.

done to resolve them. One speaker after another denounced the city's health,
sanitation, and public works regulations and the officials charged with enforcing them, noting in particular that neither the government nor the private transportation companies did anything to improve services for the poor.
In a fiery condemnation of the city administrators, one speaker charged that
it really did not seem to matter that people complained to the city authorities,
since no solution was ever forthcoming. The most outspoken and politically
conscious members of the gathering condemned the Republic, accusing it
of betraying the working man by failing in any way to improve the proletariat's living and working conditions. Noting that the public health measures,
of which the government was so proud, had not been extended to working-
class neighborhoods, participants called on the residents of the *subúrbios* to
join together in organizations and begin to pressure the government. According to one, only through organizations could they begin to ensure "liberty, equality, and fraternity" to the working class.[42]

42. *A Vanguarda*, August 12, 1911, 2.

Fig. 9.   Textile mill operator at a machine, early decades of twentieth century, Jennings Hoffenberg Collection.

    The dual problem of shortages and high prices remained a cause for complaint among the Carioca consumers for years to come, and they had been around for quite a while. Alarmed by consumer threats of violence against food stores as far back as 1905, the *Jornal do Brasil* had questioned the government's policies on meat and food distribution. The newspaper's own investigation in June of that year revealed that on any given day approximately 70,000 kilos of meat left the Matadouro slaughterhouse for sale in Rio de Janeiro, or approximately 10 grams, including bones and fat, for every person in the city (about a third of an ounce). In a follow-up editorial the paper commented that the production of meat was essential to the well-being of both the capital city and the nation, since a people's meat consumption was linked to their overall good health. Furthermore, the editor warned that Brazil's neighbors, specifically the cattle-producing nations of Argentina and Uruguay, might become powerful competitors, eventually even overtaking Brazil in her own food production and distribution.[43]

    43. *Jornal do Brasil*, June 24, 1905, 1, and June 25, 1905, 5.

Even this attempt in 1905 to prod monopolists into adequately supplying the city with meat at a reasonable price failed to solve the constant shortages. Complaints and protests persisted; apparently the *Jornal do Brasil's* warning had fallen on deaf ears in the agricultural sector. The role of the monopolies and "trusts" in causing the shortages, and the support they received from the government, were prime issues years later in the May Day demonstrations of 1917. One of the most important demands of the 1917 May Day rally, and of the general strike that followed, was the call for the abolition of the "trusts" and an end to price-fixing and shortages.

By 1912 the overall situation for Rio's poorest residents had worsened on every front: prices jumped, shortages and living conditions worsened. More than that, the city's working poor were becoming increasingly aware that nothing was going to be done for them unless they initiated more-direct action. As summed up by one irate worker, "We ought not to wait for the constituted powers, since they will never inconvenience themselves with the poor, with those that produce everything and possess nothing."[44] In November 1912 a spontaneous outcry against exorbitant food prices and frequent shortages began to spread through the *subúrbios* from Engenho Novo to Madureira. Disgruntled consumers broke into butcher shops in Madureira on the night of November 14, 1912, the eve of the national holiday commemorating the founding of the Republic, a date the demonstrators probably had in mind. Armed with cans of kerosene, they set ablaze the meat, quite possibly as punishment to the proprietor for the unreasonably high prices. When angry demonstrators charged into another butcher shop only to find no meat, they still rallied in front of the store, denounced the high prices and constant shortages, and resolved to boycott the establishment once it was stocked. Protesters attributed the problem to the protection the government granted cattle producers and packers, allowing these monopolists to withhold meat and other foodstuffs in order to drive up prices.[45]

In 1913 the anarcho-syndicalist Federação Operaria do Rio de Janeiro (FORJ) initiated a program intended to channel the spontaneous outbursts of violence against shopkeepers and the transit companies into an organized movement against the government and monopolies.[46] In February 1913 the

44. *Guerra Social*, March 6, 1912, 1.

45. *Jornal do Brasil*, November 15, 1912, 1.

46. Founded in Rio de Janeiro in 1903 as the Federação das Associações de Classe, the organization under various names centralized a number of anarchist and anarchist-influenced organizations in the city. In the mid 1920s it came under increased competition from a federation of communist-led unions and by 1928 lost its leadership role to them. Greenfield and Maram, *Latin American Labor Organizations*, 102–4.

FORJ launched the Campanha Contra a Carestia da Vida (Campaign Against the High Cost of Living) which addressed a wide spectrum of issues affecting the working class and consumers, especially high prices and poor living conditions. Although the FORJ campaign lasted no longer than a few months, it was one of the labor movement's few efforts to confront issues affecting workers as both producers and consumers. As well, the FORJ campaign attempted to build its program based on issues that touched members of an entire neighborhood or district. The campaign's demands were sufficiently broad to win support from not just industrial workers, usually seen as the standard-bearers of anarcho-syndicalism, but also from others, both those better off and those poorer, who were equally disgruntled with shoddy services and living conditions. Not since the Centro das Classes Operarias's brief intervention in the antivaccination riot of 1904 had the organized labor movement or a political party become directly involved in community-based issues.

The FORJ drew its strength from its affiliated unions, including the marble workers, tailors, painters, shoemakers, carpenters, plasterers and stonemasons, quarry workers, cabinetmakers, and graphic workers, and from associations of independent laborers and the union of those in various offices. Although a number of other unions could be counted on to support FORJ events, it was the affiliates that grounded the FORJ program in trade union politics, and it was from the perspective of organizing the working class that the FORJ launched the neighborhood campaign. There is no indication, in fact, that the FORJ ever saw the campaign against high prices as a departure from the primary task of winning recruits to the trade unions. Writing a few months after the campaign had ended, the *Voz do Trabalhador* (Voice of the worker) noted that the principal means of protecting the interests of the proletariat remained the organization of unions, since only through the trade unions could the oppressed classes hope to wrest themselves "free from the claws of the bourgeoisie."[47]

As a tactic ancillary to union organizing, the Campaign Against the High Cost of Living was quite effective. The campaign concentrated on a series of grievances, formulating a stance that integrated the FORJ's political program with complaints over living conditions, many of which had remained unresolved since 1904. If anything, conditions had worsened since 1904; thus the 1913 effort was able to capture a broad following. The campaign called for an end to customs tariffs and other protectionist policies that allowed monopolies (or "trusts") to keep prices high and make exorbitant profits on products

47. *Voz do Trabalhador*, July 15, 1913, 1.

in short supply. It opposed high municipal taxes on apartment buildings and commercial houses, which were passed on to tenants and consumers in the form of higher rents and retail prices. The platform called for across-the-board pay increases, noting that current salaries were inadequate for the needs of a family. The campaign's supporters condemned the "brutal and extremely hard work" laborers endured, which, combined with the long distances they had to travel on erratically scheduled trains and shoddy streetcar lines, made for a miserable life and brought on an early death. Finally, the campaign's platform denounced the squalid living conditions of poorer neighborhoods: houses infested with parasites, poisonous food, unpaved streets, lack of water and sanitation, the suffocating heat in living and working quarters.[48] Clearly, the campaign platform was closely tailored to conform with demands community residents had been raising for over a decade, indicating that the spontaneous and constant neighborhood protests over living conditions and prices had in large part inspired the campaign. In a sense, the transcript moved out of hiding and into the realm of direct action.

FORJ militants announced their intention to agitate throughout the country against the customs tariffs and "international taxes" and for a 40 percent reduction in municipal taxes charged on consumer goods and transportation. They called for a 30 percent reduction in rents, for an eight-hour workday, for a minimum wage of seven milreis daily, and for abolition of the law that allowed the deportation of foreigners.[49] The campaign strategy called for a series of "public meetings in the city and the suburbs, toward the goal of protesting against the negligence, alas common, from the officials in city hall, and against the national *trusts* that are the cause of the difficulties against which the people of Rio de Janeiro are now struggling."[50]

At the first rally in mid-February in Vila Isabel, residents formed a district Comité de Agitação (Committee of Agitation) and announced plans to organize future rallies, drawing in more of the area's residents. Other neighborhoods followed a similar strategy and *comités* began to crop up in working-class neighborhoods throughout the city. On February 26 the FORJ called a meeting in Gávea, a district in the Zona Sul with a number of textile plants, that drew three thousand "enthusiastic people" determined to con-

48. Ibid., February 1, 1913, 4.
49. Ibid., April 1, 1913, 3. For an explanation of the exchange value for purchases of food necessities, see Dulles, *Anarchists and Communists,* 535–40.
50. Ibid., February 1, 1913, 4.

tinue the campaign until realizing "a complete victory for the demands of the people."[51]

The second major event of the campaign was a citywide rally in late February in the downtown Largo de São Francisco, the site that had kicked off the antivaccination riot nearly a decade earlier. Cecilio Vilar, Antonio Moreira, Leal Junior, Ulisses Martins, and Candido Costa of the FORJ addressed an overflow crowd they estimated at three to four thousand demonstrators who had marched to the plaza from neighborhoods throughout the city. Each speaker lambasted a government that kept prices high, wages low, and refused to legislate an eight-hour workday. Rally speakers attributed the masses' misery to the free hand the "trusts" enjoyed in raising prices, often by withholding goods and creating artificial shortages, and to the government's protectionist policies.[52]

Large rallies continued throughout March as the FORJ successfully mobilized thousands of people against the high cost of living. A rally on March 2 in Vila Isabel attracted an "enormous mass" of men, women and children, according to the organizers.[53] Although press reports do not make continued mention of the presence of women or of children, there is reason to believe that in succeeding demonstrations both were present in substantial numbers. In the first place, issues having to do with food prices and the cost of living were of intrinsic importance to women, who were responsible for the shopping and cooking in the household. In fact, the mention of women in this demonstration echoed earlier reports on the presence of women in spontaneous and organized gatherings in front of stores, protesting shortages and high prices. In addition, for the first time both the *Voz* and the *Jornal do Brasil* carried articles discussing the particular complaints of women, articles, one may presume, that were precipitated by some active presence of women on the political scene.[54]

Regardless of the chivalry reputedly directed toward women in Brazilian culture, the presence of women and children in demonstrations did not prevent the authorities from moving quickly, and brutally, to suppress the rallies. On March 4 police units moved in to break up a crowd in downtown Rio's Praça da República, acting on orders from government officials who

51. Ibid., March 1, 1913, 1.
52. Ibid.
53. Ibid., March 15, 1913, 1.
54. Ibid., 1–2, as well as ibid., February 1, 1915, 3, refers to a program for organizing women, but does not mention whether it was of a high priority or very successful; *Jornal do Brasil*, March 2, 1915, 3.

feared that the campaign was beginning to reach, in their view, a "danger-ously large" number of the city's residents. The rally was brought to an abrupt close when mounted police units charged the crowd, killing one pro-tester, wounding others, and dispersing the rest.[55] Undaunted, the protests continued on the fifth with simultaneous rallies and meetings in the Praça Quinze and the Praça Mauá. The latter meeting spilled over into a street demonstration in which the protesters marched to the headquarters of the Sociedade de Resistencia dos Trabalhadores em Trapiches e Cafe (Resis-tance Society of Waterfront Warehouses and Coffee Workers), where a num-ber of speakers addressed the crowd.[56]

Despite police harassment, people continued to converge on the Praça Quinze de Novembro throughout the week, demanding an end to exorbitant price increases and that the government curb the power of the monopolies. Demonstrations continued in the outlying districts through the next week, drawing together thousands of angry residents. Police dispersed demonstra-tions in Catumbí and Engenho de Dentro on Sunday, March 9, reporting neither injuries nor arrests after the crowd left peacefully. Before disband-ing, however, a FORJ spokesperson proclaimed that the meeting was "closed down because in Brazil there is no freedom of thought."[57]

It is difficult to know how broad a following the campaign amassed, but the *Voz do Trabalhador* spoke as optimistically of these rallies as it had any of its other organizing efforts. Looking toward building an organization "of the entire working class, which [would] be prepared for a genuine battle with the capitalists," the movement's leaders enthusiastically reported on neigh-borhood committee meetings and rallies.[58] The FORJ called a number of the rallies, some with the express purpose of building the Confederação Oper-aria Brasileira (Brazilian Workers Confederation) as well as fighting the high cost of living, a clear indication of the links it was attempting to forge be-tween the union and community movement. The *Voz do Trabalhador* re-ported that by March 16 "the agitation against the high cost of living initiated in this capital by the Federação Operaria in accord with the Confederação Operaria Brasileira [had] assumed huge proportions . . . and [stood] as one of the major victories of the Confederação and of the proletariat."[59]

55. *Voz do Trabalhador*, March 15, 1913, 1–2.

56. The participation of this so-called yellow union, a moderate reformist organization that generally supported the government, indicates the extent of the frustration enveloping the en-tire working class of the city as the crisis deepened. Greenfield and Maram, *Latin American Labor Organizations*, 117–18.

57. *Voz do Trabalhador*, March 15, 1913, 1.

58. Ibid.

59. Ibid., April 1, 1913, 3.

In fact, there was throughout the campaign a conscious overlap of trade union issues, such as strike support and calls for the eight-hour workday and higher wages, with broader demands for a reduction in living costs and an end to the government's protectionist policies. And while constructing its immediate strategy around the mass demonstrations, the FORJ continually stressed that the meetings and rallies were part of a process of showing the working class the advantages and necessity of forming organizations. It was only through organizations, trade unions and the Brazilian workers federation, they argued, that the working class would be able to achieve victory. Dividing the population into two classes—the exploited and the exploiters— FORJ leaders placed the Campaign Against the High Cost of Living at the top of their agenda, considering it as essential to the proletariat's cause as the struggle for the eight-hour workday.

In spite of claims at the campaign's outset to bring the fight against high prices "to every city in the country,"[60] FORJ intentions fell short of that outcome, on this round at least. The May Day rally in the Largo de São Francisco seemed almost anticlimactic after the stream of marches and demonstrations in March and April. Although reported with the enthusiasm typical of accounts in the *Voz,* the absence of exuberance, the failure to mention the size of any of the demonstrations, and the low-key announcement of the speakers bespoke a slump in the cost-of-living campaign. There was, in fact, no more than a short paragraph summarizing everything that took place throughout the city.[61] The June 1 issue of the *Voz do Trabalhador* made no mention of the campaign that only a few months before had been heralded as the proletariat's stepping stone to state power. Despite the clearly demarcated set of domestic issues on which the campaign had been founded, and despite the web of grassroots organizations that had successfully brought thousands of bodies into the streets in protest against living costs, it was ultimately the effects of Brazil's place within the broader, international economic system that disrupted the campaign and eventually halted it entirely.

The prosperity Brazil had experienced from 1906 to 1913 had been based on healthy coffee exports. Aided by the creation of a centralized investment bank and a financial strategy that poured more coffee-revenue profits into domestic manufacturing and infrastructure, the country had enjoyed six years of growth at 5 percent or more. It was, however, an economic expansion built on borrowed foundations. The percentage of Brazil's economic growth dependent on foreign investment climbed, reducing the domestic

60. Ibid., March 15, 1913, 1.
61. Ibid., May 15, 1913, 2.

A VOZ DO TRABALHADOR

ORGAM DA CONFEDERAÇÃO OPERARIA BRAZILEIRA

ANO VI   RIO DE JANEIRO — BRAZIL — 1 DE MAIO DE 1913   N. 30

PRIMEIRO DE MAIO

LIBERDADE

BURGUEZIA • MILITARISMO • ARISTOGRACIA

CLERO • CAPITALISMO

Dia grande e cruel á memoria operaria,
Hinos brancos de Paz, hinos rubros de Guerra,
A Bandeira do Amor que se fez incendiaria...

Data fatal que em si ao mesmo tempo encerra
A promessa do Bem ao coração do Pária
E juramentos de Odio aos senhores da Terra!

Olhar perdido além, num horizonte vago,
Num sonho em que se vê o Mundo Comunista,
Ou se lembram talvez os mortos de Chicago!

Grande marco miliario á suprema conquista
Do Pa..; Ideal onde se esplaina o Lago
Verde-azul da Concordia a consolar a vista...

Calendimaio! o Sol que te ilumina seja
O ultimo a iluminar as grades da Prizão,
Os muros do Quartel e as fachadas da Igreja;

E amanhã, ao brotar do grande Astro o clarão,
Que aos seus raios triunfais o Homem por fim se veja
Sobre a Terra, a cantar, liberto do patrão!...

MAX DOS VASCONCELOS

Fig. 10.   Front page of *Voz do Trabalhador* newspaper marking May Day 1913.

portion of the federal debt and increasing the part to foreign lenders.[62] When economic depression swept Europe in 1913, accompanied by heightened political tensions and predictions of imminent war, foreign investment in Brazil's economy dropped off sharply. Combined with a decrease in coffee consumption abroad—coffee was still seen as a semiluxury—the impact on Brazil's export revenues was disastrous. By late 1913 Brazil had entered an economic crisis that left the country "politically, financially, and economically bankrupt."[63] The crisis-ridden financial structure of the Old Republic, which had seen the national debt consume over one-quarter of the federal budget and produce deficits most years, merely worsened during the First World War. The financial house of cards collapsed on its own mortgage.

The intensity of the crisis devastated the protest movement. *Comités* that had spearheaded demonstrations against high prices early in the year disappeared; factories went on a three-day workweek; many closed their doors entirely. Plans to expand public works and construct new buildings were suspended, especially those on state-sponsored projects. More than four thousand public employees were dismissed by the end of the year; banks closed or stopped extending credit; and the national treasury was nearly empty.[64] While the crisis reduced employment and curtailed the already limited buying power of the laboring classes, most of all it enforced quiescence. A period of intense protest against consumer prices and against the unchallenged authority of the transportation companies and trusts drew to a close by the end of 1913.

By early 1914 Brazil was in a severe crisis, owing to a drastic drop in world coffee prices on the international market, which set off a chain reaction in Brazilian finances. Domestic industries and commercial houses, counting on an ever-expanding export market, had borrowed money to finance improvements and expansion, only to find themselves facing foreclosure as banks called in their loans during the 1914 slump. Attempting to recoup losses, many firms stopped meeting the payroll, thereby shifting the burden of the crisis to the workers. Office workers at Trajano de Medeiros & Cia., a leading commercial firm, struck on November 21, 1914, claiming that the owner was fifteen months behind in paying their wages.[65] In December of that same year meatcutters at the Matadouro slaughterhouses walked off the job be-

62. Steven Topik, *The Political Economy of the Brazilian State, 1889–1930* (Austin: University of Texas Press, 1987), 50–51; Mauricio A. Font, *Coffee, Contention, and Change in the Making of Modern Brazil* (Cambridge, Mass.: Basil Blackwell, 1990), chap. 1.

63. *Voz do Trabalhador*, November 1, 1913, 1.

64. Ibid.

65. Ibid., December 1, 1914, 4; *Jornal do Brasil*, November 21, 1914, 1.

cause they had not been paid for over four months.[66] In both cases workers returned under the promise of receiving back pay. Whether they did, or for how long, is impossible to say.

Despite these strikes, the *Voz do Trabalhador* lamented the appearance of "a certain apathy among the working class in the face of organization, principally in this capital, among the comrades that have the greatest responsibility for the movement."[67] The newspaper was not coming out regularly; the leadership was reportedly tired and discouraged; the labor movement was in a slump; and apart from an admonition to the most conscious workers to step up the agitation, no one seemed to have any solution to the malaise spreading through the working class. As the crisis deepened, unemployment climbed, and the labor leadership turned inward, replacing the open agitation of the year before with long, tedious meetings and strategy sessions.

In August 1914 the anarchist leadership turned toward opposing the outbreak of war, the "universal calamity" and "bloodbath" that had struck Europe. In a particularly poignant comment, the paper noted that we live "today in a permanent state of fratricide. We consider as savages the cannibals who eat each other for necessity. But among the civilized we kill each other and abandon the rest."[68] Unfortunately, the presence of the crisis and the repeated condemnation of the war and its effect on the international working class did not translate into an effective strategy to combat the inflationary spiral in prices that was its chief effect in Brazil. To say the working class was paying for the war and being internationally slaughtered in it was rather empty rhetoric when divorced from any political program to counter the effects.

By mid-1914 the intensity of street protests had fallen off to the point that the FORJ was able to gather no more than six hundred people to its traditional May Day demonstration in the Largo de São Francisco. Although proclaiming this rather pathetic showing a "grand success for the class," it was apparent that the larger economic crisis was destroying the workers' movement. The following October the FORJ reported that there was no money to print the *Voz do Trabalhador* and that union organizing was at a standstill.[69]

The pall that had fallen over the protest movement lasted through most of 1914, but some signs of agitation reappeared briefly on November 29, 1914,

66. *Jornal do Brasil*, December 7, 1914, 1.
67. *Voz do Trabalhador*, June 20, 1914, 2.
68. Ibid., August 5, 1914, 3.
69. Ibid., October 1, 1914. The *Voz* was a biweekly publication, but it came out monthly most of 1914, with the exception of May, June, July, and August, when it came out only twice.

and continued into the early months of 1915. Beginning with a series of meetings designed "to organize the working class by neighborhood," the FORJ called together groups in Vila Isabel and Catumbí. The year before, the FORJ had reported that women and children were in attendance at the rallies, but in 1915 they boasted that their meetings had "attracted large numbers of women," both working women and those who came to the meetings out of concern for issues in the neighborhood. Again, the FORJ spoke enthusiastically of the results of their organizing efforts, indicative of a level of success from this strategy. On January 1, 1915, the *Voz do Trabalhador* reported that the local neighborhood meetings initiated by the FORJ were enjoying the greatest success of any recent organizing strategy.[70] Even if they overstated their successes, this was certainly a different tone from the discouraging reports of widespread apathy and failure six months earlier. FORJ organizers continued to stress that the neighborhood meetings were not an end in themselves, that it was not enough merely to protest against high prices and rents but that the protests also should be considered as a support for union-organizing drives. Again, as in 1913, the meetings stopped as quickly as they had begun. By February 1915 the FORJ seemingly abandoned the community organizing campaign and, without reporting any major gains, closed once again the spontaneous and organized popular protest movement.

The constancy of opposition from the city's suburban communities during the eleven-year-long period following the 1904 antivaccination riot had alarmed government officials. The latter barely hesitated to call out mounted police against assemblies of protesters. Similar to the protests that erupted during the years before the Yellow Fever Campaign and the heated opposition to the campaign itself, these later protests involved both literate and articulate residents, as well as the poor and working class. They raised their complaints in the traditional form of middle-class protest: they sent letters to the newspaper, they signed petitions, they alerted government officials. Others who eventually took to the streets were not literate petitioners but the poor and destitute whose only recourse was direct action. However, frustrated with the government's inattention to their just demands, they protested in one voice. The extent to which organized and spontaneous protests punctuated the years from 1905 through 1915 calls into question conclusions that Rio's popular classes passively accepted their lot. Certainly the constancy of protests over transportation costs, routes, and service indicates that

70. Ibid., December 1, 1914, 4, and January 1, 1915, 1.

people who normally traveled to and from work did not always accept the unpredictable transportation costs and service, unjust price hikes, and miserable living conditions.

This intersection, or fusion, of protests by salaried and articulate residents with those from the laboring poor and the emergent working class appeared fleetingly in the 1913 Campaign Against the High Cost of Living. While the *suburbanos* never united into a single movement or brought their demands to the government and monopolies in a consistent manner, their protests indicate a united, if spontaneous, level of willingness to protest against unjust conditions.[71] In this context the FORJ took the first step toward fusing its class-conscious, anticapitalist program with the spontaneous demands of the residents of the Zona Norte and the *suburbanos* against prices and services. These anarcho-syndicalists were, to use Antonio Gramsci's term, the "organic intellectuals" of the Rio laboring classes.[72] That the FORJ's first steps were short-lived, that their program lacked depth and consistency, does not alter the fact that they made attempts. Through a maze of ups and downs, community-based, popular protests moved more solidly into the orbit of FORJ's influence in the third period, culminating in the 1917 May Day rally and general strike. The special significance of the May Day events and the subsequent strike wave rests with the emergence of a working-class program and working-class leaders at the forefront of what had been the long-standing demands of a less differentiated class of community residents.

71. Sheldon Maram, "The Immigrant and the Brazilian Labor Movement, 1890–1920," in *Essays Concerning the Socioeconomic History of Brazil and Portuguese India,* ed. Dauril Alden and Warren Dean (Gainesville: University Presses of Florida, 1977), 191.

72. Gramsci's definition is worked out in several of his essays, but most concisely it is as follows: "Every social group, coming into existence on the original terrain of an essential function in the world of economic production, creates together with itself, organically, one or more strata of intellectuals which give it homogeneity and an awareness of its own function not only in the economic but also in the social and political fields." Antonio Gramsci, "The Intellectuals" in *Selections from the Prison Notebooks,* trans. and ed. Quintin Hoare and Geoffrey Nowell Smith (New York: International Publishers, 1971), 5. For a discussion of a different interpretation and use of Gramsci's definition, see Florencia E. Mallon, *Peasant and Nation: The Making of Postcolonial Mexico and Peru* (Berkeley and Los Angeles: University of California Press, 1995), 9–10.

6

The General Strike

Down with the high cost of living! We want bread and work!
—Slogans from the May Day demonstration, 1917

In his discussion of urban movements, Ira Katznelson makes the point that
the proletariat's protests have been the most effective and have had the greatest impact on those occasions when the ties between the trade unions and
communities have been the strongest.[1] On a theoretical level, Katznelson's
argument shows not only that urban community movements have constituted a key component of the class struggle but also that the very existence
of the working-class community (the spatial production of class, in Castells's
words) has itself been a product of the class struggle. Thus, the popular
classes' resistance to the control of capital, its combat, if you will, always
takes place in the *community* as well as on the shop floor. Not only is one
arena of struggle inextricably linked to the other, but as evidenced in Rio de
Janeiro, especially in 1913, 1915, and 1917, the working class launches its

---

1. Ira Katznelson, *City Trenches: Urban Politics and the Patterning of Class in the United States*
(Chicago: University of Chicago Press, 1981), 212.

most widespread and successful attack on governmental and economic policies when it most effectively fuses community and workplace demands.

Except in broad discussions of "working-class culture," labor history has
tended to see the "community" as simply an appendage or natural extension
of the work relations established at the point of production. As this study has
argued all along, a point that is abundantly clear on examining the events of
1917, combining the struggle at the point of production (the strike) with that
in the community (protests against the cost of living, food, rent, and mass
transit service) provided the Rio working class with its most potent formula
against the demands of capitalism. From 1904 through 1916 the masses
chipped away at the structure; in mid-1917 they tried to take the roof off.

Brazil's economy remained depressed through 1915, suffering along with
all of Latin America the effects of the war: disruption in government finance,
decline in local commercial transactions, shortages in supplies of food and
fuel, reduced industrial output and concomitant escalating unemployment.
The Great War was starkly demonstrating the disastrous effects of the nation's heavy reliance on European markets for goods and on European investors for capital.[2] On the other hand, the crisis likewise opened the window of
opportunity for Brazil to pull itself out of both its economic slump and its
dependence on foreign commerce and investment.

In mid-1916 the economy, based on two factors, began to show a few feeble
signs of revival. First, the federal government initiated an import-substitution
plan, particularly in textile manufacturing, which succeeded in revitalizing
lagging industrial output. In 1916 textile production soared to its highest
level, and Brazilian manufacturers began to capture a share of the internal
market previously dominated by Great Britain, now embroiled in war. Second, the devastation to European fields caused by the war increased the demand for Brazilian foodstuffs, leather goods, grains, and other products.
Since Brazilian suppliers could reap higher profits for their products on the
European market than from impoverished domestic workers, they increased
exports, causing acute shortages and high prices on the local market. John
W. F. Dulles states that the "foreign demand for Brazilian leather was said to
have doubled the price of footwear."[3] He goes on to quote a poor Brazilian
widow who lamented, "If I want to buy a meter of cloth to make clothing for
my children, I have to spend 900 or 1,000 reis instead of the 300 reis I used

2. Bill Albert, *South America and the First World War: The Impact of the War on Brazil, Argentina, Peru, and Chile* (Cambridge: Cambridge University Press, 1988), 38.

3. John W. F. Dulles, *Anarchists and Communists in Brazil, 1900–1935* (Austin: University
of Texas Press, 1973), 57.

to pay."[4] The modest resurgence in the Brazilian economy did not meet with a corresponding increase in workers' wages, however. Anxious to maximize profits and faced with an impoverished and temporarily acquiescent working class, manufacturers showed no willingness to grant labor a share in their wartime profits.

Popular resistance reappeared in 1916. As in the past, the crowds' anger over problems with the transportation system and high food prices led to the outbreak of spontaneous, undirected demonstrations. In April 1916 over a hundred people rioted against a proposal by the Central to terminate the Linha Circular, a rail line running from the outskirts to the downtown and back. Angry commuters gathered along the railroad track, stoned the cars, placed barricades on the tracks, and set fire to a few cars. Although the press reported that damage was relatively minor, the police and cavalry intervened to defend the company, arrested "about a dozen" demonstrators, and dispersed the crowds.[5]

A few weeks later another protest broke out when the Central stopped issuing free passes to children during commuter hours. The company argued that the new policy would stop parents from taking children on the trains during the crowded commuter hours, thereby providing more space to passengers traveling to and from work. Few passengers accepted the company's reasoning, since they were aware, as was the Central most likely, that children on the trains during rush hours, like the adults, were commuting to work. Since children's wages were already very low, the cost of the train tickets to and from their jobs threatened to wipe out the benefit of their employment to their families. Considering the slim margin of subsistence at which most working-class families existed, the loss of a child's income could prove disastrous. Finally, commuters were outraged at the Central's greed. By charging for children the railroad company was attempting to increase its revenue just at a time when its passengers could least afford to pay. In response, train passengers gathered in the stations and demanded that authorities reinstate the free rides for children. When station attendants attempted to collect the fare from the children, they were pushed out of the way, knocked down, and practically trampled. Adults pushed children past the gates and boarded the trains in defiance of the new regulation.[6]

Child labor had been a conflictual issue in the protests, in the labor press, even in the bourgeois newspapers. To some extent child labor was a micro-

4. Ibid., quoting from *Correio da Manhã*, December 27, 1916.
5. *Jornal do Brasil*, April 18, 1916, 1.
6. Ibid., May 4, 1916, 1.

cosm of the ills of Rio's industrializing society, as it may well be in any society, and conflicting attitudes toward it mirrored class divisions. In January 1891, under Deodoro Fonseca's tenure, the provisional government had passed a rudimentary child labor law establishing a minimum age for working children, limiting the number of hours they could work, and protecting them from specific jobs and dangers. Periodically stories appeared in the press lambasting the government for refusing to enforce the law, denouncing the textile mill owners, in particular, for massively violating it, and chiding the working class for failing to protest against the abuses children were suffering.[7]

According to the law, no male children under thirteen years of age and no females under eleven were to work in the mills for longer than six hours daily. All of the children were to know how to read, write, and count before being allowed to work in the factories; they were to be protected from abusive conditions; and the owners were subject to fines upon violation of the law. Despite these regulations on paper, accidents were so common that it seems doubtful that children were kept from the most dangerous jobs or prevented from working long hours. This announcement in the *Jornal do Brasil* was all too typical: "The minor Luiz de Araújo Nelson, Brazilian, fourteen years old, textile worker at Fabrica de Tecidos Carioca, while working yesterday afternoon at this factory, was caught in the gears of one of the machines, receiving grave wounds on the right leg and over various parts of his body."[8]

While condemning the existence of child labor on the one hand, the labor press had on the other hand consistently argued that children's wages were essential to the maintenance of the working-class family. In that light, the 1916 protest was a continuation of a long-standing call on the part of the labor movement, echoed in the popular protests of the last two decades, for the government to end the hypocrisy of turning a blind eye to the widespread violations of the child labor laws and then moving to penalize the children even more by charging them to take the train. However, there is little indication that the labor press in this case, or in any other, ever condoned the labor of children. The Associação Graphica (Association of Graphic Workers) at one point argued that the laws prohibiting child labor would only be enforced if the unions pressured the government to penalize those factory owners who ignored it, and that, failing government action, the union itself

7. *Guerra Social*, June 29, 1911, 3.

8. *Jornal do Brasil*, April 4, 1903, 1. Although the account listed the youth's age as fourteen, it still noted him as a "minor." Since, by law, boys over the age of thirteen were considered adults, the newspaper may have used the term "minor" descriptively.

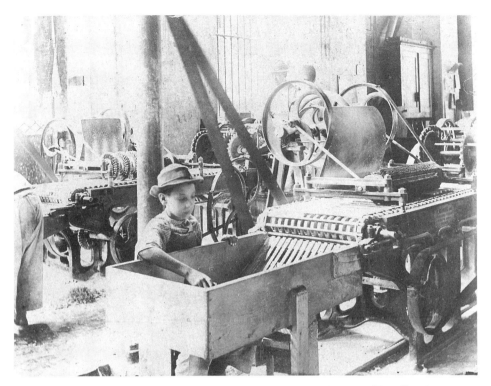

Fig. 11.   A child laboring at a milling machine, a common feature of Brazilian factories during the First Republic. Rio de Janeiro, c. 1910. Jennings Hoffenberg Collection.

should attempt to collect the fine.[9] Rui Barbosa, in his 1919 treatise on the "social question," pointed to the long-standing violation of the child labor laws, passed thirty years earlier supposedly to prevent the country from "sacrificing its children for the sake of prosperity."[10] One may assume that Rui was responding to the repeated demand to end child labor raised in the protests of 1913, 1915, and again in 1917.

9. *O Graphico*, January 11, 1917.
10. Rui Barbosa, "A questão social e política no Brasil," in *Escritos e discursos selectos* (Rio de Janeiro: Editora José Aguilar, 1960), 86–110. In addition to this and other reports cited earlier, a major study of the effects of child labor and abandonment of children appeared in 1905, which was referred to in subsequent reports on schools, child labor, reform schools, and orphanages: Ministerio da Justiça e Negocios Interiores, *Relatório apresentado ao Ministro da Justiça pela Comm. Inspectoria dos estabelecimentos de alienados, públicos e particulares no Districto Federal*, Annexo 7 (February 14, 1905), vol. 2 of *Relatório apresentado ao Presidente da República pelo Dr. J. J. Seabra* (March 1905), 59–133.

Beyond child labor, however, other issues came to the foreground throughout 1916 and 1917 as the spiraling cost of essential food and subsistence commodities became the central concern for most Carioca consumers.[11] In January 1917 signs of organized protest against the high cost of living resurfaced when the anarcho-syndicalists once again attempted to channel spontaneous mass protests in a single direction. The FORJ distributed a leaflet at several factories and commercial establishments announcing a meeting for all those interested in organizing against the "cost of living that is by now becoming unbearable."[12] In response, over fifty people gathered for an initial meeting at the FORJ headquarters in Vila Isabel on January 4. In a near repeat of the 1913 initiation of the Campaign Against the High Cost of Living, speakers denounced the government's policies and called for a renewed consumer campaign against high prices.[13] Throughout February and especially during March the FORJ held rallies every few days in the working-class neighborhoods of the city. Once again, as it had in 1913 and briefly in 1915, the FORJ attempted to reestablish the network of neighborhood *comités*. In contrast to the campaigns of earlier years, however, the 1917 protests began to develop a momentum that far outstripped the FORJ's ability, or desire, to channel into organized committees the mounting discontent arising from the streets.[14]

Clearly it was this series of community-based protests that underlay the revitalization of the working class and the labor movement in 1917. In discussing the 1917 rebirth of labor militancy, Sheldon Maram explains: "To reactivate the proletariat, organizers resorted once again to demonstrations against the high cost of living, child labor, and other issues of concern to the working class."[15] Rather than "resort" to the issues of the community protest movement, the FORJ actually was building on a tradition, one that had developed as a central component of Carioca political culture. Recognized or not by the FORJ leadership, the popular protests had been an inspiration to the general movement, in turn compelling the organization's men to intervene in protests that up until this point had only sporadically come under the

11. Eulalia Maria Lahmeyer Lobo, *História do Rio de Janeiro: Do capital commercial ao capital industrial e financeiro* (Rio de Janeiro: Instituto Brasileiro de Mercado de Capitais, 1978), 2: 516, 521.

12. *Jornal do Brasil*, January 5, 1917, 7.

13. Reports of the January 1917 demonstrations appeared in the *Jornal do Brasil* (1917): January 9, p. 7; January 15, p. 5; January 17, p. 7; January 22, p. 6; January 29, p. 5; February 1, p. 9.

14. Ibid., February 4, p. 5; February 5, p. 7; February 12, p. 7; February 26, p. 5; March 6, p. 1.

15. Sheldon Maram, "Anarchists, Immigrants, and the Brazilian Labor Movement, 1890–1920" (Ph.D. diss., University of California, Santa Barbara, 1972), 168.

control of the labor movement; more often they had simply churned along on their own. The FORJ's intervention was effective. Their work against high prices increased the federation's membership to thirty thousand in a matter of a few months, bolstered participation in industrial unions, and infused militancy into the trade union movement, leading to a wave of strike activity in textiles. Quite aware of the concerns that were pushing forward this new wave of trade union militancy, FORJ leaders declared the fight against the rising cost of living the centerpiece of the capital's May Day protest that year.[16]

On May Day 1917 the working class poured into the street, bringing to the traditional workers' day celebration a list of grievances against the policies of the Brazilian government and the elite it represented. The FORJ and the Centro Cosmopólita provided the leadership, planned the marches, and fanned out organizers to bring entire neighborhoods and workplaces to downtown Rio on the international workers' day. The event condemned the "capitalists, landlords, politicians, and other parasites" who produce nothing but are able to live in "opulence and laziness" through their exploitation of the workers.[17] Protesters who had traveled, many on foot, from distant *subúrbios* converged into a massive march down Rio's main street, the Avenida Rio Branco, at three o'clock in the afternoon. There over six thousand workers and their families, unemployed people, and disgruntled consumers denounced the high cost of living and shouted slogans, calling for "bread and work!"[18]

In spite of government prohibitions and threats of reprisals, demonstrators carried signs prepared by the FORJ that read "Down with the High Cost of Living, We Want Bread and Work!" Arguing that the slogans were too inflammatory, the police department had prohibited the display of these banners, but their attempted restriction only drew more attention to the signs. The *Jornal do Brasil* carried a front-page photograph of about a dozen FORJ supporters holding the signs, with the caption "Placards prohibited by the police that figured in the workers' demonstrations."[19]

The May Day crowd listened to FORJ speakers Maximiliano de Macedo, Paschoal Gravina, and José Madeira loudly denounce the war in Europe and the government's economic policies that supported the sending of foodstuffs

16. *Jornal do Brasil*, March 6, 1917, 1; Timothy Harding, "The Political History of Organized Labor in Brazil" (Ph.D. diss., Stanford University, 1973), 42.

17. *Jornal do Brasil*, May 1, 1917, 1.

18. *Correio da Manhã*, May 2, 1917, 1.

19. *Jornal do Brasil*, May 2, 1917, 1.

and materials to the Allied powers. While emphasizing their willingness to
defend Brazil from outside attack, the anarchist leaders noted that Brazilian
workers had no reason to fight against their fellow workers in Europe and
that Brazil should not take sides in this little-understood conflict, whose only
purpose was to fill the tills of the war-profiteering industrialists. The day's
main speaker was José Caizzo, president of the FORJ. Caizzo, in a lengthy
address, spoke against the high cost of living, the misery caused the working
class by the policies of capricious and indifferent public officials, and the
continual scarcity of consumer goods. Caizzo's fiery speech was frequently
interrupted by applause and shouts against the government and its policies.
He finished with a loud denunciation of the war, labeling the conflagration a
"manifestation of backwardness, of barbarity, and of inhumanity" perpetu-
ated by the "international bourgeoisie." Caizzo's closing appeal to those present to join in unified action to oppose high prices, to demand an eight-hour
workday, and to resist involvement in the war met with cheers and thunder-
ous applause from the crowd.[20]

Alarmed by the size of the May Day demonstration, and especially by the
apparent anger of the demonstrators, Chief of Police Aurelino de Araújo Leal
sought instructions from his superiors in the Ministry of Justice. As in all
past protests, the full repressive powers of the state were placed at the service of the powerful utility and transit companies, the factory owners, and
commercial interests. Police and army cavalry units were dispatched to
guard key government buildings, utility installations, transportation terminals, and food-storage warehouses throughout the city. The guard was doubled in front of police stations, while military forces were placed on alert
throughout the capital. In many previous demonstrations, a show of massive
police presence had provoked protesters, though the police themselves had
not intentionally instigated a melee; however, May Day 1917 ended peacefully. While the speakers issued fiery denunciations against the government
and manufacturers, they continually cautioned the crowd to remain calm, to
organize, and to prepare for further rallies and strikes. For its part, the government prepared to confront the assemblies with repression, to ignore or
disregard the legitimacy of the Carioca citizenry's demands, and to demonstrate that no matter what the issue or how numerous the protesters, the
government would stay firmly on the side of the monopolists, the utility companies, the manufacturers, and the transit bosses.[21]

20. Ibid., May 1, 1917, 1; *Correio da Manhã*, May 1, 1917, 1.
21. *Jornal do Brasil*, May 1 and 2, 1917, 1; *Correio da Manhã*, May 2, 1917, 1.

In the days, weeks, and months following the May Day rally, the Rio de Janeiro proletariat confronted the capital's economic and political elite with ferocity. Rallies against the high cost of living continued through the week after the May Day convocation; a strike at a major textile mill erupted in violence; and a number of other strikes followed in June and July. By July 24 the Rio de Janeiro labor movement was in the midst of its first general strike. This surge of labor militancy drew its strength from several factors. First, a tradition of consumer resistance against high food, housing, and transportation costs was now converging with the nascent labor movement's demand for an eight-hour workday and better working conditions. Second, the Rio de Janeiro general strike was drawing its inspiration from the far more militant strike and uprising that was shaking São Paulo during the same period.

In São Paulo, on June 10, women workers at the Rudolfo Crespi textile mill initiated a job action that was then joined by men, demanding a 25 percent wage increase. In spite of the Crespi's formidable profits, along with those of other industries, the workers' request was summarily dismissed, and the latter voted to strike. Over the next month, under the coordination of the São Paulo Comité de Defesa Proletaria (Committee in Defense of the Proletariat), a near total general strike closed down all urban activity; troops loyal to the workers resisted orders to intervene against the strikers; and military units from outside the state of São Paulo had to be called in to restore calm. At the high point of the strike the *comité* governed the city for two days. The São Paulo *comité*'s fifteen demands to the government and factory owners combined consumer and workplace demands, including lower rents and prices on basic commodities, an end to hoarding and speculation, regulations to stop the sale of adulterated and falsely labeled foods, the right to unionize, an eight-hour workday, shorter workweek, an end to child labor, higher salaries, freedom for imprisoned protesters, and reinstatement of all strikers with no reprisals.[22]

Notably, while the São Paulo strike began as a walkout in a textile mill and more directly drew its strength from a militant and growing trade union movement, Rio's protests built from the cost-of-living marches of May Day. This points to a difference in the development pattern of the two cities: São Paulo developed more as a manufacturing center, while Rio was more impor-

---

22. *Estado de São Paulo*, July 9–12, 1917, 5–6; Joel Wolfe, *Working Women, Working Men: São Paulo and the Rise of Brazil's Industrial Working Class, 1900–1955* (Durham: Duke University Press, 1993), 16–27; Evararado Dias, *História das lutas sociais no Brasil* (São Paulo: Editora Edglit, 1962), 230–31; Maram, "Anarchists, Immigrants, and the Brazilian Labor Movement," 169–70.

tant as a commercial city, to a lesser extent dependent on its manufacturing base. In industrial São Paulo trade unions were an organic form of organization and a vehicle of proletarian resistance. The city's massive textile mills were ringed by working-class communities often directly tied to the mills; thus, slight alterations in the workday, in happenings in the mill, in wage rates, and in working conditions directly affected the surrounding communities. This pattern of mills coupled to adjacent "mill towns" more closely resembled early industrialization in the northeastern United States, where, not surprisingly, one finds patterns of unionization similar to those in São Paulo.[23]

By contrast, in the federal capital factories were smaller than in São Paulo, communities were more diverse, and the factory system not so intensely dominated working-class life. The city's importance as a center of banking, commerce, and international trade, and its role as the capital of the Republic, meant that the lower-class communities were composed of people who worked in many different shops, often long distances from their homes. As shown in the pattern of community protests, neighborhood residents came together to demonstrate against transportation services or high prices less than to object to the regimentation and misery of factory life. This difference helps to explain why the two general strikes followed separate paths. In São Paulo, trade union demands and shop-floor issues dominated from the outset. In Rio the strike fused community and workplace demands, drawing its trade union inspiration more from the São Paulo workers than from a tradition of militancy organic to Rio's own union movement. In Rio de Janeiro strike demands paralleled the demands that had been raised in earlier community protests.

Although workers in Rio de Janeiro did not carry out a general strike and protest movement to match the one in São Paulo, the events from May through August nevertheless were unprecedented in the federal capital's history. Beginning with the May Day demonstration, the capital witnessed widespread and violent demonstrations against high prices and low wages. Speakers from the FORJ addressed three different rallies in scattered parts of the city on Sunday, May 6, pressing ahead with their demand for lower

23. John D. French, *The Brazilian Workers' ABC: Class Conflict and Alliances in Modern São Paulo* (Chapel Hill: University of North Carolina Press, 1992), 31–47; Wolfe, *Working Women, Working Men*, 25–27; Sheldon Maram, "Labor and the Left in Brazil 1890–1921: A Movement Aborted," *Hispanic American Historical Review* 57, no. 2 (1977): 268–69; Boris Fausto, *Trabalho urbano e conflito social* (São Paulo: DIFEL, 1976), 59–60; Leôncio Martins Rodrigues, "Classe operaria e sindicalismo no Brasil," in *Sindicalismo e sociedade*, ed. Leôncio Martins Rodrigues (São Paulo: Difusão Européia do Livro, 1968), 345.

prices and protesting Brazil's involvement in the war. Commenting on the speeches, the *Jornal do Brasil* observed that the workers' protests against "the critical situation in which they find themselves because of high prices on essential commodities and goods produced nationally have now extended to opposing Brazil's entrance into the European bloodbath."[24]

It is hard to pinpoint just how much the FORJ's antiwar stance affected workers who flocked to rallies and later walked out on strike. Whereas FORJ speakers were wildly applauded at rallies throughout the city, it is unclear just what aspect of their speeches was eliciting the crowds' response. What is clear is that the demands strikers raised in the following weeks pertained to the economic crisis and complaints over living conditions. Moreover, the general strike in Rio developed spontaneously: one event built on another, and unrelated grievances came together into a strike movement at a time when frustrations were high. Since the strike grew out of a series of events rather than a coordinating plan, it is doubtful that the FORJ's antiwar political program was key to the workers' anger with the government and monopolies.

Historical accounts and interpretations of the protests in Rio from May through August have varied, quite possibly because the strike wave developed out of a series of seemingly unconnected events. For instance, Maram states that, "unlike [in] São Paulo, where textile operatives spearheaded the walkouts, in Rio they remained working until the strike was virtually over."[25] By contrast, Dulles writes that during "the first half of May 1917 order was maintained in Rio only with difficulty. Strikes broke out in the textile plants following some threatened dismissals."[26] Edgard Carone lists several textile mills where strikes broke out, though he does not state whether the capital's numerically important textile workers were key to the success of the general strike.[27] Why this confusion? Quite possibly the reason for these differing accounts has to do with the way one interprets both the strike and its place within the longer history of protests in Rio de Janeiro. Maram, for example, separates events in May and June from the outbreak of the general strike in July. He discusses the general strike according to its place solely within Rio's trade union tradition and then debates its success or failure according to the role of one or another key union, political ideology, or trade union confederation.

24. *Jornal do Brasil*, May 7, 1917, 1.
25. Maram, "Anarchists, Immigrants, and the Brazilian Labor Movement," 174.
26. Dulles, *Anarchists and Communists*, 44.
27. Edgard Carone, *A República Velha: Instituições e classes sociais* (São Paulo: DIFEL, 1975), 231–32.

Stepping outside the parameters of the trade union movement and examining the general strike more broadly, a different picture emerges. In June, July, and August 1917 Rio's tradition of spontaneous protests involving community residents and workers as consumers was combining with the workers' trade union struggles to form a new type of protest: the general strike. In São Paulo, on the other hand, while the strikers' demands touched on issues that affected workers as consumers and producers, the strike drew its strength more directly from a trade union tradition, drawing in workers whose political culture was dominated by their consciousness as workers more than as consumers. Community protests and riots against the high cost of living had not been as central to the Paulistas' resistance movement as it had been in Rio.[28] Nevertheless, though events in Rio de Janeiro during May and June 1917 did not equal the militant struggles of São Paulo, the masses of Brazil's capital city could hardly be described as acquiescent.

In addition, the strike ushered in a new era of popular protest in the city. Consider some of the changes. On May 11 the calm of the federal capital was broken by a police attack on a peaceful picket line of workers striking the Corcovado textile mill. Textile workers at the São Felix and the Carioca mills, immediately outraged at the police attack on the Corcovado workers, walked off their jobs at 11:30 that morning in solidarity. Workers at the Carioca mill returned to work the next day, while negotiators in the Corcovado strike announced a possible settlement and return to work two days later, on May 14.[29] Strikes in textiles and other industries continued to break out during the next month. On June 13 shoemakers at the Braga Costa firm walked off the job when management refused to raise wages and to negotiate employees' complaints over their treatment by a foreman.[30] The next week the workers at the Carioca textile mill announced a strike over unhealthy working conditions, including complaints that the factory was poorly ventilated, that bathrooms were primitive outhouses, and that on his infrequent visits the director of hygiene "inspects no further than the inside of the factory manager's office." Stating that they worked from 6:00 A.M. to 9:00 P.M. for 300 to 500 reis daily, workers demanded shorter hours and more money.[31]

By mid-July the capital was on the brink of a major confrontation between labor and capital—a confrontation that had been steadily building since May Day. On the evening of July 14 the FORJ issued a statement declaring com-

28. Fausto, *Trabalho urbano*, 58–61.
29. *Jornal do Brasil*, May 7, 12, 14, 1917, 1–2.
30. Ibid., June 14, 1917, 1.
31. Ibid., June 23, 1917, 1.

plete solidarity with the demands and tactics of the São Paulo strikers. So as adequately to respond to the changing strike situation in both Rio and São Paulo, the FORJ declared itself in permanent session. Crowds jammed the FORJ headquarters on the evening of July 17 to hear reports on the happenings in São Paulo and listen to speakers denounce the high cost of living in Rio de Janeiro.[32] On the same day two so-called yellow unions, the Sociedade Resistencia de Trabalhadores em Trapiches e Cafe (Resistance Society of Waterfront Warehouse and Coffee Workers) and the Federação Marítima (Maritime Federation) announced, after meeting with police chief Aurelino Leal, their intent to continue working during the strike.[33] Other unions, however, remained on strike or joined the agitation.

On July 16 seamstresses in a sack factory struck for higher pay. Some of the most poorly paid workers in the city, these women toiled in sweatshops such as this one and in textile mills under miserable conditions.[34] In her account of work in the textile mills in Rio, where she began working during World War I at the age of seven, Luiza Ferreira de Medeiros paints a picture of the deplorable conditions. The regular workday began at 6:00 A.M. and ended at 5:00 P.M., but very often the women were forced to work longer hours, without receiving overtime pay. With no place to eat, no set lunch time, filthy washrooms, and no drinking fountains, the workers stood at their machines for hours on end until some of them literally dropped. Accidents were common, and Luiza recounted seeing women die or lose arms when they were caught in the machines. Not only did the company not compensate victims or their families for loss of life and limb, but the workers themselves had to collect money to pay for the funerals. Working conditions for men were comparable, but women were paid less and suffered sexual abuse at the hands of the foremen and managers. "Foreman Claúdio Batista shut girls up in his office in order to force them to have sex with him. Many of the mill hands became prostitutes because of that scoundrel!"[35]

32. *Correio da Manhã*, July 18, 1917; *Jornal do Brasil*, July 18, 1917, 1.

33. The Warehouse and Coffee Workers was a moderate union that enjoyed good relations with the government and the police. Founded in the early 1900s, it had been initially weakened because of tensions between workers of African and those, mostly immigrants, of Portuguese background, which resulted in violent confrontations. Gerald Michael Greenfield and Sheldon L. Maram, *Latin American Labor Organizations* (Westport, Conn.: Greenwood Press, 1987), 117–18.

34. *Correio da Manhã*, July 18–19, 1917; *Jornal do Brasil*, July 19, 1917, 1.

35. "Recollections of a Rio Textile Worker, by Luiza Ferreira de Medeiros," from Edgar Rodrigues, *Alvorado operário: Os congressos operários no Brasil,* cited in June E. Hahner, *Emancipating the Female Sex: The Struggle for Women's Rights in Brazil, 1850–1940* (Durham: Duke University Press, 1990), 220–21.

As June Hahner shows, women and children not only labored under the worst conditions for the least pay but were also among the least organized of the city's workforce. There were few strikes in which women participated; neither the labor press nor daily press discussed the participation of women in unions, as representatives to labor congresses, or as spokespersons in the labor movement. For example, the front page of the October 1, 1913, *Voz do Trabalhador* was devoted to photographs heralding the successful Second Brazilian Labor Conference. In none of the four photos showing seated delegates in session and the head table of labor leaders is a single woman visible.[36] Until early 1914 the labor press was all but silent on women as factory workers and on the need to organize them into unions; however, the *Voz* did mention that women were joining the community protests in "substantial numbers."[37] By the beginning of the next year, the participation of women in community protests and their importance to the future of the labor movement were considered significant enough to warrant a special column in the paper devoted to organizing women. Jaime Fernandes's first "woman's column" ("A Mulher") hinted at the terrain the labor movement was crossing. He spent most of the column exhorting his fellow workers to consider women who took jobs in factories and shops as workers and potential comrades, not as prostitutes.[38] Not surprisingly, then, the pivotal role of this most oppressed sector of the Carioca workforce in the outbreak of the 1917 general strike was reported in the *Jornal do Brasil,* complete with a photograph, but nothing more was said about it. Actually, the events in Rio paralleled those in São Paulo in that women workers were at the forefront of both strikes.[39]

Despite the seamstresses' strike, most accounts state that the Rio general strike began with the walkout by furniture workers in the Syndicato dos Marceneiros e Artes Correlativas (Union of Cabinetmakers and Related Crafts) on July 18, since, in contrast to the seamstresses, the furniture workers supposedly were the first in Rio to strike in solidarity with their São Paulo comrades. In the next week thousands of other workers joined the general strike, demanding changes in working conditions as well as living conditions. Strikers' demands in July 1917 were the same as those raised in earlier community and workplace protests.[40]

36. *Voz do Trabalhador*, October 1, 1913, 1–4.

37. Ibid., December 1, 1914, 4.

38. Ibid., February 1, 1915, 3. For a general discussion of women workers, see Hahner, *Emancipating the Female Sex*, chap. 3.

39. Wolfe, *Working Women, Working Men*, 16–20.

40. *Correio da Manhã*, July 18–19, 1917; *Jornal do Brasil*, July 19, 1917, 1.

On Monday morning, July 23, an estimated fifty thousand were striking in Rio. Later in the day about twenty thousand metalworkers left their jobs. In the evening the tailors and bread carriers decided to join the movement. On July 24 shoemakers founded the União dos Cortadores de Calçado (Union of Shoemaker Cutters) and demanded the eight-hour workday and a 20 percent wage increase.[41] Strikers at the América Fabril textile company were demanding a 30 percent wage increase and schools for their children. Workers at another textile company, Fabrica de Tecidos Aliança, wanted a 30 percent wage increase and an end to corporal punishment.[42]

The strikes in Aliança and América Fabril, considered alongside the July 16 walkout in the sack factory, raise the important question of women's participation in the labor movement in the 1917 demonstrations. Whereas the reports do not specifically mention whether many women were involved, textile factories employed large numbers of women workers, many of them, as in the América Fabril plant, concentrated in spinning, where they were paid by the hour and had less security than the men in weaving.[43] If textile workers struck, then large numbers of women must have walked out. Not only did textiles employ the largest concentration of female factory workers, 70 percent (double the 33.4 percent of male workers), but the factories themselves had high percentages of women employees. As in other industrializing countries, textile manufacturers preferred to hire women and children because the plants were mechanized and the work required dexterity and agility rather than great strength. Most important, however, women and children were paid less and, as the most unskilled and worst paid sector of the workforce, could be forced to accept the dangerous, loud. and dirty conditions that prevailed in textiles. Along with recent immigrants and migrants from the countryside, women formed the core of the textile industry, but they, unlike men, were usually locked into these low-paying positions, unable to climb into more highly skilled and better-remunerated jobs.[44] When on July 26 the FORJ announced that "all workers in this capital, without distinction of class, are on strike," by "class" they meant occupation, but they may

41. These workers were probably from the União Geral dos Trabalhadores em Calçado (General Union of Shoemakers) or associated with it, since that particular anarchist-influenced shoemakers union was known to have played a strong role in the 1917 strike; Greenfield and Maram, *Latin American Labor Organizations*, 86.

42. *Correio da Manhã*, July 24, 1917, 1–2.

43. Hahner, *Emancipating the Female Sex*, 109.

44. Hahner, *Emancipating the Female Sex*, 99–106. See Joel Wolfe's discussion of the importance of women workers in the organizing drives in São Paulo's labor movement, *Working Women, Working Men*.

even have meant gender in an undefined sense.[45] Moreover, if "all workers" were out on strike, their ranks must have included significant numbers of women from the factories, even if they were not specifically mentioned.

Following the traditional pattern, sporadic clashes between strikers and their supporters, on one side, and the police and military units, on the other, erupted during the last week of July and first few days of August. The anarchist labor federation announced that it and the Centro Cosmopólita labor organization were coordinating the strike and negotiations with management. Beyond the bounds of the FORJ, however, street demonstrations seemed to erupt spontaneously throughout the city, targeting those sites and institutions against which the Carioca lower classes had always vented their anger. Reports of vandalism against trolley companies, the Companhia de Light e Power, and the train station caused Aurelino Leal to call for special police and military protection of all utility and transportation installations in the city.[46] Although, as in many previous demonstrations, workers were quick to vent their frustration against the transit and utility companies, strikers may also have disrupted streetcar and train service to prevent scabs from reaching work, and set upon the light and gas companies in hopes of cutting power to factories.

Except for this vandalism, and the actions a few gangs of demonstrators who roamed through the downtown district waving red banners and denouncing the government, the strike in Rio remained relatively calm and never approached the level of violent confrontation of its counterpart in São Paulo. Nevertheless, naval units on ships in Guanabara Bay were put on alert, and police and cavalry units patrolled the streets of the capital. On July 27 several important unions individually began to negotiate with police chief Leal for an end to the strike. By early August most workers were back on the job, having won a few significant concessions. On August 2 textile workers and manufacturers reached an agreement that granted strikers a 10 percent wage hike, a nine-and-a-half-hour workday, a fifty-six hour workweek, amnesty for strikers, and the right to organize. All issues pertaining to job safety and unhygienic working conditions, as well as lower prices, control of the monopolies, and miserable living conditions, were referred to the government for action.[47]

When workers returned to their jobs in early August 1917, could they sum

45. *Jornal do Brasil*, July 27, 1917, 1.

46. *Correio da Manhã*, July 25–26, 1917, 2–3.

47. Ibid., July 27–28, 1917, 1–2; Dias, *História das lutas sociais*, 302–5; Maram, "Anarchists, Immigrants, and the Brazilian Labor Movement," 175.

up the agitational wave that had swept the city in the previous few months as having improved their situation or not? As is often the case, the lessons of the general strike and the estimation of what was gained by it remained concealed for a considerable period. In terms of immediate gains, the 10 percent wage increase was wiped out by rampant price increases in the weeks during and following the strikes. No doubt hoping to bury the issues entirely, the government agencies charged with investigating working conditions and job safety promptly relegated many of the workers' demands to a commission. The authorities closed the FORJ and Centro Cosmopólita headquarters, rounded up labor leaders, and, when possible, deported them. Finally, on October 26, 1917, in response to the German's sinking of one of its ships, the Brazilian government officially entered the war.[48]

Did the Rio de Janeiro working class lose more than it gained from the general strike? The answer is complex, since the strike's significance only stands out when evaluated against the backdrop of the many years of protest that had preceded it. In 1917 the Rio proletariat's long-standing complaints against high prices, poor services, and miserable living conditions burst forth in organized protest and found their expression in their most modern form: the general strike. The appearance of the general strike as a tactic for militant working-class protest was a radical departure from the disparate, spontaneous, and short-lived street demonstrations and strikes that had dominated the masses' protest movement in the capital before 1917. The general strike was a major step, and a lesson, in the popular classes' education in modern class conflict. Nevertheless, as a tactic it was reliant on the community protest struggles from which it had drawn its inspiration. Both the strike and the neighborhood riot were interchangeable forms of a common struggle that had for decades thrown divergent sectors of the popular classes into temporary and informal alliances against an intransigent power elite.

By contrast, a number of studies have highlighted only the movement's ineffectiveness. Arguing that there is "scant evidence of labor activities reflecting a militancy born from an awareness of common class interests that were opposed to the interests of the bourgeoisie," Eileen Keremitsis based her conclusions on the obvious lack of cohesion, unity, and militancy demonstrated by the Rio workforce in traditional "shop-floor" confrontations with management.[49] As she ably explained, factors such as the availability of labor

---

48. *Jornal do Brasil*, October 27, 1917, 1; Fausto, *Trabalho urbano*, 218–30.

49. Eileen Keremitsis, "The Early Industrial Worker in Rio de Janeiro, 1870–1930" (Ph.D. diss., Columbia University, 1982), 184.

and capital resources, the number and level of skill of workers in a given
enterprise, and the high rates of geographic mobility played decisive roles in
determining the leverage labor was able to exert. Artisan shoemakers, before mechanization, and drivers for the Companhia de Light e Power and for
some trolley lines enjoyed considerable bargaining strength because they
were relatively skilled and could not easily be replaced, whereas textile workers, whose work was highly mechanized but required little skill, were in a
less advantageous position. These factors, however, much as they may have
inhibited labor union organizing efforts, did not necessarily enforce passivity. The same textile workers who may have had enormous difficulties
holding together a union seized the opportunity to make their discontent
known in the days and months after May Day 1917, in the general strike that
year, and in the abortive insurrection of 1918.[50]

Another consequence of the strike was that for the first time the Brazilian
elite began to realize the capital's urban problems were not going to disap-
pear, since the urban renewal project that had removed the lower classes
from the Old City still had not isolated the problems to the Zona Norte and
subúrbios. In sum, urban renewal had not ensured social control. In a newspaper interview in 1918 President-elect Rodrigues Alves admitted that the
Brazilian lower classes suffered serious deprivations, something he had long
refused to concede. Ironically, the Brazilian president who eventually was
forced to recognize the legitimacy of the complaints from the city's poor had
been the architect of Rio's urban renewal project and the promulgator of the
public health campaign.[51]

These were not sentiments that came easily to Alves; rather, his concilia-
tory remarks came at the end of a close and often heated presidential campaign against Rui Barbosa. As the spokesperson for the urban liberal bourgeoisie, Barbosa had campaigned relentlessly. Speaking before crowds of
urban workers, the liberal candidate condemned the absence of a social
policy to address the needs of the working class and poor, and promised, if
elected, to fight for a better life for the urban worker. Throughout the hotly
contested presidential campaign, Barboso relied on his considerable oratori-
cal skills to "inform" the working poor of the misery in their lives, which
they knew all too well, though for years he too had ignored the frequent
complaints from the *suburbanos*, workers, and urban poor for better living
and working conditions.[52]

50. Ibid., 185–87.
51. *A Razão*, November 18, 1918, 1.
52. Barbosa, "A questão social."

Although Alves emerged victorious, the vehemence of Barbosa's campaign, along with existing pressures from the workers' movement, forced the president-elect to modify his elitist disregard for the plight of the poor. In one of the ironies in which history abounds, Rodrigues Alves, the public health president, died in the great "Spanish flu" epidemic of 1918 before he was to reassume the presidency; nevertheless, his campaign speeches represented more than his own opinion and signified a shift away from the previous intransigence of the planter-controlled government. Barbosa's stance likewise revealed a changed attitude on the part of the liberal reformers who had in the past rarely objected to the planter government's conservatism, so long as Rio's civilized veneer remained intact. Not until 1919 would laws protecting labor be included in the civil code, since, despite frequent demands, neither the constitution of 1891 nor the 1892 Civil Code had recognized the freedom for labor unions.[53]

The events of 1917 and the demonstrations in following years proved to the Republican ruling class, irrespective of political persuasion, that their ideal of a Europeanized, civilized capital remained elusive. The elite had actually traveled a distance in ideological terms from the "personalized hierarchies of patronage and power" that predominated in the city before the abolition of slavery in 1888.[54] In the wake of the decline of patron-client relationships, the city had established a police force, a bureaucracy for apprehending criminals, and system for meting out punishment, thereby transferring to the *state* and away from the *individual* the role of civil administration. As Thomas Holloway notes, the rationale was not simply to maintain control but "to increase control through state structures."[55] The urban renewal and public health plan, intended as it was to facilitate the containment of crime and the criminal element, was an additional step in the evolution of state structures to serve the interests of the ruling class.

But if threats to order and property, as well as of the "classic urban riot," had been minimized by the massive relocation of the working class, the poor, and commercial and government workers out of the downtown after 1904, class conflict now arose from another front: working-class strikes. The few months of agitation in 1917 opened up a period of unprecedented strike activity in Rio de Janeiro. The following year began with demonstrations and strikes against price increases and ended with an attempted workers' insur-

53. Harding, "Political History of Organized Labor," 36–37.
54. Thomas H. Holloway, *Policing Rio de Janeiro: Repression and Resistance in a Nineteenth-Century City* (Stanford: Stanford University Press, 1993), 289.
55. Ibid., 288.

170 Civilizing Rio

rection against the government.[56] It was, as Hobsbawm would have conceived it, a period in which the issues remained much the same, while the *mechanisms* of protest began to show signs of change. "It is the discovery that modern organization is better suited to the struggle in a modern society, rather than the discovery of modern ideology, which accounts for the decline of pre-political movements in the modern world."[57] Additionally, the mechanisms of so-called premodern, as well as modern, protest shaped Rio's emergent industrial society.

Although the failed anarchist insurrection of November 1918 could be considered the second, higher, and more militant stage of the uprising that began with the general strike the year before, it was more like the beginning of the end of this era of urban protest in Rio's history. Politically, the events of 1918 differed markedly from the general strike, as the seat of insurgency moved away from the anarchist-dominated trade union federations and a political program based on mass rallies, strikes, and demonstrations toward a more tightly controlled insurrectionist strategy. With the Bolshevik Revolution of October 1917 now firmly established as the model for achieving political power, complete with the premise that revolution could succeed in the less industrialized nations, Brazil's working-class leaders no longer looked toward the mass rally and march as the best means of enacting change. They opted instead for a conspiratorial insurrection and coordinated general strike designed to paralyze the capital economically while militarily overpowering the police and army.

Beginning on November 18, 1918, the anniversary week of the founding of the Republic and the period traditionally set aside for political protests in Rio, workers in textiles, metallurgy, and civil construction walked off the job and gathered in small rallies at various points around the city. A coordinated insurrection, led by a council of anarchist and labor leaders, disaffected military officers, and academics, was planned for November 18. Intending to invade and hold hostage the Senate and House of Deputies, capture key arsenals, occupy the factories, paralyze the city, and take power, the conspirators met several times during the first week of November to plan their strategy. Jorge Elias Ajus, an army lieutenant who joined the conspiracy to coordinate the military uprising, was actually a spy for the government and succeeded in sabotaging the entire operation. Although a partial general

56. Moniz Bandeira, Clovis Melo, and A. T. Andrade, *O ano vermelho: A Revolução Russa e seus reflexos no Brasil* (Rio de Janeiro: Editora Civilização Brasileira, 1967), 115–47.
57. Eric Hobsbawm, "Pre-political Movements in Peripheral Areas" (paper presented at the Conferencia sobre História e Ciencias Sociais, Campinas, Brazil, May 26–30, 1975), 23.

strike began, with workers at Bangu and Fabrica de Tecidos Confiança textile plants, the metalworkers, and construction workers adhering to the
planned work stoppage, the army moved quickly to arrest the plot's leaders,
disrupt union assemblies, and disperse demonstrations. The police managed
to prevent the unions from meeting to issue demands, thereby stalemating
the strike effort before it could get off the ground.[58]

The anarchist uprising of 1918 ended with no clear gains. The quick action
of the police and military prevented the labor leaders from mobilizing the
mass of Rio's disaffected citizens, who in the past had taken to the streets in
protest against high prices, low wages, and poor working conditions. Once
the government succeeded in isolating, imprisoning, and deporting the leadership, the movement was doomed. The following May Day 1919 demonstration, organized by the newly formed Communist Party, was probably the
best-organized workers' day event in Rio's history; however, in contrast to
the event two years before, neither strike wave nor mass protests followed in
its wake. On the other hand, the dramatic series of events from May Day
1917 through the attempted uprising in November 1918 and May Day rally
the next year finally had forced Brazil's elite to acknowledge the misery and
deprivation they had long attempted to ignore. Partially in response to internal strife, and partially as a result of international pressure, President Delfim
Moreira called on the Brazilian Congress to pass labor-protection legislation.
It was then, for the first time, that the Congress debated the question of
legislação social (social legislation). As a signatory of the International Labor
Charter, included in the Treaty of Versailles that ended World War I, Brazil
was committed to pass legislation ensuring workers a maximum number of
working hours, accident protection, and other minimal labor protections.[59]
Although most of the suggested reforms were shelved or intentionally ignored, the political leaders finally conceded that "social problems" might be
the responsibility of the legislature, not just the police.[60]

During the 1920s, strikes and job actions at the point of production formed
an expanding part of working-class political culture, although trade unionism
never developed to the point of entirely replacing spontaneous consumer

58. *Jornal do Brasil* (1918): November 19, p. 5; November 20, p. 5; November 23, p. 5; November 24, p. 5; November 27, p. 5; November 30, p. 5; December 5, p. 7.

59. Harding, "Political History of Organized Labor," 44.

60. Directoria do Interior, *Relatório apresentado ao Presidente da República dos Estados Unidos
do Brasil pelo Ministro da Justiça e Negocios Interiores, Dr. Alfredo Pinto Vieira de Mello* (Rio de
Janeiro: Imprensa Nacional, 1921), v–vi. For a summary of the 1919 debate and its contending
sides, see *Jornal do Brasil* (1919): January 21, pp. 3–4; May 7, p. 6; May 11, p. 6; May 12, p. 9;
May 17, p. 6; May 21, p. 5; July 13, p. 4.

Fig. 12.   Vista of Rio de Janeiro with the Castelo Hill (Morro de Castello) before its
destruction in 1921; Lapa in the foreground, Guanabara Bay on the right, c. 1890.
Jennings Hoffenberg Collection.

protests. There are two reasons why consumers' demands for better living
conditions and lower prices persisted in the 1920s alongside the increasingly
audible cry for union recognition and the eight-hour workday. The first had
to do with the government's continued failure to meet the *suburbanos'* demands for better public services and transportation facilities, while the second had to do with the fragility of the trade union movement and the fact that
the majority of Rio's laboring poor remained untouched by political and
union organizations even after the turbulent events of the late teens.[61]

Although it would be nice to report that Rio's authorities in the 1920s
turned their attention toward the plight of the poor, they did not. In this
regard, Alves, as well as Barbosa, mouthed the necessary political slogans
so common to electoral campaigns. As Michael Conniff shows in his study
of the rise of populist politics, during the 1920s living and working conditions
in the *subúrbios* worsened. "Unlike the pattern in most major cities, land values and quality of life decreased with distance from downtown. In remote
areas land was cheaper, utilities scantier, contact with the city more tenuous,
and dependence on agrarian vocations more common."[62] During the 1920s,

61. *Jornal do Brasil* (1920): May 30, p. 5, June 2, p. 5, June 5, p. 6, July 16, p. 5, August 1–2, p. 5.
62. Michael Conniff, *Urban Politics in Brazil: The Rise of Populism, 1925–1945* (Pittsburgh:
University of Pittsburgh Press, 1981), 27. For contrast with development patterns in the advanced industrialized world, see Manuel Castells, *The Urban Question: A Marxist Approach*,
trans. Alan Sheridan (Cambridge, Mass.: MIT Press, 1977), 40–48.

Fig. 13.   Dwellings and shops on Castelo Hill, July 29, 1921. Photograph by Augusto Malta, Jennings Hoffenberg Collection.

street repair, school construction, improvements to the commuter rail lines and the transportation networks in general, and maintenance of hospitals, clinics, and social services came to a halt, while the urban problems that called out for solutions were either forgotten or simply ignored.

Moreover, the city followed a set of priorities not dissimilar to the ones that had guided the 1904 urban renewal project. In 1920 the city borrowed $20 million to electrify the aged and inefficient Central railroad, the main commuter artery from the *suburbios* to the downtown. But rather than follow through on that project, the mayor used the money to level the oldest region of the city, Castelo Hill, on whose slopes lived the only remaining poor residents of the downtown district.[63] In 1922, on the wide stretch of land where the hill had risen, the city hosted the National Centenary Exposition, a trade fair that attracted foreign visitors and investors. Reasons for the renovation

63. Luiz Edmundo, *O Rio de Janeiro do meu tempo* (Rio de Janeiro: Imprensa Nacional, 1938), 207–18; *Jornal do Brasil*, March 16, 1914, 1, and December 16, 1914, 1.

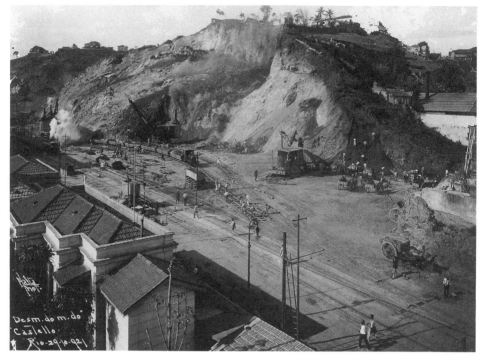

Fig. 14.   Leveling of Castelo Hill, October 29, 1921. Photograph by Augusto Malta,
Jennings Hoffenberg Collection.

were outlined in a 1921 government report that called for a continuation and
deepening of the renovation plan and its civilizing goals throughout the
1920s.[64] Similar to the outcome of the 1904 Yellow Fever Campaign, the destruction of Castelo Hill intensified the plight of the poor. In a comment that
could as easily have described the urban renewal project early in the century
as the 1921 diversion of moneys from the needed repairs on the Central,
Conniff notes that the Carioca consumers viewed the demolition of Castelo
Hill as "a project of dubious value" that "condemned tens of thousands of
persons to isolation and deteriorating quality of life."[65]

In the 1920s public and private moneys were poured into developing housing and transportation facilities in the fashionable Zona Sul beach communi-

64. Ministerio da Justiça e Negocios Interiores, *Relatório, 1921* (Rio de Janeiro: Imprensa
Nacional, 1921), xvii–xx.
65. Conniff, *Urban Politics in Brazil*, 25.

ties of Copacabana, Ipanema, Leblon, and Jardim Botânico. Between 1925 and 1929 middle- and upper-income-housing starts accounted for almost all new assessments, while lower-income housing accounted for almost none.[66] Deterioration in the *suburbios* and the government's continued bias toward Rio's upper class meant that the consumers' demands remained key components in working-class protests.

During the 1920s the trade union movement floundered. After the general strikes of 1917 and the worker uprising in 1918, the 1920s was a period of intensified labor-management conflict coupled with highly charged infighting between different wings of the labor movement.[67] Constant bickering and conflicts between anarchists and Communists during the 1920s undermined the emergence of political leadership and an expanded trade union movement. Commenting on the developing stagnation in the labor movement, Dulles notes that most unions "had so few members that Astrogildo Pereira spoke of general staffs without troops. To make matters worse, the anarchist-communist schism sometimes split original unions into two new rival unions."[68] The economic climate of the 1920s was disastrous: prices rose without a corresponding increase in workers' wages, and labor organizations, unions, and political parties turned on each other, sometimes to the point of physical combat.[69]

The founding of the Brazilian Communist Party in 1922 signaled the major attempt by the most militant sections of the organized labor movement to exert leadership over the strikes and demonstrations that had broken out in Brazil's major cities since 1917. Most individuals and members of the anarchist organizations that had led strikes and demonstrations throughout the Republic joined the Communist Party; a smaller group, mostly intellectuals, formed a Socialist Party the same year. Neither force on the Left exhibited much strength during the twenties. Political upheaval, economic downturns, failed alliances between the military and labor, and infighting between the various political tendencies all combined to eclipse the Left's effectiveness, despite the conscientious efforts of some leaders and rank-and-file members.[70] Rather than lend leadership to a movement that could build on the

66. "Ordem pública," in Ministerio da Justiça, *Relatório, 1921*, xvii–xx.
67. *Jornal do Brasil* (1919): May 12, p. 9; May 27, p. 9; ibid. (1920): January 29, p. 5; March 11, p. 7; March 23–30, pp. 5 and 7; "Ordem pública," in Ministerio da Justiça, *Relatório, 1921*, 104–6; Harding, "Political History of Organized Labor," 45.
68. Dulles, *Anarchists and Communists*, 185.
69. *Jornal do Brasil*, November 26, 1920, 5.
70. Maurício de Lacerda, *Entre duas revoluções* (Rio de Janeiro: Leite Ribeiro, 1927), 61–67; Edgard Carone, *Revoluções do Brasil contemporáneo, 1922–1938* (Rio de Janeiro: DIFEL, 1977).

common interests of workers as producers and consumers, disgruntled train riders, victims of disease and pollution, recipients of the worst in food, housing, and services the city had to offer, the organized labor movement left the masses bereft of program, leadership, and strategy at the moment they most desperately needed it.

Conclusion

"Did all the vigor, heroism and violence recounted and dissected in these chapters lead to any positive results?"[1] asked George Rudé in the conclusion to his pathbreaking study of the English and French crowds of the eighteenth and nineteenth centuries. It is a question that could apply as readily to Rio de Janeiro as it did to Europe. Arguing against the view that riots are merely temporary moments with negligible lasting effects, Rudé demonstrated that the crowds' accomplishments varied. Some protests succeeded in ensuring permanent change; others resulted in short-term gains that were quickly rescinded; and still others, no matter how militantly staged nor heroically executed, ended in repression, defeat, and disillusionment.[2]

Similarly, in Rio de Janeiro the near constant war that the lower classes waged against the manufacturers, the transit companies, and the government during the Old Republic resulted in many losses, a few short-lived victories, and a number of changes that are only apparent when viewed in historical perspective. For example, the 1904 antivaccination riot succeeded in calling off the obligatory vaccination plan, even if that was only one of the protesters' goals and even if vaccination, for all its benefits, was reintroduced a few years later. In the wave of repression following the November uprising,

---

1. George Rudé, *The Crowd in History, 1730–1848* (New York: John Wiley & Sons, 1964), 259.
2. Rudé notes that the Luddites failed to stop the steam loom but won temporary concessions from the Yorkshire clothiers, as well as the reduction of tolls on some turnpikes and the establishment of county boards. Ibid., 260.

working-class leaders were arrested and deported or exiled to the distant territories, while the centers of popular resistance and labor organizing were closed. Since the government characteristically acceded to those demands that least interfered with established property rights, the city's poorest residents, especially when confronting the interests of foreign investors, lost housing, never got sanitation, saw their transit costs escalate, and endured abysmal living and working conditions no matter how forcefully they protested. Moreover, the housing crisis intensified in the decades following the Yellow Fever Campaign, while sanitation, health care, and transportation for the urban poor either remained the same or worsened.

After 1905, especially in the years of heightened street disorders from 1909 through 1915, protesters won and lost demands in almost equal numbers. In Campos in August of 1908 a riot against an increased fare on a streetcar line produced no gains for the passengers, but the demonstration against the city's trolley and utility company, the omnipresent Companhia de Light e Power, the following year did force the owners to reduce the fare in accordance with commuters' demands. Likewise, residents from Rio das Pedras saw their petition for lower fares and better service on the notoriously inefficient Central ignored in 1910, but when the passengers rioted against the same rail line the next year, the government agreed to lower the fare. Defeat for the city's working poor meant more than simply losing a battle, however. Defeat was delivered along with severe repression, imprisonments, deportations, not to mention bruises, broken limbs, bloodied and mutilated bodies, or even loss of life, suffered under the hooves of cavalry horses and at the butts of bayonets and rifles. The stakes in any confrontation were always higher for the protesters than for the owners or the government, which only makes the record of continual resistance all the more impressive.

It is unclear whether organized protests were more successful in the short-term than the more frequent, spontaneous outbreaks of street violence that erupted in front of stores and on the trains or that escalated out of control during or after planned, peaceful demonstrations. For example, the FORJ's 1913 Campaign Against the High Cost of Living, which the federation briefly resurrected in 1915, was an orderly series of rallies and marches, spiced up with some vitriolic denunciations of the government and the monopolies. Nonetheless, the campaign failed to bring down prices and, in the short term, may have accomplished little more than the ubiquitous and spontaneous demonstrations in front of stores to protest the meat monopoly, or the attacks on train stations and transit lines to roll back a fare hike.

But in 1913 the FORJ did more than simply initiate and implement a strategy of popular resistance. By harnessing the collective protests that already permeated the city, the working-class leadership had adopted, as its own, the preexistent political culture of the masses, reformulating its tactics, merging the spontaneous street tactics with those of the organized labor movement. The ongoing ferment in working-class neighborhoods had raised to the foreground a set of demands and issues that needed to be addressed by working-class leaders. As a result of this agitation, by 1913 the FORJ had placed the issues of the popular crowds on par with its demands for higher pay and better working conditions, and it is doubtful they would have done so apart from the pressure of the riots. In that regard, the success of the FORJ's agitation against high prices, over the long term, lay in the groundwork it established for the intervention of working-class leadership in the popular protest movement. A case in point: the 1913 Campaign Against the High Cost of Living was a valuable learning experience *for both* the masses and the labor movement leadership, which, unbeknownst to most everyone, had begun to lay the foundation for the general strike and worker uprising four years later.

During the Old Republic street violence became a viable method for expressing discontent and, given the insensitivity of the Republican elite, produced nearly the same results as orderly petitioning, peaceful marches, and respectful letters to the editor. Moreover, while protesters sought redress of their grievances from municipal and federal authorities, from private utility and transportation companies, or from manufactures and entrepreneurs, actually their meetings, demonstrations, and riots informed a wider audience. They brought the urban poor's grievances to the attention of everyone in the city, many of whom were in the same situation as the protesters. It was only as a result of continual disorders in the *subúrbios* that established organs such as the *Jornal do Brasil* began to report to its readership the misery in which the city's poor lived. At the same time, protests in one part of Rio served to educate those similarly afflicted in another area. When news of a protest in Campos reached people in Rio das Pedras, for example (and word of these upheavals traveled), the latter recognized that they suffered under the same conditions and were often inspired to take up similar action. In a geographically dispersed society, where communities were cut off one from another by distance and by inadequate or nonexistent communication and transportation networks, and where poor and illiterate workers passed long hours in small, noisy mills and factories, protests served as the vehicle through which large numbers of Rio's residents learned that they shared grievances with thousands of others around them.

Mass demonstrations—the only mechanism of resistance available to the disenfranchised and isolated urban poor—were the means by which the popular classes developed their political consciousness. The organized, albeit sporadic, intervention of working-class groups such as the Centro das Classes Operarias and the FORJ was invaluable in driving home the lesson to the ordinary resident of the city that protests were legitimate forms of expression, that the working poor were justified in voicing their discontent with the established order, and that much could be gained by uniting these disparate grievances under the umbrella of collective actions. In 1917 they stood on the precipice, closest to the edge of understanding just how formidable a power that was.

The events of 1917 linked the consumers' struggles against high prices and poor living conditions to the call for trade union recognition and higher wages. It was under this banner that the FORJ called the May Day rally, as a result of this platform that the subsequent general strike broke out, and from this ripple that the wave of trade union militancy swept the late teens. In retrospect, however, it seems that the anarcho-syndicalists adapted their program to meet the demands raised in the street disorders but that their motivation was more pragmatic than ideological. For instance, despite continual price increases and worsening living conditions for the working class and urban poor in the 1920s, labor militants and political organizers focused their attention on the trade unions and lost themselves in bitter arguments over competing political ideologies. Combined with the constant repression the state unhesitatingly served out to the Communists, socialists, and unaffiliated Left, the economic crises of the twenties undercut labor's programs and the socialist cause.[3]

On the surface what is striking about the twenties is the trade union leadership's inattention to complaints over living conditions and price rises. Instead, the working-class leaders, whose organizations were indeed ripped with repression, remained embroiled in political intrigue and abortive revolts. Rather than working-class political power, the 1920s foreshadowed the rise of Brazil's most important populist leader, Getúlio Vargas. When Vargas came to power in October 1930, he ushered in a period of personalist, populist rule unequaled in Brazilian history. In his discussion of Vargas's success,

3. John W. F. Dulles, *Anarchists and Communists in Brazil, 1900–1935* (Austin: University of Texas Press, 1973), 176–275; Boris Fausto, *Trabalho urbano e conflito social* (São Paulo: DIFEL, 1976), chap. 7. For a discussion of the importance of the urban protests to the general strike in 1917, see James M. Malloy, "Social Security Policy and the Working Class in Twentieth-Century Brazil," *Journal of Interamerican Studies and World Affairs* 19, no. 1 (1977): 35–60.

Michael Conniff shows how the populist leader effectively managed modern urban politics and the modern crowd to the extent that his persona dominated the political scene through his various and intermittent administrations from 1930 until his suicide in 1954. He enacted, or promised to enact, the reforms urban consumers had been demanding for years: construction of the long-delayed workers' housing, even if inadequate for the need; improved medical care; and social legislation, albeit on a limited scale, the Republicans had been debating for years.[4]

Populist ideology therefore took hold among a people discontent with "the elitist, unrepresentative government instituted under the First Republic."[5] Although Vargas eventually turned against the principles and the rhetoric that had won him such popularity in 1930—promises to improve the lives of the urban poor—he initially addressed the broad range of consumer demands the Republican elite had failed to meet. That is his legacy. In Rio de Janeiro today pilgrims continue to leave their requests for better living conditions, complaints against landlords and employers, as well as bouquets and gifts, at the foot of Vargas's statue in downtown Rio. Clearly, there are those among the ordinary people who remain under the impression that "Getúlio" cared about them, that he was genuinely concerned with their problems, and that, if they could only reach him, he would help them. Whether he actually cared is a subject beyond this study.[6]

But this analysis of crowd behavior, of the issues and slogans the Rio masses raised in the opening decades of the century, reveals much more than a simple tally of what was won and what was lost in either the short or the long term. As Rudé emphasized, a riot peels back the cover and leaves exposed the traditions, contradictions, and tensions prevalent in the society in which it occurs. The Rebecca riots, the Captain Swing group, London's Gordon riots, and "Church and King," all of which Rudé and Hobsbawm describe in such fascinating detail, go a long way toward explaining the tran-

4. Michael Conniff, *Urban Politics in Brazil: The Rise of Populism, 1925–1945* (Pittsburgh: University of Pittsburgh Press, 1981), 14–15. Getúlio Vargas served first as provisional president of a constitutional government (1930–37), next as dictator under the Estado Novo (New State, 1937–45), and finally as an elected president (1951–54); Thomas E. Skidmore, *Politics in Brazil, 1930–1964: An Experiment in Democracy* (New York: Oxford University Press, 1967).

5. Conniff, *Urban Politics in Brazil*, 14.

6. Skidmore's *Politics in Brazil* remains the most complete study of the politics of the Vargas era. See also Joel Wolfe, "'Father of the Poor' or 'Mother of the Rich'? Getulio Vargas, Industrial Workers, and Constructions of Class, Gender, and Populism in São Paulo, 1930–1954," *Radical History Review* 58 (Winter 1994): 88–111, for a discussion of the messages workers sent to Vargas and the way in which they interpreted the leader's responses, or lack thereof.

sitional character of eighteenth- and early-nineteenth-century English society, toward telling us how the old order was changing and what was at stake,
and for whom, in those changes.[7] Similarly, Roderick Barman's account of
the Quebra-Quilo revolt in late 1874 disputed the view that Brazil lacked a
peasantry and a system of rural traditions. In Rio de Janeiro, the antivaccination riot, similar to the Quebra-Quilo riot, signaled the masses' resistance to
the changes their society was undergoing. Just as Pernambuco's peasants
invaded the backlands marketplaces and smashed the metric scales as a way
of opposing the Empire's taxation and record-keeping policies, so too Rio's
urban masses exploded over one aspect of the public health project—smallpox vaccination—as a way of resisting the far-reaching grasp of the urban
renewal plan, which would soon leave them homeless.[8]

An analysis of the popular protests of the Old Republic, and of the causes
that precipitated them, reveals the way Rio de Janeiro developed—that its
geographic sprawl and separation of richer, well-serviced areas from poorer,
neglected ones was not accidental. Ultimately this bit of information matters
more than whether a particular riot was a success or failure for its participants, since through this analysis we see the history of urban growth. Rio
developed as a city in which the sprawling neighborhoods of the urban poor,
as well as the *informal* economy those neighborhoods generated, existed in
close relationship with the *formal* economy, the state, and its culture but only
experienced that formal sector as brutal and abusive.

The majority of Rio's residents lived to toil and die in the workplace, to
move morning and night in an undulating mass from rickety shacks on
muddy streets to dirty, slow, and costly trains and trolleys; they fell victim to
the epidemics, to tuberculosis and dysentery, and tried to make a living in
whatever way they could in an economy that held out little hope for a stable
job and secure future. They were not, and were not to be, educated, sanitized,
cultivated, Europeanized, and civilized, as was formal, official, international
Rio de Janeiro, the capital of an emerging great nation. Nonetheless, the
working poor were elements of the same system comprising the bankers,
transit authorities, entrepreneurs, and government officials: they were all
members, in their own specific urban spaces, of a dependent city, of a depen-

7. Eric Hobsbawm and George Rudé, *Captain Swing* (New York: W. W. Norton, 1968), 15.
8. Roderick J. Barman, "The Brazilian Peasantry Re-examined: The Implications of the
Quebra-Quilo Revolt, 1874–1875," *Hispanic American Historical Review* 57, no. 3 (1977): 404.
For an analysis of a wide number of issues that congealed in the class struggle inherent in the
Contestado Rebellion, see Todd A. Diacon, *Millenarian Vision, Capitalist Reality: Brazil's Con-
testado Rebellion, 1912–1916* (Durham, N.C.: Duke University Press, 1991).

dent state, of a dependent economy. It was a situation, or an "ecological form," as Manuel Castells notes, in which every resident's dependency upon the political system and that system's place within the world market was at the very core of his or her social condition.[9]

Rio's poor, and even not-so-poor, never accepted passively their social condition. In the riot against vaccination and the Yellow Fever Campaign in 1904, and in the continuing string of protests over living and working conditions and transportation costs and services in the decades that followed, Rio's residents voiced their disagreements with the state's formal economic, political, and cultural priorities, at least with regard to the distribution of city services and the living space to which they were relegated. To understand those disagreements, to peel back the cover on the combat, so to speak, is to understand the workings of the class struggle, not just at the point of production, where it has usually been analyzed, but also in the neighborhood, in the community, and on the train to work. If the fight over the allocation of urban space has been integral, not tangential, to the class struggle, then this analysis of the way that space got parceled out deepens our conception of the war between labor and management, as well as broadens the arena in which we examine the individual battles.[10]

In this light, one could not say that "there is scant evidence of labor activities reflecting a militancy born from an awareness of common class interests that were opposed to the interests of the bourgeoisie,"[11] nor could one argue that the Brazilian lower classes have been "surprisingly passive, resigned and tolerant."[12] Recently, Ruth Berins Collier and David Collier have resurrected the argument of labor's passivity, blaming it on the far-reaching tentacles of the interventionist Latin American state. In a highly sophisticated and exhaustive study the Colliers have attempted to show that the state in

9. Manuel Castells, *The City and the Grassroots: A Cross-Cultural Theory of Urban Social Movements* (Berkeley and Los Angeles: University of California Press, 1983), 212.

10. Ira Katznelson, *City Trenches: Urban Politics and the Patterning of Class in the United States* (Chicago: University of Chicago Press, 1981), 203.

11. Eileen Keremitsis, "The Early Industrial Worker in Rio de Janeiro, 1870–1930" (Ph.D. diss., Columbia University, 1982), 184.

12. Charles Wagley, *An Introduction to Brazil* (New York: Columbia University Press, 1963), 133. See also James L. Busey, "Brazil's Reputation for Political Stability," in *A Century of Brazilian History Since 1865*, ed. Richard Graham (New York: Alfred A. Knopf, 1969), 199–213; José Honório Rodrigues, *Conciliação e reforma* (Rio de Janeiro: Civilização Brasileira, 1965). In "Oswaldo Cruz and the Impact of Yellow Fever," *Bulletin of Tulane University Medical Faculty* 26 (February 1967): 51, Donald Cooper remarks that the antivaccination riot occurred in a nation "that historically has escaped the tradition of violence that has characterized many Latin American countries."

Latin America has effectively intervened to redirect the feeble appearances of worker solidarity toward state-sponsored patronage.[13]

There are two reasons why this analysis of quiescence has prevailed and why labor's tradition of resistance has remained so ignored in Brazilian history. The first has to do with the fact that popular protests have been seen as premodern, or prepolitical, protests, and thereby of less importance than modern strikes and job actions. The second has to do with the notion that since work relations constitute the essential core of society, the economic and political struggle at the level of work has had a tangible effect on the balance of power, whereas the struggle at the level of the community has been seen to have had little effect on the basic economic relationship between labor and capital or has been considered of less importance simply because it is difficult to judge how the outcome of a community struggle has essentially altered the power relationship.[14] Both of these points need to be considered separately in order to understand the theoretical implications of Brazil's protest movements and the role of protest movements in determining the built form of Rio de Janeiro.

In many historical accounts street protests, consumer riots, and cost-of-living demonstrations have been considered premodern, or prepolitical, protests, whose effectiveness has been of shorter or longer duration but whose existence *as a form of protest* has been historically short-lived. Rudé comments that just as "the sans-culotte, small freeholder, and cottager have given way to the factory worker and farm laborer, so the machine wrecker, rick burner, and 'Church and King' rioter have given way to the trade unionist, labor militant, and organized consumer of the new industrial society."[15] Charles Tilly notes that premodern protest was local in scope, motivated by a popular resistance to the demands of a central authority, and sometimes backward looking: for example, food riots, tax rebellions, and machine-breaking sprees. In France, he argues, this earlier premodern protest even-

13. Ruth Berins Collier and David Collier, *Shaping the Political Arena: Critical Junctures, the Labor Movement, and Regime Dynamics in Latin America* (Princeton: Princeton University Press, 1991). For an interesting critique of Berins Collier and Collier based on a summary of working-class movements in three Latin American countries, see Jeremy Adelman, "Latin American Labour at the Crossroads: State and Labour in Argentina, Brazil, and Mexico, 1916–1922" (unpublished paper in author's possession).

14. Katznelson argued in *City Trenches* that protests at work and those in residence communities were viewed as separate because the former involved the base and the latter the superstructure. Moreover, Katznelson (203) asserted that there was no reason for this differentiation, which necessarily lent priority to struggle at the base over struggle for the superstructure. Katznelson, in his later *Marxism and the City* (Oxford: Oxford University Press, 1993), no longer stresses this point.

15. Rudé, *The Crowd in History*, 268.

tually gave way to collective violence that was "highly organized, more regularly based on associations, more in pursuit or defense of a political program. It was modern." [16] The discourse on modernity aside, these comments implicitly assume that in the modern industrial society trade unions, or some form of organized groupings, have replaced the disorganized crowds, and that modern protest, if not preferable, has been at least more effective in bringing about real social change in the modern era. Supposedly, the effect of the strike is tangible; that of the local, community protest is not.

There are two problems here. It is unclear that in a developed industrial society, such as Rio's, protests, fitting the description of these so-called premodern collective actions (food riots, rent strikes, machine-breaking sprees, local neighborhood-based riots), have disappeared in the face of expanded capitalist relations of production and consumption. In fact, in Rio, as in similar cities in similar societies, rioting and street disorders continued during the First Republic just as advanced capitalist relations of production—characterized by a fragile labor market and unstable employment opportunities—were taking root. In Rio, contention between management and worker, between government and citizen, between elite and poor, did not simply spill over the factory gates into the community; it erupted from the neighborhood, from the street, just as readily as it did from the shop floor, because the whole interdependent matrix (neighborhood as well as factory) was an arena of struggle. And it stayed there.

So long as neither Rio nor Brazil moved out of the dependent social relationship (export-oriented economy beholden to international capital at every step), then neither did the arena from which resistance to that domination was launched. Contrary to the form Rudé indicates protests assumed in the emerging capitalist societies of England and France, resistance to the new order in Brazil did not follow an orderly route from food riots and machine breaking to demonstrations by organized consumers and trade unionists. A portion of laborers did indeed form unions, went on strike, and adopted "modern" forms of protest, but the huge size of Rio's marginal and unstable workforce forced modern and so-called premodern protests to erupt in tandem, to fuse into one form of resistance that broke out as readily on the shop floor as in front of the local meat market.[17]

On closer scrutiny it is apparent that the very terms "premodern," "prein-

16. Charles Tilly, "The Changing Place of Collective Violence," in *Workers in the Industrial Revolution,* ed. Peter N. Stearns and Daniel J. Walkowitz (New Brunswick, N.J.: Transaction Books, 1974), 133.
17. When Castells states that "urban marginality can be defined as the inability of the market economy, or of state policies, to provide adequate shelter and urban services to an increasing

dustrial," and "prepolitical" are shallow descriptive categories at best, certainly not rigorous concepts corresponding to the forms of resistance in precapitalist and capitalist societies, as they have been used.[18] What does one call the riots that have broken out in the most advanced capitalist societies in those enclaves where people have not been incorporated into the stable economic and political relationships of the dominant society, where labor is casual, where the line between stable, "respectable" employment and the underworld of vice and corruption is continually crossed? These urban communities have emerged as the pockets of resistance where essentially modern collective action has assumed the form of, or has borne a similarity to, premodern protests of centuries earlier.

In the Brixton section of London, or Liberty City, Miami, in Watts, Newark, and Detroit, and most recently south-central Los Angeles, significant numbers of poor and working people—for reasons of discrimination; lack of education, skill, and opportunity; the devastations of alcohol and drug use; or the fluctuations in a declining industrial economy—have never been incorporated into the stable workforce and have despaired of ever being called into it. In those cases, as in Rio de Janeiro early in this century, the only mechanism of resistance that has offered itself has been the community protest. Those protests, in south-central Los Angeles in 1992, just as in Rio de Janeiro in 1917, or Paris in the 1840s, or all over the East and South of England in 1830, have always erupted when the formal, official society refused to meet basic human demands, when the prices on essential goods climbed too high and no manner of polite complaint brought relief, when the train was too slow, when there was no decent school in miles, when the chances for viable employment proved nonexistent year after year, when the police entered a neighborhood only to quell a riot, when parents watched children die from preventable diseases, when people lay awake nights listening to gunshots, or when their voice at the ballot box went unheard. An event trig-

---

proportion of city dwellers," he accounts for the expansion of the marginalized sector as modern, industrial capitalism consolidated. It is, especially in Latin America but elsewhere as well, a key aspect of the very relations of capitalist development; and it is growing. Rather than a simple feature of the transition to capitalism, it is basic to the form. Castells, *City and the Grassroots*, chaps. 18 and 19.

18. Too often paradigms developed to explain advanced capitalist societies have been uncritically applied to the Third World, or non-European societies, especially theories of capitalist development and Marxist revolution. My criticism of the theory of premodern protests as developed primarily by the European and U.S. historians thus contributes, if only in a small way, to the rectification of that paradigm, since, when one attempts to describe premodern protest in Latin America, the inadequacy of the concept as it has been used to explain protests in European and U.S. society becomes glaringly apparent.

gered a riot—a late train, a fare hike, a vaccination law, a verdict—and the resultant melee has maintained the same pattern for centuries. These are not premodern protests; they are as integral a part of the capitalist system as is the urban structure that has spawned them and the official intractability that has ignored the misery of the poor.[19]

But the second issue raised in this false dichotomy between premodern and modern protest is the implication that modern protest has been more effective because it represents an attack on capitalism at the point of production, where work and capital have been consolidated. Accordingly, the undifferentiated protests at the level of the community, those which arise from the day-to-day oppressive life of the street or from the ever-present grievances that simply explode into confrontations from time to time, are considered of far less importance and only tangential to the class struggle. This narrow conception of the class struggle derives first from an economic and reductionist definition of working class—that it is somehow only defined by an individual's relationship to work or, even more narrowly, by the individual as a producer of surplus value.[20] By arguing that class must be understood on four levels, Katznelson explodes the restrictions entailed by this view and, in so doing, broadens the base from which the class struggle—collective action in this case—can be interpreted. He notes that although class is primarily that relationship elaborated on the basic level of production, it is also the way people live actual lives, including the features of life "at work and off work."

19. Grounded in the dispute over the distribution of the fruits of labor, for which both owners and laborers perpetually contend, urban protest movements have actually proliferated in the modern era as urban centers have grown. In that regard, urban protests, many of which assume forms similar to protests in the early and precapitalist era, have become an increasingly common phenomenon in the gigantic urban centers of Latin America. To label a protest "premodern" because it looks like something from an earlier era but has really emerged as an effect of the structural properties of advanced capitalism only compounds the error. For a discussion of social movements in Latin American cities, see David Slater, *New Social Movements and the State in Latin America* (Cinnamininson, N.J.: Foris Publications, 1985).

20. The main proponent of the distinction between productive and unproductive labor as the dividing line for the structural determination of the working class was Nicos Poulantzas. See esp. *Classes in Contemporary Capitalism* (London: New Left Books, 1976), 14–35. For a review of the criticisms of Poulantzas's argument, as well as a lucid explanation of what Poulantzas himself meant by productive/unproductive labor, see Andor D. Skotnes, "Structural Determination of the Proletariat and the Petty Bourgeoisie: A Critique of Nicos Poulantzas," *Insurgent Sociologist* 9, no. 1 (1979): 34–54, esp. n. 12; see also Katznelson, *Marxism and the City*, 260; Terry Johnson, "What Is to Be Known? The Structural Determination of Social Class," *Economy and Society* 6, no. 2 (1977): 218–27. For Marx's own discussion of the production of surplus value, which I do not think supports Poulantzas's narrow definition, see *Capital: A Critical Analysis of Capitalist Production*, vol. 1, ed. Frederick Engels (New York: International Publishers, 1967), chap. 16.

Third, it exists at the level of "cognitive and linguistic dispositions," or the way people interpret and represent their life experiences; and finally, at the level of collective action, or the way a class moves to pursue its common objectives.[21]

The outcome of any "class-based action," therefore, from community-based protest to factory-based strike, differs according to which aspect of class identity predominates and what issues have most directly come into contention in a specific historical time and place. During the First Republic in Rio, the labor market on the one hand was joined by the housing market on the other as the two fundamental elements of working-class life and identity—work and community—which, in turn, elaborated the two basic components of the class struggle. People lived in a society that was based not simply on buying and selling their labor but also on governing and distributing land, housing, labor, and capital.[22] As a consequence, the fight over housing, prices, and transportation was not peripheral to the battle between capital and labor over the work process, wages, and hours; rather, these forms were linked and complemented each other, contributed to the very definition of class, and, as a combined entity, have provided a picture of the full range of class-conscious activity in Rio's early-twentieth-century history.[23]

Furthermore, in the two basic arenas, work and community, it bears remembering that job actions may or may not have resulted in better wages, working conditions, and union recognition, while community protests may or may not have resulted in better housing, transportation, health care, and a visible change in the "built form of the city." But following any form of collective action there was an outcome, and it was measurable. Just as the working class of Rio de Janeiro contended for its own space and for its own livelihood in community protests, so too the existence of the highly differentiated neighborhoods separating rich from poor, middle class from working class, business from residence, provides proof of the results of hundreds of urban protests involving thousands of the city's residents.

If, as I have argued here, the definition and conception of working-class collective action is expanded, and if that expanded definition contains, under the rubric of the class struggle, those battles in the community along with

21. Katznelson, *Marxism and the City*, 208–9.

22. Ibid., 230.

23. I do see struggle at the point of production as central and ultimately determinant, but not *always* determinant. But what this analysis does is to provide the "linkage between the economic system and the social and spatial specificity of the structuring of working-class lives." Katznelson, *Marxism and the City*, 230.

those in the workplace, then the picture of working-class protesters likewise changes. Who were, in fact, the key players in the formation of classes and class consciousness in Rio de Janeiro? On the one hand, the community protests drew participants from a group far broader than the industrial working class and involved as well wide swatches of the marginally employed urban poor and the unemployed. In addition to European immigrants and their descendants, who predominated in trade union activities, community protesters included women, children, recent migrants from the rural plantations, and others who were neither steadily employed nor prone to join unions. Looking back over the decades of protest during the First Republic, the culprits reported over and over in police accounts were residents of the *cortiços*, riders on the trains, shoppers at the markets, as well as laborers. The accounts of the disturbances both in the bourgeois and labor press, in the police reports, and in government records support the conclusion that the rallies and marches included a cross section of the urban population— men, women, children; immigrant, black, white, and mulatto Brazilians.

Because women were known to have participated in the demonstrations against high prices, shortages, and the monopolies, as well as in the anti-vaccination revolt in 1904, the cost of living rallies in 1913, and the general strike in 1917, their role as agents of social change on a local level needs to be underscored, rather than ignored, as has too often happened. Moreover, rather than simply searching the archives for evidence of women's participation in a narrowly defined trade union movement, expanding the whole arena of the class struggle allows for the inclusion of women as crucial actors on the historical stage in those areas that most concerned them, and avoids the tokenism that necessarily results from attempts to hammer the very few female participants into significant roles in the labor movement, if they were not there. In sum, although at no time did the social movements in Rio's early history ever hold gender relationships at the core of the conflict, the very broadening of the conception of class analysis outlined above does foreground gender as an issue in Rio's class conflict by enhancing the particular contribution of women.[24]

24. My observation here is based on reading the evidence, but it stands, as well, as a minor intervention in the dispute between Joel Wolfe and John French regarding the role of women, and community organizations in general, in the 1917 São Paulo general strike. In their argument both Wolfe and French are trapped in a narrow definition of working-class organizing: Wolfe finds women, as opposed to the anarchists, in factory commissions serving as the vanguard of the 1917 strike, whereas French upholds the role of the anarchists (male) as the primary organizers both in the community and on the shop floor. Neither one, however, links the female role in community organizations with the male- or female-led shop-floor rebellions. Both men and

Over the years a number of historians have argued that Latin American labor history needs to take greater account of the relationship of local struggles to the place of labor in the development of the world economy.[25] They are right. But such a task requires more than connecting the conventional struggle of the working class and the trade union movement to the mechanisms of the export sector or the demands of foreign capital on the labor process. Likewise the task involves more than just appraising the considerable resources multinational corporations have used to diffuse and repress the Latin American labor movement.[26] Operating from a restricted definition of the class struggle and finding always the Latin American urban proletariat lacking, social scientists have advanced many reasons to explain this acquiescence, including state repression, the rise of a powerful labor aristocracy linked to multinational capital, the co-optation of the workforce by charismatic corporatist/populist leaders, low levels of skill, oversupply of labor, high and low levels of technology, and primitive political consciousness fed by widespread illiteracy and poverty.[27] It seems appropriate to abandon the assumption that the Brazilian labor movement has demonstrated little militancy. Quite the contrary, when judged at the level of the shop floor *and* the broader community during the Old Republic, the record is one of impressive resistance and constant turbulence.

Edward Thompson, George Rudé, Eric Hobsbawm, and the first wave of Marxist labor historians sought to recover the lost history of the European peasantry and working class, or, as Thompson stated it, "to rescue the

women, in the factory and in the community, were codependent agents in the formation of working-class consciousness. Joel Wolfe, "Anarchist Ideology, Worker Practice: The 1917 General Strike and the Formation of São Paulo's Working Class," *Hispanic American Historical Review* 71, no. 1 (1991): 809–46; idem, "Response to John French," ibid., 856–58; John French, "Practice and Ideology: A Cautionary Note on the Historian's Craft," ibid., 847–55. For a more theoretically sound solution to the problems raised in the Wolfe-French debate, see Castells, *City and the Grassroots,* 268, 335.

25. See, e.g., Charles Bergquist, "Labor History and Its Challenges: Confessions of a Latin Americanist," *American Historical Review* 98, no. 3 (1993): 757–62; Emilia Viotti da Costa, "Experience Versus Structures: New Tendencies in the History of Labor and the Working Class in Latin America—What Do We Gain? What Do We Lose?" *International Labor and Working Class History* 36 (Fall 1989): 3–24; and responses to this article in the same issue: Barbara Weinstein, "The New Latin American Labor History: What We Gain," 25–30; Perry Anderson, "The Common and the Particular," 31–36; Hobart A. Spalding, "Somethings Old and Somethings New," 37–43; June Nash, "Gender Issues in Latin American Labor," 44–50.

26. Bergquist, "Labor History and Its Challenges," 762–63. See also Jeremy Adelman's critique, "Against Essentialism: Latin American Labour History in Comparative Perspective: A Critique of Bergquist," *Labour/Le Travail* 27 (Spring 1991): 175–84.

27. Berins Collier and Collier, *Shaping the Political Arena,*

poor stockinger, the Luddite cropper, the 'obsolete' hand-loom weaver, the 'utopian' artisan, and even the deluded follower of Joanna Southcott, from the enormous condescension of posterity."[28] These eloquent historians opened up to us the stories of the valiant resistance of thousands of common people against the onslaught of capitalist regulation and regimentation. They showed us the logic in seemingly illogical uprisings, the ideals behind fantastic schemes, and the pain in the lost causes. Those first inspirational labor histories have been succeeded by generations of monographs, articles, papers, and conferences recounting the militant actions of various working classes in small towns, in individual factories, and in combined industries. Less well studied and in need of more are the forms of resistance in the working-class communities far from the metropolitan centers of capitalist development. In addition to those well-chronicled opponents of the ruthless sweep of industrial capitalism in Europe and the United States, millions of others in Rio de Janeiro and throughout the world have resisted in similar fashion and with similar logic what the spread of the market economy and ultimately capitalism's own brand of "civilization" meant for them. Alongside the rick burner of Rudé's English countryside stands the kerosene courier of Rio de Janeiro, just as alongside Thompson's Luddite stands the antivaccination rioter.

Although rescuing the history of unknown collective actions and seemingly illogical riots, along with the nameless historical actors themselves, from obscurity, or the "condescension of posterity," is in itself a worthy task, that has not been my primary concern. I have instead tried to understand the importance of a group of seemingly unconnected collective actions in determining the particular configuration of capitalist development in one city, Rio de Janeiro. Far more study is needed in order to understand fully how the city developed, who developed it, where people worked, how well they lived, and how they explained their lives. However, it is only within a broader world context that the individual actions of a few people in Rio de Janeiro make sense, since it is only, ultimately, on the level of the world system that the development of any major city can be understood.

Lewis Pyenson's observation, that even well-meaning doctors of tropical medicine or railway engineers, who in no way saw themselves as agents of imperialism, carried out an activity whose ultimate goal was to ensure that

---

28. Edward Thompson, *The Making of the English Working Class* (New York: Random House, 1966), 12. I agree with Joan Wallach Scott's criticism that Thompson too easily dismisses South-cott's followers as "deluded"; see "Women in the *Making of the English Working Class*," in *Gender and the Politics of History* (New York: Columbia University Press, 1988), 74.

peripheral territory was secure for metropolitan investment, can as well be turned on its head.[29] Those who rioted against the vaccination plan and the urban renewal project; those who protested the lack of water, the dirty streets, the trains that never came, and the fares that always went up; those who denounced a government that relegated most of its citizens to the worst sections of the city, where they retreated "after a day of badly paid labor,"[30] and reserved for the elite, for foreign visitors, merchants, and investors, the center of the city as a showcase of European civilization—all those nameless people may have in no way seen themselves as resisting imperialism's plan for the built form of their city, but that was their ultimate task. They protested that powerful force with all that they had, but that was really only themselves.

29. Lewis Pyenson, "The Limits of Scientific Condominium: Geophysics in Western Samoa, 1914–1940," in *Scientific Colonialism: A Cross-Cultural Comparison,* ed. Nathan Reingold and Marc Rothenberg (Washington, D.C.: Smithsonian Institution Press, 1987), 251.
30. *Novo Rumo,* July 20, 1906, 1.

Bibliography

I. Archives

Arquivo da Fundação Getúlio Vargas, Rio de Janeiro.
Arquivo de Patrimonio Histórico e Artístico do Estado do Rio de Janeiro.
Arquivo do Instituto Histórico e Geográfico Brasileiro, Rio de Janeiro.
Arquivo Edgard Leuenroth da Universidade Estadual de Campinas, Campinas, São Paulo.
Arquivo Nacional, Rio de Janeiro.
Biblioteca Nacional do Rio de Janeiro.
Library of Congress, Washington, D.C.
National Archives, Washington, D.C.
New York Public Library, New York.
Wellcome Institute for the History of Medicine, London.

II. Public Documents

Backheuser, Evarardo. "Habitações Populares." In *Relatório apresentado ao Dr. J. J. Seabra, Ministro da Justiça e Negocios Interiores*. Rio de Janeiro: Imprensa Nacional, 1906.
Brazil. Directoria da Justiça. Article 80. Rio de Janeiro: Imprensa Nacional, 1891.
———. Directoria do Interior. "O Abándono Material." Pt. 1 of *Relatórios apresentado ao Ministro da Justiça pela Commissão Inspectora dos estabelecimentos de alienados, públicos e particulares, no Districto Federal, e pelos membros das respectivas Commissões Inspectoras nos Estados de Minas Geraes e Rio Grande do Sul*. Rio de Janeiro: Imprensa Nacional, 1905.
———. Directoria do Interior. "O Abándono Moral." Pt. 2 of *Relatórios apresentado ao Ministro da Justiça pela Commissão Inspectora dos estabelecimentos de alienados, públicos e particulares, no Districto Federal, e pelos membros das respectivas Commissões Inspectoras nos Estados de Minas Geraes e Rio Grande do Sul*. Rio de Janeiro: Imprensa Nacional, 1905.

———. Directoria do Interior. *Relatório apresentado ao Presidente da República dos Estados Unidos do Brasil pelo Ministro da Justiça e Negocios Interiores, Dr. Alfredo Pinto Vieira de Mello.* Rio de Janeiro: Imprensa Nacional, 1921.

———. Directoria do Interior. *Relatório apresentado ao Presidente da República dos Estados Unidos do Brasil pelo Ministro de Estado da Justiça e Negocios Interiores, Dr. Rivadavia da Cunha Correa.* Rio de Janeiro: Imprensa Nacional, 1911.

———. Directoria Geral de Estatística. *Apuração das Cadernetas Empregadas no Recenseamento Geral da República dos Estados Unidos do Brazil en 31 de Dezembro de 1890, Districto Federal.* Rio de Janeiro: Imprensa Nacional, 1895.

———. Directoria Geral de Estatística. *Recenseamento do Brazil Frealisado em 1 de Stetembro de 1920, População do Rio de Janeiro (Districto Federal).* Vol. 2. Rio de Janeiro: Imprensa Nacional, 1923.

———. Directoria Geral de Estatística. *Recenseamento do População do Imperio do Brazil a que se Procedeu no Dia 1 de Agosto de 1872.* Rio de Janeiro: Imprensa Nacional, 1873–76.

———. Directoria Geral de Estatística. *Recenseamento do Rio de Janeiro Realisado em 20 de Setembro de 1906. Rio de Janeiro: Imprensa Nacional, 1907.*

———. Directoria Geral de Estatística. *Recenseamento Geral da República dos Estados Unidos do Brazil em 31 de Dezembro de 1890, Districto Federal.* Rio de Janeiro: Imprensa Nacional, 1895.

———. Directoria Geral de Saúde Pública. *Os serviços de saúde pública no Brazil.* 2 vols. Rio de Janeiro: Imprensa Nacional, 1904.

———. Directoria Geral de Saúde Pública. *Relatório apresentado ao Dr. Cruz pelo Delegado Alvaro Graça. 9 Districto Sanitário.* Vol. 5. Rio de Janeiro: Imprensa Nacional, 1907.

———. Directoria Geral de Saúde Pública. *Relatório apresentado ao Dr. Cruz pelo Theophilo Torres, Inspector Geral Districto 8 Sanitário.* Vol. 5, app. 10. Rio de Janeiro: Imprensa Nacional, 1906.

———. Directoria Geral de Saúde Pública. *Relatório apresentado ao J. J. Seabra, Ministro da Justiça pelo Director Geral de Saúde Pública, Annexos ao Relatório do Director Geral de Saúde Pública. Rio de Janeiro: Imprensa Nacional, 1904.*

———. Directoria Geral de Saúde Pública. *Relatório apresentado ao Presidente de República dos Estados Unidos do Brasil pelo Sr. Sabino Barrosa Junior, Ministro da Justiça e Negocios Interiores.* Rio de Janeiro: Imprensa Nacional, 1902.

———. Directoria Geral de Saúde Pública. Placido Barbosa e Cassio Barbosa de Rezende. *Os serviços de saúde pública no Brasil especialmente na cidade do Rio de Janeiro de 1808 a 1907.* 2 vols. Rio de Janeiro: Imprensa Nacional, 1909.

———. Directoria Sanitária da Capital Federal. *Exposição apresentada ao Generalissimo Chefe do Governo Provisorio dos Estados Unidos do Brazil pelo Dr. José Cesario de Faria Alvim, Ministro e Secretário de Estado dos Negocios do Interior.* Rio de Janeiro: Imprensa Nacional, 1890.

———. Directoria Sanitária da Capital Federal. *Relatório ao Presidente da República pelo Dr. Amaro Cavalcanti, Ministro dos Negocios Interiores.* Rio de Janeiro: Imprensa Nacional, 1897.

———. Directoria Sanitária da Capital Federal. *Relatório ao Presidente da República pelo Dr. Antonio Gonçalves Ferreira, Ministro dos Negocios Interiores.* Rio de Janeiro: Imprensa Nacional, 1896.

———. Directoria Sanitária da Capital Federal. *Relatório apresentado ao Ministro dos Negocios Interiores de Agostinho José de Souza Lima, Inspector Geral de Hygiene.* Rio de Janeiro: Imprensa Nacional, 1891.

———. Directoria Sanitária da Capital Federal. *Relatório do Encarregado do Serviço de Estatística Demografo-Sanitário.* Rio de Janeiro: Imprensa Nacional, 1893.

————. Directoria Sanitária da Capital Federal. *Relatório do Instituto Sanitário Federal ao Presidente da República.* Rio de Janeiro: Imprensa Nacional, 1895.

————. Junta Commercial. *Relatório apresentado ao Presidente da República pelo Dr. Antonio Gonçalves Ferreira, Ministro dos Negocios Interiores.* Rio de Janeiro: Imprensa Nacional, 1895.

————. Junta Commercial da Capital Federal. *Relatório apresentado ao Vice-Presidente da República pelo Dr. Fernando Lobo Leite Pereira, Ministro do Negocios Interiores.* Rio de Janeiro: Imprensa Nacional, 1892.

————. Ministerio da Justiça e Negocios Interiores. *Relatório ao Presidente da República pelo Dr. J. J. Seabra, Ministro da Justiça e Negocios Interiores.* 2 Vols. Rio de Janeiro: Imprensa Nacional, 1906.

————. Ministerio da Justiça e Negocios Interiores. *Relatório apresentado ao Ministro da Justiça e Negocios Interiores, Barão de Lucene, pelo Secretária da Policia da Capital Federal, Pedro Antonio de Oliveira Ribeiro.* Rio de Janeiro: Imprensa Nacional, 1891.

————. Ministerio da Justiça e Negocios Interiores. *Relatório apresentado ao Ministro da Justiça e Negocios Interiores pelo Dr. Epitacio Pessôa.* Rio de Janeiro: Imprensa Nacional, 1899.

————. Ministerio da Justiça e Negocios Interiores. *Relatório apresentado ao Presidente da República de Antonio Luiz Affonso Carvalho, Chefe da Policia da Capital Federal, Dezembro, 1890.* Rio de Janeiro: Imprensa Nacional, 1891.

————. Ministerio da Justiça e Negocios Interiores. *Relatório apresentado ao Presidente da República pelo Dr. Antonio Gonçalves Ferreira, Ministro da Justiça e Negocios Interiores.* Rio de Janeiro: Imprensa Nacional, 1895.

————. Ministerio da Justiça e Negocios Interiores. *Relatório apresentado ao Presidente da República pelo Dr. J. J. Seabra, Ministro da Justiça e Negocios Interiores.* Rio de Janeiro: Imprensa Nacional, 1905.

————. Ministerio da Justiça e Negocios Interiores. *Relatório 1921* (no author given). Rio de Janeiro: Imprensa Nacional, 1921.

————. Tratamento de variolosos. Decreto do Instituto Vaccinogenico, 1888–1906. Arquivo de Patrimonio Histórico e Artistico do Estado do Rio de Janeiro.

Estatutes da Companhia de Saneamento do Rio de Janeiro, 1888–1906. Arquivo de Patrimonio Histórico e Artistico do Estado do Rio de Janeiro.

Records of the Department of State Relating to the Internal Affairs of Brazil, 1910–29. National Archives, Washington, D.C.

III. Newspapers and Journals

Brazilian Business (American Chamber of Commerce for Brazil).
Clarté (Rio de Janeiro).
Correio da Manhã (Rio de Janeiro).
Estado de São Paulo (São Paulo).
Gazeta de Notícias (Rio de Janeiro).
O Graphico (Rio de Janeiro).
A Guerra Social (Rio de Janeiro).
Jornal do Brasil (Rio de Janeiro).
Jornal do Commércio (Rio de Janeiro).
Latin American Labor News (Miami).
A Noite (Rio de Janeiro).
Novo Rumo (Rio de Janeiro).

O Paiz (Rio de Janeiro).
A Razão (Rio de Janeiro).
A Vanguarda (Rio de Janeiro).
A Voz do Povo (Rio de Janeiro).
A Voz do Trabalhador (Rio de Janeiro).

IV. Books, Articles, and Unpublished Manuscripts

Adamo, Sam. "The Broken Promise: Race, Health, and Justice in Rio de Janeiro, 1890–1940." Ph.D. diss., University of New Mexico, 1983.
Adelman, Jeremy. "Against Essentialism: Latin American Labour History in Comparative Perspective: A Critique of Bergquist." *Labour/Le Travail* 27 (Spring 1991): 175–84.
———. "Latin American Labour at the Crossroads: State and Labour in Argentina, Brazil, and Mexico, 1916–1922." Unpublished paper in author's possession.
Albert, Bill. *South America and the First World War: The Impact of the War on Brazil, Argentina, Peru, and Chile.* Cambridge: Cambridge University Press, 1988.
Althusser, Louis. *Lenin and Philosophy and Other Essays.* New York: Monthly Review Press, 1971.
Amado, Jorge. *The Violent Land.* Translated by Samuel Putnam. New York: Alfred A. Knopf, 1945.
Anderson, Perry. "The Common and the Particular." *International Labor and Working Class History* 36 (Fall 1989): 31–36.
Andrews, George Reid. *The Afro-Argentines of Buenos Aires, 1800–1900.* Madison: University of Wisconsin Press, 1980.
———. *Blacks and Whites in São Paulo, Brazil, 1888–1988.* Madison: University of Wisconsin Press, 1991.
Arnold, B. In *Powers, Possessions, and Freedom: Essays in Honour of C. B. Macpherson,* edited by Alkis Kontos. Toronto: University of Toronto Press, 1979.
Azevedo, Aluizio. *A Brazilian Tenement.* Translated by Harry W. Brown. New York: Robert M. McBride, 1928.
Bandeira, Moniz, Clovis Melo, and A. T. Andrade. *O ano vermelho: A Revolução Russa e seus reflexos no Brasil.* Rio de Janeiro: Editora Civilização Brasileira, 1967.
Barbosa, Rui. *Obras completas de Rui Barbosa.* Rio de Janeiro: Ministério da Educação e Saúde, 1947.
———. "A Questão Social e Política no Brasil." In *Escritos e discursos selectos.* Rio de Janeiro: Editora José Aguilar, 1960.
Barman, Roderick J. "The Brazilian Peasantry Re-examined: The Implications of the Quebra-Quilo Revolt, 1874–1875." *Hispanic American Historical Review* 57, no.3 (1977): 401–24.
Bell, Alured Gray. *The Beautiful Rio de Janeiro.* London: William Heinemann, 1914.
Bello, José Maria. *A History of Modern Brazil, 1889–1964.* Translated by James L. Taylor. Stanford: Stanford University Press, 1966.
Benchimol, Jaime Larry. "Pereira Passos, um Haussmann tropical: As transformações urbanas na cidade do Rio de Janeiro no inicio do seculo XX." Master's thesis, Universidade Federal do Rio de Janeiro, 1982.
Bergquist, Charles. *Labor in Latin America: Comparative Essays on Chile, Argentina, Venezuela, and Colombia.* Stanford: Stanford University Press, 1986.
———. "Labor History and Its Challenges: Confessions of a Latin Americanist." *American Historical Review* 98, no. 3 (1993): 757–62.

Borges, Thomas Pompeu Accioly. "Relationships Between Economic Development, Industrialization, and the Growth of Urban Population in Brazil." In *Urbanization in Latin America,* edited by Philip M. Hauser. New York: International Documents Service, 1961.

Bresciani, Maria Stella M. *Londres e Paris no seculo XIX: O espetaculo da pobreza.* São Paulo: Editora Brasiliense, 1982.

Burns, E. Bradford. "Cultures in Conflict: The Implication of Modernization in Nineteenth-Century Latin America." In *Elites, Masses, and Modernization in Latin America, 1850–1930,* edited by Virginia Bernhard. Austin: University of Texas Press, 1979.

———. *A History of Brazil.* 2d ed. New York: Columbia University Press, 1980.

Busey, James L. "Brazil's Reputation for Political Stability." In *A Century of Brazilian History Since 1865,* edited by Richard Graham. New York: Alfred A. Knopf, 1969.

Butterworth, Douglas, and John K. Chance. *Latin American Urbanization.* New York: Cambridge University Press, 1981.

Cannadine, David. "The Context, Performance, and Meaning of Ritual: The British Monarchy and the 'Invention of Tradition,' c. 1820–1977." In *The Invention of Tradition,* edited by Eric Hobsbawm and Terence Ranger. Cambridge: Cambridge University Press, 1983.

Cardoso, Fernando Henrique. "The City in Politics." In *Urbanization in Latin America: Approaches and Issues,* edited by Jorge E. Hardoy. New York: Doubleday, 1975.

———. "Dos governos militares a Prudente—Campos Sales." In *Historia geral da civilização brasileira,* vol. 8, *O Brasil repúblicano: Estrutura de poder e economia, 1889–1930,* edited by Boris Fausto. São Paulo: Difusão Editorial, 1975.

Carone, Edgard. *A República Velha: Evolução politica.* São Paulo: DIFEL, 1964.

———. *A República Velha: Instituições e classes sociais.* São Paulo: DIFEL, 1975.

———. *Revoluções do Brasil contemporáneo, 1922–1938.* Rio de Janeiro: DIFEL, 1977.

Carvalho, José Murilo de. *Os bestializados: O Rio de Janeiro e a república que não foi.* São Paulo: Editora Schwarcz, 1987.

———. "Brazil, 1870–1914: The Force of Tradition." *Journal of Latin American Studies* 24 (Quincentenary Supplement, 1992): 145–62.

Castells, Manuel. *The City and the Grassroots: A Cross-Cultural Theory of Urban Social Movements.* Berkeley and Los Angeles: University of California Press, 1983.

———. *The Urban Question: A Marxist Approach.* Translated by Alan Sheridan. Cambridge, Mass.: MIT Press, 1977.

———. "Urban Social Movements and the Struggle for Democracy: The Citizens' Movement in Madrid." *International Journal of Urban and Regional Research* 2 (March 1978): 133–46.

Caulfield, Sueann. "In Defense of Honor: The Contested Meaning of Sexual Morality in Law and Courtship, Rio de Janeiro, 1920–1940." Ph.D. diss., New York University, 1994.

Chalhoub, Sidney. "Medo branco de almas negras: Escravos, libertos e republicanos na cidade do Rio." *Revista Brasileira de Historia* 8, no. 16 (1988): 83–105.

———. "Slaves, Freedmen, and the Politics of Freedom in Brazil: The Experience of Blacks in the City of Rio." *Slavery and Abolition* 10, no. 3 (1989): 64–84.

———. *Trabalho, lar e botequim: O cotidiano dos trabalhadores no Rio de Janeiro da belle epoque.* São Paulo: Editora Brasiliense, 1986.

Chance, John K. "Recent Trends in Latin American Urban Studies." *Latin American Research Review* 15, no. 1 (1980): 183–88.

Chevalier, Louis. *Laboring Classes and Dangerous Classes in Paris During the First Half of the Nineteenth Century.* Translated by Frank Jellinek. New York: Howard Fertig, 1973.

Clarke, Colin G. *Kingston, Jamaica: Urban Development and Social Change, 1692–1962.* Berkeley and Los Angeles: University of California Press, 1975.

Coaracy, Vivaldo. *Memórias da cidade do Rio de Janeiro.* Vol. 88 of *Coleção Documentos brasileiros.* Rio de Janeiro: Libraria José Olympio Editora, 1955.

Collier, Ruth Berins, and David Collier. *Shaping the Political Arena: Critical Junctures, the Labor Movement, and Regime Dynamics in Latin America.* Princeton: Princeton University Press, 1991.

Conniff, Michael. *Urban Politics in Brazil: The Rise of Populism, 1925–1945.* Pittsburgh: University of Pittsburgh Press, 1981.

Conrad, Robert. *The Destruction of Brazilian Slavery, 1850–1888.* Berkeley and Los Angeles: University of California Press, 1972.

Cooper, Donald B. "The New 'Black Death': Cholera in Brazil, 1855–1856." *Social Science History* 10, no. 4 (1986): 467–88.

———. "Oswaldo Cruz and the Impact of Yellow Fever on Brazilian History." *Bulletin of Tulane University Medical Faculty* 26 (February 1967): 49–52.

Cruls, Gastão. *Aparencia do Rio de Janeiro: Noticia histórica e descriptiva da cidade.* 2 vols. Rio de Janeiro: Livraria José Olympio Editora, 1965.

Cueto, Marcos, ed. *Missionaries of Science: The Rockefeller Foundation and Latin America.* Bloomington: Indiana University Press, 1994.

da Cunha, Euclides. *Rebellion in the Backlands.* Translated by Samuel Putnam. Chicago: University of Chicago Press, 1944.

Davis, Diane E. *Urban Leviathan: Mexico City in the Twentieth Century.* Philadelphia: Temple University Press, 1994.

Davis, John Emmeus. *Contested Ground: Collective Action and the Urban Neighborhood.* Ithaca: Cornell University Press, 1991.

Della Cava, Ralph. *Miracle at Joaseiro.* New York: Columbia University Press, 1970.

Diacon, Todd A. *Millenarian Vision, Capitalist Reality: Brazil's Contestado Rebellion, 1912–1916.* Durham, N.C.: Duke University Press, 1991.

———. "Peasants, Prophets, and the Power of a Millenarian Vision in Twentieth-Century Brazil." *Comparative Studies in Society and History* 32, no. 3 (July 1990): 488–514.

Dias, Evararo. *História das lutas sociais no Brasil.* São Paulo: Editora Edglit, 1962.

Dulles, John W. F. *Anarchists and Communists in Brazil, 1900–1935.* Austin: University of Texas Press, 1973.

Dunlop, C. J. *Chrônicas, fatos, gente e coisas da nossa história.* Rio de Janeiro: Companhia Editora Americana, 1972.

Eakin, Marshall C. "Race and Identity: Sílvio Romero, Science, and Social Thought in Late-Nineteenth Century Brazil." *Luso-Brazilian Review* 22, no. 2 (1985): 151–74.

Eckstein, Susan. *The Poverty of Revolution: The State and the Urban Poor in Mexico.* Princeton: Princeton University Press, 1977.

———, ed. *Power and Popular Protest: Latin American Social Movements.* Berkeley and Los Angeles: University of California Press, 1989.

Edmundo, Luiz. *O Rio de Janeiro do meu tempo.* Rio de Janeiro: Imprensa Nacional, 1938.

Erickson, Kenneth Paul, Patrick V. Peppe, and Hobart A. Spalding Jr. "Dependency vs. Working Class History: A False Contradiction." *Latin American Research Review* 15, no. 1 (1980): 177–81.

Ernani, Silva Bruno. *História do Brasil—geral e regional.* Vol. 4. São Paulo: Editora Cultrix, 1967.

Fausto, Boris. *Trabalho urbano e conflicto social.* São Paulo: DIFEL, 1976.

——, ed. *O Brasil repúblicano: Estructura de poder e economia, 1889–1930.* Vol. 8 of *História geral da civilização brasileira.* São Paulo: Difusão Editorial, 1975.

——, ed. *O Brasil repúblicano: Sociedade e instituições, 1889–1930.* Vol. 9 of *História geral da civilização brazileira.* Sao Paulo: Difusão Editorial, 1977.

Fernandes, Florestan. *The Negro in Brazilian Society.* New York: Atheneum, 1969.

——. *A revolução burguesa no Brazil: Ensaio de interpretação sociologica.* Rio de Janeiro: Zahar Editores, 1976.

Ferreira da Rosa, Francisco. *Rio de Janeiro.* Rio de Janeiro: Edição Official da Prefeitura, 1905.

Ferreira Lima, Heitor. *História politico—econômica e industrial do Brasil.* São Paulo: Companhia Editora Nacional, 1970.

Font, Mauricio A. *Coffee, Contention, and Change in the Making of Modern Brazil.* Cambridge, Mass.: Basil Blackwell, 1990.

Foucault, Michel. *The Birth of the Clinic: An Archeology of Medical Perception.* Translated by A. M. Sheridan Smith. New York: Vintage Books, 1975.

French, John D. *The Brazilian Workers' ABC: Class Conflict and Alliances in Modern São Paulo.* Chapel Hill: University of North Carolina Press, 1992.

——. *Latin American Labor Studies: A Bibliography of English Publications Through 1989.* Miami: Center of Labor Research and Studies, Florida International University, 1989.

——. *Latin American Labor Studies: An Interim Bibliography of Non-English Publications.* Miami: Center of Labor Research and Studies, Florida International University, 1989.

——. "Practice and Ideology: A Cautionary Note on the Historian's Craft." *Hispanic American Historical Review* 71, no. 1 (1991): 847–55.

Gersón, Brasil. *História das ruas do Rio de Janeiro.* Rio de Janeiro: Editora Souza, 1954.

Graham, Lawrence S. *Civil Service Reform in Brazil: Principles Versus Practice.* Austin: University of Texas Press, 1968.

Graham, Richard. *Britain and the Onset of Modernization in Brazil, 1850–1914.* Cambridge: Cambridge University Press, 1968.

——, ed. *The Idea of Race in Latin America, 1870–1940.* Austin: University of Texas Press, 1990.

Graham, Sandra Lauderdale. *House and Street: The Domestic World of Servants and Masters in Nineteenth-Century Rio de Janeiro.* Cambridge: Cambridge University Press, 1988.

——. "The Vintem Riot and Political Culture: Rio de Janeiro, 1880." *Hispanic American Historical Review* 60, no. 3 (1980): 431–49.

Gramsci, Antonio. *Selections from the Prison Notebooks.* Translated and edited by Quintin Hoare and Geoffrey Nowell Smith. New York: International Publishers, 1971.

Greenfield, Gerald Michael. "Lighting the City: A Case Study of Public Service Problems in São Paulo, 1885–1913." In *Essays Concerning the Socioeconomic History of Brazil and Portuguese India,* edited by Dauril Alden and Warren Dean. Gainesville: University Presses of Florida, 1977.

Greenfield, Gerald Michael, and Sheldon L. Maram, eds. *Latin American Labor Organizations.* Westport, Conn.: Greenwood Press, 1987.

Guimaraes, Alberto Passos. *As classes perigosas: Banditismo urbano e rural.* Rio de Janeiro: Edições Graal, 1982.

Gutman, Herbert G. *Work, Culture, and Society in Industrializing America.* New York: Random House, 1977.

Guy, Donna J. "Medical Imperialism Gone Awry: The Campaign Against Legalized Prostitution in Latin America." In *Science, Medicine, and Cultural Imperialism,* edited by Teresa Meade and Mark Walker. New York: St. Martin's Press, 1991.

Hahner, June E. *Emancipating the Female Sex: The Struggle for Women's Rights in Brazil, 1850–1940.* Durham, N.C.: Duke University Press, 1990.

———. *Poverty and Politics: The Urban Poor in Brazil, 1870–1920.* Albuquerque: University of New Mexico Press, 1986.

Hall, Michael. "The Italians in São Paulo, 1880–1920." Paper presented at the annual meeting of the American Historical Association, December 28, 1971.

———. "The Origins of Mass Immigration in Brazil, 1871–1914." Ph.D diss., Columbia University, 1969.

Harding, Timothy. "The Political History of Organized Labor in Brazil." Ph.D. diss., Stanford University, 1973.

Hardoy, Jorge E., ed. *Urbanization in Latin America: Approaches and Issues.* New York: Doubleday, 1975.

Hauser, Philip M., ed. *Urbanization in Latin America* (proceedings of a seminar of the United Nations Bureau of Social Affairs, ECLA, and UNESCO, Santiago, Chile, July 6–18, 1959). New York: International Documents Service, 1961.

Helg, Aline. "Race in Argentina and Cuba, 1880–1930: Theory, Policies, and Popular Reaction." In *The Idea of Race in Latin America, 1870–1940,* edited by Richard Graham. Austin: University of Texas Press, 1990.

Hilton, Rodney. Introduction to *The Transition from Feudalism to Capitalism.* London: NLB, 1976.

Hobsbawm, Eric. *The Age of Empire, 1875–1914.* New York: Pantheon Books, 1987.

———. "Pre-political Movements in Peripheral Areas." Paper presented at the Conferencia sobre História e Ciencias Sociais, Campinas, Brazil, May 26–30, 1975. Revised and reprinted as "Pre-Political Movements in Modern Politics." In *Powers, Possessions, and Freedom: Essays in Honour of C. B. Macpherson,* edited by Alkis Kontos. Toronto: University of Toronto Press, 1979.

Hobsbawm, Eric, and Terence Ranger, ed. *The Invention of Tradition.* Cambridge: Cambridge University Press, 1983.

Hobsbawm, Eric, and George Rudé. *Captain Swing.* New York: W. W. Norton, 1968.

Holloway, Thomas H. *The Brazilian Coffee Valorization of 1906: Regional Politics and Economic Dependence.* Madison, Wis.: State Historical Society, 1975.

———. *Immigrants on the Land: Coffee and Society in Sao Paulo, 1886–1934.* Chapel Hill: University of North Carolina Press, 1980.

———. *Policing Rio de Janeiro: Repression and Resistance in a Nineteenth-Century City.* Stanford: Stanford University Press, 1993.

Ianni, Octavio. *As metamorfoses do escravo.* São Paulo: Difusão Europeia do Livro, 1962.

Jakobson, Leo, and Ved Prakash, eds. *Urbanization and National Development: South and Southeast Asia Urban Affairs Annuals.* Vol. 1. Beverly Hills: Sage Publications, 1971.

Johnson, Terry. "What Is to Be Known? The Structural Determination of Social Class." *Economy and Society* 6, no. 2 (1977): 194–233.

Karasch, Mary C. *Slave Life in Rio de Janeiro, 1808–1850.* Princeton: Princeton University Press, 1987.

Katzman, Martin T. *Cities and Frontiers in Brazil: Regional Dimensions of Economic Development.* Cambridge, Mass.: Harvard University Press, 1977.
Katznelson, Ira. *City Trenches: Urban Politics and the Patterning of Class in the United States.* Chicago: University of Chicago Press, 1981.
———. *Marxism and the City.* Oxford: Oxford University Press, 1993.
Keremitsis, Eileen. "The Early Industrial Worker in Rio de Janeiro, 1870–1930." Ph.D. diss., Columbia University, 1982.
Knight, Alan. "Racism, Revolution, and *Indigenismo*: Mexico, 1910–1940." In *The Idea of Race in Latin America, 1870–1940,* edited by Richard Graham. Austin: University of Texas Press, 1990.
Kowarick, Lucio. "Capitalismo, dependencia e marginalidade urbana na America Latina: Uma contribuição teorica." *Estudos CEBRAP* 8 (April–June 1974): 77–96.
———. *Capitalismo e marginalidade na America Latina.* Rio de Janeiro: Editora Paz e Terra, 1975.
Lacerda, Maurício de. *Entre duas revoluções.* Rio de Janeiro: Leite Ribeiro, 1927.
Lafuente, A., A. Elena, and M. L. Ortega, eds. *Mundialización de la ciencia y cultura nacional: Actas del congreso internacional "Ciencia, descubrimiento y mundo colonial."* Madrid: Ediciones Doce Calles, 1993.
Leff, Nathaniel H. *Economic Structure and Change, 1822–1947.* Vol. 1 of *Underdevelopment and Development in Brazil.* Boston: George Allen & Unwin, 1982.
Lesser, Jeffrey. *Welcoming the Undesirables: Brazil and the Jewish Question.* Berkeley and Los Angeles: University of California Press, 1995.
Levine, Robert M. "'Mud-Hut Jerusalem': Canudos Revisited." *Hispanic American Historical Review* 68, no. 3 (1988): 525–72.
———. *Vale of Tears: Revisiting the Canudos Massacre in Northeastern Brazil, 1893–1897.* Berkeley and Los Angeles: University of California Press, 1992.
Lima Barreto, Afonso Henriques. *Clara dos anjos.* Rio de Janeiro: Mérito, 1949.
Lobo, Eulalia Maria Lahmeyer. *História do Rio de Janeiro: Do capital commercial ao capital industrial e financeiro.* 2 vols. Rio de Janeiro: Instituto Brasileiro de Mercado de Capitais, 1978.
Lobo, Eulalia Maria Lahmeyer, Octavio Canavarros, Zakia Feres, Sonia Gonçalves, and Lucena Barbosa Madureira. "Evolução dos preços e do padrão de vida no Rio de Janeiro, 1820–1930: Resultados preliminares." *Revista Brasileira de Economia* 26 (October–December 1971): 235–65.
Lobo, Eulalia Maria Lahmeyer, and Eduardo Navarro Stotz. "Flutuações cíclicas da economia, condições de vida e movimento operario—1880 a 1930." *Revista Rio de Janeiro* 1 (December 1985): 61–86.
Love, Joseph L. *São Paulo in the Brazilian Federation, 1889–1937.* Stanford: Stanford University Press, 1980.
Mallon, Florencia E. *Peasant and Nation: The Making of Postcolonial Mexico and Peru.* Berkeley and Los Angeles: University of California Press, 1995.
Malloy, James M. "Social Security Policy and the Working Class in Twentieth-Century Brazil." *Journal of Interamerican Studies and World Affairs* 19 (February 1977): 35–60.
Manchester, Alan K. *British Pre-eminence in Brazil, Its Rise and Decline: A Study in European Expansion.* Chapel Hill: University of North Carolina Press, 1933.
Maram, Sheldon. "Anarchists, Immigrants, and the Brazilian Labor Movement, 1890–1920." Ph.D. diss., University of California, Santa Barbara, 1972.
———. "The Immigrant and the Brazilian Labor Movement, 1890–1920." In *Essays*

Concerning the Socioeconomic History of Brazil and Portuguese India, edited by Dauril Alden and Warren Dean. Gainesville: University Presses of Florida, 1977.

———. "Labor and the Left in Brazil, 1890–1921: A Movement Aborted." *Hispanic American Historical Review* 57, no. 2 (1977): 242–72.

Marx, Karl. *Capital: A Critical Analysis of Capitalist Production.* Vol. 1, edited by Frederick Engels. New York: International Publishers, 1967.

Marx, Karl, and Frederick Engels. *The German Ideology.* Edited by R. Pascal. New York: International Publishers, 1947.

Meade, Teresa. "The Transition to Capitalism in Brazil: Notes on a Third Road." *Latin American Perspectives* 5 (Summer 1978): 7–26.

Meade, Teresa, and Gregory Alonso Pirio. "In Search of the Afro-American 'Eldorado': Attempts by North American Blacks to Enter Brazil in the 1920s." *Luso-Brazilian Review* 25, no. 1 (1988): 85–110.

Moisés, José Alvaro, and Verena Martinez-Alier Stolcke. "Urban Transport and Popular Violence: The Case of Brazil." *Past and Present* 86 (February 1980): 174–92.

Monteiro, Duglas Teixeira. "Um Confronto entre Juazeiro, Canudos e Contestado." In *História geral da civilização brasileira,* vol. 9, *O Brasil repúblicano: Sociedade e instituições, 1889–1930,* edited by Boris Fausto. São Paulo: Difusão Editorial, 1977.

Morse, Richard M. *From Community to Metropolis: A Biography of São Paulo, Brazil.* Gainesville: University of Florida Press, 1958.

———. "São Paulo: Case Study of a Latin American Metropolis." In *Latin American Urban Research,* vol. 1, edited by Francine F. Rabinowitz and Felicity M. Trueblood. Beverly Hills: Sage Publications, 1971.

Nabuco, Caroline. *The Life of Joaquim Nabuco.* Translated and edited by Ronald Hilton. New York: Greenwood Press, 1968.

Nabuco, Joaquim. *Abolitionism: The Brazilian Anti-Slavery Struggle.* Translated and edited by Robert Conrad. Urbana: University of Illinois Press, 1977.

Nachman, Robert G. "Positivism and Revolution in Brazil's First Republic: The 1904 Revolt." *The Americas* 24, no. 1 (1977): 20–39.

———. "Positivism, Modernization, and the Middle Class in Brazil." *Hispanic American Historical Review* 57, no. 1 (1977): 1–23.

Nash, June. "Gender Issues in Latin American Labor." *International Labor and Working Class History* 36 (Fall 1989): 44–50.

Needell, Jeffrey D. "The *Revolta Contra Vacina* of 1904: The Revolt Against Modernization in *Belle-Epoque* Rio de Janeiro." *Hispanic American Historical Review* 67, no. 2 (1987): 233–69.

———. *A Tropical Belle Epoque: Elite Culture and Society in Turn-of-the-Century Rio de Janeiro.* Cambridge: Cambridge University Press, 1987.

Neves, Maria Cecília Baeta. "Greve dos sapateiros de 1906 no Rio de Janeiro: Notas de pesquisa." *Revista de Administração de Empresas,* June 2, 1973, 49–68.

Noble, David F. *Forces of Production: A Social History of Industrial Automation.* New York: Alfred A. Knopf, 1984.

Padilha, Sylvia F. "Da 'Cidade Velha' a periferia." *Revista Rio de Janeiro* 1, no. 1 (1985): 17–19.

Pearse, Andre. "Some Characteristics of Urbanization in the City of Rio de Janeiro." In *Urbanization in Latin America* (proceedings of a seminar of the United Nations Bureau of Social Affairs, ECLA, and UNESCO, Santiago, Chile, July 6–18, 1959), edited by Philip M. Hauser. New York: International Documents Service, 1961.

Pechman, Robert Moses, and Luís César Queiroz Ribeiro. "A companhia de Saneamento do Rio de Janeiro." *Revista Rio de Janeiro* 1, no. 1 (Dezembro 1985): 105–13.

Perlman, Janice E. *The Myth of Marginality: Urban Poverty and Politics in Rio de Janeiro.* Berkeley and Los Angeles: University of California Press, 1976.

Petrone, Maria Tereza Schorer. "Imigração." In *História geral da civilização brasileira,* vol. 9, *O Brasil repúblicano: Sociedade e instituições, 1889–1930,* edited by Boris Fausto. São Paulo: DIFEL, 1977.

Pimentel, Antonio Martins de Azevedo. *Quaes os Melhoramentos Hygienicos que Devem ser introduzidos no Rio de Janeiro para tornar esta cidade mais saudavel.* Rio de Janeiro: Imprensa Nacional, 1895.

Pinheiro, Paulo Sérgio. "Classes Medias Urbanas: Formação, Natureza, Intervenção na vida politica." In *História geral da civilização brasileira,* vol. 9, *O Brasil repúblicano: Sociedade e instituições, 1889–1930,* edited by Boris Fausto. São Paulo: 1977.

———. "Trabalho industrial no Brasil: Uma revisão." Paper presented at the twenty-seventh annual reunion of the Sociedade Brasileira para O Progresso da Ciencia, Belo Horizonte, July 14, 1975.

———, ed. *Crime, violncia e poder.* São Paulo: Editora Brasiliense, 1983.

Pinheiro, Paulo Sérgio, and Michael M. Hall, eds. *A Classe Operária no Brasil: Condições de vida e de trabalho, relações com os empresários e o estado, 1889–1930, Documentos.* São Paulo: Editora Brasiliense, 1981.

Platt, D.C.M. "The Anatomy of 'Autonomy' (Whatever That May Mean): A Reply." *Latin American Research Review* 15, no. 1 (1980): 147–49.

———. "Dependency in Nineteenth-Century Latin America: A Historian Objects." *Latin American Research Review* 15, no. 1 (1980): 113–30.

———. *Latin American and British Trade, 1806–1914.* New York: Harper & Row, 1973.

Porto, Rubens d'Almeida H. de. *O problema das casas operarias e os institutos e caixas de pensões.* Rio de Janeiro: Imprensa Nacional, 1938.

Poulantzas, Nicos. *Classes in Contemporary Capitalism.* London: New Left Books, 1976.

Prado, Caio, Jr. *História econômica do Brasil.* São Paulo: Editora Brasiliense, 1945.

Pyenson, Lewis. "The Limits of Scientific Condominium: Geophysics in Western Samoa, 1914–1940." In *Scientific Colonialism: A Cross-Cultural Comparison,* edited by Nathan Reingold and Marc Rothenberg. Washington, D.C.: Smithsonian Institution Press, 1987.

Quijano, Anibal. "The Urbanization of Latin American Society." In *Urbanization in Latin America: Approaches and Issues,* edited by Jorge E. Hardoy. New York: Doubleday, 1975.

Raphael, Alison. "Samba and Social Control: Popular Culture and Racial Democracy in Rio de Janeiro." Ph.D. diss., Columbia University, 1981.

Ribeiro, Candido Barata. *Quaes as medidas sanitárias que devem ser aconselhadas para impedir o desenvolvimento e propagação da febre amarela na cidade do Rio de Janeiro.* Rio de Janeiro: Imprensa Nacional, 1877.

Ridings, Eugene W. "Business, Nationality, and Dependency in Late-Nineteenth-Century Brazil." *Journal of Latin American Studies* 14, no. 1 (1982): 55–96.

Rodrigues, José Honório. *Conciliação e reforma.* Rio de Janeiro: Civilização Brasileira, 1965.

Rodrigues, Leôncio Martins. "Classe operaria e sindicalismo no Brasil." In *Sindical-*

ismo e sociedade, edited by Leôncio Martins Rodrigues. São Paulo: Difusão Européia do Livro, 1968.
————. *Sindicalismo e conflito industrial no Brasil.* São Paulo: Difusão Européia do Livro, 1966.
Rudé, George. *The Crowd in History, 1730–1848.* New York: John Wiley & Sons, 1964.
Saes, Decio. *Classe media e politica na Primeira República Brasileira, 1889–1930.* Petropolis: Vozes, 1975.
Sarmiento, Domingo Faustino. *Life in the Argentine Republic in the Days of the Tyrants; or, Civilization and Barbarism.* Translated from the Spanish. New York: Hafner Publishing Co., 1868.
Scenna, Miguel Angel. *Cuando murió Buenos Aires, 1871.* Buenos Aires: Ediciones La Bastilla, 1974.
Scobie, James R. *Buenos Aires: Plaza to Suburb, 1870–1910.* New York: Oxford University Press, 1974.
Scott, James C. *Domination and the Arts of Resistance: Hidden Transcripts.* New Haven: Yale University Press, 1990.
Scott, Joan Wallach. *Gender and the Politics of History.* New York: Columbia University Press, 1988.
Sevcenko, Nicolau. *Literatura como missão: Tensões sociais e criação cultural na Primeira República.* São Paulo: Editora Brasiliense, 1985.
————. *A revolta da vacina: Mentes insanas em corpos rebeldes.* São Paulo: Editora Brasiliense, 1984.
Silva, Fernando Nascimento, ed. *Rio de Janeiro em seus quatrocentos anos: Formação e desenvolvimento da Cidade.* Rio de Janeiro: Distribuidora Record, 1965.
Skidmore, Thomas E. *Black into White: Race and Nationality in Brazilian Thought.* Durham, N.C.: Duke University Press, 1993.
————. *Politics in Brazil, 1930–1964: An Experiment in Democracy.* New York: Oxford University Press, 1967.
————. "Workers and Soldiers: Urban Labor Movements and Elite Responses in Twentieth-Century Latin America." In *Elites, Masses, and Modernization in Latin America, 1850–1930,* edited by Virginia Bernhard. Austin: University of Texas Press, 1979.
Skotnes, Andor D. "Structural Determination of the Proletariat and the Petty Bourgeoisie: A Critique of Nicos Poulantzas." *Insurgent Sociologist* 9, no. 1 (1979): 34–54.
Slater, David. *New Social Movements and the State in Latin America.* Cinnamininson, N.J.: Foris Publications, 1985.
Smithburn, Kenneth C. *Yellow Fever Vaccination.* World Health Organization Monograph Series, no. 36. Geneva: World Health Organization, 1956.
Sodré, Nelson Werneck. *História da burguesia brasileira.* Rio de Janeiro: Editora Civilização Brasileira, 1976.
Sofer, Eugene. "Recent Trends in Latin American Labor Historiography." *Latin American Research Review* 15, no. 1 (1980): 167–76.
Solis, Sidney Sérgio F., and Marcus Venício T. Ribeiro. "O Rio onde o sol não brilha: Acumulação e pobreza na transição para o capitalismo." *Revista Rio de Janeiro* 1, no. 1 (1985): 45–59.
Spalding, Hobart A. "Somethings Old and Somethings New." *International Labor and Working Class History* 36 (Fall 1989): 37–43.
Spitzer, Leo. *Lives In Between: Assimilation and Marginality in Austria, Brazil, and West Africa, 1780–1945.* New York: Cambridge University Press, 1989.

————. "The Mosquito and Segregation in Sierra Leone." *Canadian Journal of African Studies* 2 (Spring 1968): 49–61.

Stedman Jones, Gareth. "Class Expression Versus Social Control: A Critique of Recent Trends in the Social History of 'Leisure.'" *History Workshop* 4 (Autumn 1977): 162–70.

————. *Outcast London: A Study in the Relationship Between Classes in Victorian Society.* New York: Oxford University Press, 1971.

————. "Working-Class Culture and Working-Class Politics in London, 1870–1900: Notes on the Remaking of a Working Class." *Journal of Social History* 7, no. 4 (Summer 1974): 460–508.

Stein, Stanley J., and Barbara H. Stein. *The Colonial Heritage of Latin America: Essays on Economic Dependence in Perspective.* New York: Oxford University Press, 1970.

————. "D.C.M. Platt: The Anatomy of 'Autonomy.'" *Latin American Research Review* 15, no. 1 (1980): 131–46.

Stepan, Nancy. *Beginnings of Brazilian Science: Oswaldo Cruz, Medical Research and Policy, 1890–1920.* New York: Science History Publications, 1976.

Stepan, Nancy Leys. *"The Hour of Eugenics": Race, Gender, and Nation in Latin America.* Ithaca: Cornell University Press, 1991.

Tannuri, Luiz Antonio. *O Encilhamento.* São Paulo: Editora Hucitec, 1981.

Taylor, Quintard. "Frente Negra Brasileira: The Afro-Brazilian Civil Rights Movement, 1924–1937." *Scholarly Journal of Black Studies* 2 (Spring 1978).

Thompson, Edward. *The Making of the English Working Class.* New York: Random House, 1966.

————. "The Moral Economy of the English Crowd in the Eighteenth Century." *Past and Present* 50 (February 1971): 76–136.

Tilly, Charles. "The Changing Place of Collective Violence." In *Workers in the Industrial Revolution,* edited by Peter N. Stearns and Daniel J. Walkowitz. New Brunswick, N.J.: Transaction Books, 1974.

————. *The Contentious French.* Cambridge, Mass.: Harvard University Press, 1986.

————, ed. *An Urban World.* Boston: Little, Brown, 1974.

Tilly, Charles, and Louise A. Tilly, eds. *Class Conflict and Collective Action.* Beverly Hills: Sage Publications, 1981.

Topik, Steven. *The Political Economy of the Brazilian State, 1889–1930.* Austin: University of Texas Press, 1987.

Touraine, Alain, and Bernard Mottez. "Classes operarias e sociedade global." In *Sindicalismo e sociedade,* edited by Leôncio Martins Rodrigues. São Paulo: Difusão Europeia do Livro, 1968.

Urquidi, Victor L. "The Underdeveloped City." In *Urbanization in Latin America: Approaches and Issues,* edited by Jorge E. Hardoy. New York: Doubleday, 1975.

Van Onselen, Charles. *Studies in the Social and Economic History of Witwatersrand, 1886–1914.* 2 vols. New York: Longman, 1982.

Viotti da Costa, Emilia. *Da senzala a colonia.* São Paulo: Difusão Europeia do Livro, 1966.

————. "Experience Versus Structures: New Tendencies in the History of Labor and the Working Class in Latin America—What Do We Gain? What Do We Lose?" *International Labor and Working Class History* 36 (Fall 1989): 3–24.

Wagley, Charles. *An Introduction to Brazil.* New York: Columbia University Press, 1963.

Weinstein, Barbara. "The New Latin American Labor History: What We Gain." *International Labor and Working Class History* 36 (Fall 1989): 25–30.

Wellisz, Stanislaw. "Economic Development and Urbanization." In *Urbanization and National Development,* vol. 1. Beverly Hills: Sage Publications, 1971.

Williams, Greer. *The Plague Killers.* New York: Charles Scribner's Sons, 1969.

Wolfe, Joel. "Anarchist Ideology, Worker Practice: The 1917 General Strike and the Formation of São Paulo's Working Class." *Hispanic American Historical Review* 71, no. 1 (1991): 809–46.

———. "'Father of the Poor' or 'Mother of the Rich'? Getulio Vargas, Industrial Workers, and Constructions of Class, Gender, and Populism in São Paulo, 1930–1954." *Radical History Review* 58 (Winter 1994): 80–111.

———. "Response to John French." *Hispanic American Historical Review* 71, no. 1 (1991): 856–58.

———. *Working Women, Working Men: São Paulo and the Rise of Brazil's Industrial Working Class, 1900–1955.* Durham, N.C.: Duke University Press, 1993.

Index